THE OTHER
BLACK
BOSTONIANS

THE OTHER

WEST INDIANS

BLACK

IN BOSTON

BOSTONIANS

1900–1950

VIOLET SHOWERS JOHNSON

Indiana University Press
Bloomington & Indianapolis

This book is a publication of

Indiana University Press
601 North Morton Street
Bloomington, Indiana 47404-3797 USA

http://iupress.indiana.edu

Telephone orders   800-842-6796
Fax orders   812-855-7931
Orders by email   iuporder@indiana.edu

The paper used in this publication meets the minimum
requirements of American National Standard for Information
Sciences—Permanence of Paper for Printed Library
Materials, ANSI Z39.48-1984.

Manufactured in the United States of America

Library of Congress Cataloging-in-Publication Data

Johnson, Violet Showers.
   The other Black Bostonians : West Indians in Boston, 1900–1950 /
Violet Showers Johnson.
       p. cm. — (Blacks in the diaspora)
   Includes bibliographical references and index.
   ISBN 0-253-34752-1 (cloth : alk. paper)
   1. West Indian Americans—Massachusetts—Boston—History—
20th century. 2. West Indian Americans—Massachusetts—Boston
—Social conditions—20th century. 3. Blacks—Massachusetts—
Boston—History—20th century. 4. Blacks—Massachusetts—Boston
—Social conditions—20th century. 5. Immigrants—Massachusetts
—Boston—Social conditions—20th century. 6. West Indians—Mi-
grations—History—20th century. 7. Blacks—Migrations—History
—20th century. 8. Boston (Mass.)—Race relations—History—20th
century. 9. Boston (Mass.)—Social conditions—20th century.   I.
Title. II. Series.
   F73.7.W54J64 2006
   305.8009744'61—dc22

                                                                    2006005254

1 2 3 4 5 11 10 09 08 07 06

TO MY MOTHER,

EDNA TAIWO SHOWERS,

AND TO THE MEMORY OF MY FATHER,

SAMUEL DANDESON SHOWERS.

CONTENTS

ACKNOWLEDGMENTS

This book has the imprints of several contributors. Andrew Bunie suggested the topic and served as advisor for my dissertation from which this work grew. Judith Smith and Marilyn Halter, the other members of my dissertation committee, offered valuable suggestions for developing and articulating my arguments. Marilyn Halter's friendship and continued interest in my scholarly development influenced some of the post-dissertation revisions. Her seemingly effortless ability to deftly interweave narrative and analytical history continues to serve as a model.

Many scholars who are also my friends offered unwavering support and critical feedback. They include Tina and Clarence Johnson, Cathy Scott, Paul Spickard, and Patrick Miller. The humor, ideas, and encouragement from Paul Breines, a kind and genuine friend, were valuable, especially during the low points of the project. Members of the history department of Agnes Scott College were very supportive. Kathy Kennedy, as chair and a friend, was an advocate for an environment conducive for combining teaching and scholarship. Former colleague and friend Michele Gillespie, as the other Americanist in the department, shared her knowledge and offered valuable insights based partly on her own experiences in the field. Outside the traditional academic circles, the interest and confidence of friends helped sustain my enthusiasm for this work. Sylvia Ashong, Adeline Johnson, Rhoda Spence, and Deborah Bradford encouraged me to talk about my ideas, materials, and evolving interpretations.

Family support was crucial. My mother, Edna Showers, courageously ventured out of Africa for the first time at the age of sixty to assist me. She provided child care and moral support during the early stages of data collection. My husband's niece, Charida Dumbuya, also helped with child care. My brothers Moses, Henry, Cyril, and David Showers showed steadfast interest and confidence in this work, as they have in everything I have pursued. My husband, Percy Johnson, was a tower of strength throughout the long span of this project. As my number one fan, he willingly served as my sounding board, offering the kindest yet most candid critiques. My son, P. J., made numerous sacrifices. Never picky about food or anything, he made it so much easier for me to delve into intensive research and writing without feeling guilty about neglecting him.

Much of the content of this book is the result of the generosity of people like Mel King and David Nelson, who willingly shared details of their lives and provided valuable contacts in the community. Unfortunately some of the people who were so instrumental in providing and helping me locate materials have passed and are not around to see the outcomes of their efforts: Victor Bynoe, Elma Lewis, Amanda Houston, and George Commissiong. Others who helped me with oral history, too many to mention here, are acknowledged in endnotes and in the bibliography.

The staffs of various libraries and archives helped me locate and use sources: the Microfilm Division and Aaron Schmidt of the Print Division of the Boston Public Library; the National Archives, Waltham, Massachusetts, branch; the Archives of Northeastern University; Public Records Office, Kew, England; Jamaica National Archives, Spanish Town; Special West Indies Collections of the University of the West Indies, Mona; and the Jamaica National Library. Susan Dougherty, manager of faculty services at Agnes Scott College, in addition to diligently preparing several drafts of the manuscript, was one of my staunchest supporters. Her words of encouragement and confidence in what came to be "our project" were vital to the completion of this book. Nell Ruby and her graphics team suggested images for the book cover, and Calvin Burgamy of Agnes Scott Information Technology scanned some of the illustrations. Casey Yannella, history department student assistant, worked hard in finding and compiling information for the final submission of the manuscript. Students who took my courses, "Race, Ethnicity and Immigration" and "The African Diaspora," showed genuine interest in my work. Many of them, even after leaving Agnes Scott, continued to check when my book will be published, assuring me that I had something valuable to contribute to these fields. Robert J. Sloan, editorial director, Indiana University Press, showed great enthusiasm and gave his hearty support from our first contact. Managing editor Miki Bird and copy editor Drew Bryan were generous with useful editorial advice that helped enhance the effect of several analyses and discussions.

This project would not have been possible without much-needed financial support. The United States Junior Fulbright Foundation provided the scholarship that enabled me to pursue my doctoral program during which the life of this book began. A dissertation fellowship from the Boston College Graduate School of Arts and Sciences enabled me to conduct research. Awards from the Agnes Scott College Professional Development Committee supported travel to and research in Jamaica and Boston.

These sources of support from family, friends, and institutions have their imprints subtly and conspicuously in this work, and I am most grateful. This support notwithstanding, I take full responsibility for any errors.

THE OTHER
BLACK
BOSTONIANS

Introduction

The Afro-Caribbean diaspora has shaped Black America in subtle and conspicuous ways. From Hubert Harrison's stepladder oratory to Marcus Garvey's Black nationalism and Claudia Jones' communism, it has influenced Black American discourses on race, racism, protest, and Black advancement. Through rotating credit associations, food enterprises, the carnival, Rastafarianism, steel drums, and reggae, it has diversified Black community and culture. Undeniably, the dispersal of people and ideas from the Caribbean has played a big part in the evolution of modern Black America. The impact of this component of the modern Black diaspora on America began to be profound and more easily recognizable in the first decades of the twentieth century. During that time, especially after the outbreak of World War I, people of African descent, mostly from the British Caribbean colonies, began to migrate to America in significant numbers. In this influx, Boston was the third most popular destination behind only New York and Miami.[1]

The Boston that the Black foreigners came to, by 1910, was not exactly the Bible Commonwealth of John Winthrop and John Cotton,[2] but it was still steeped in the legacies of its Puritan past. The Brahmin hegemony was at the core of that past and, in the early twentieth century, was still a crucial driving force of life in that city. No aspect of Boston's history can be meaningfully analyzed without considering the "Brahmin factor." By the time of the American Revolution, the leading families like the Hancocks, Lowells, Cabots, and Appletons, to name a few, had established an economic-cum-political oligarchy. As prominent Boston historian Thomas O'Connor explained: "Like the priestly Brahmin class of the ancient Hindus, who performed the sacred rites and set the moral standards, the new leaders of Boston society emerged as self-styled 'Brahmins' of a modern caste system in which they were clearly and undisputedly the superior force."[3] This Brahmin aristocracy was quite cognizant of the importance of party politics, the power of the popular vote, and the influence of public opinion. Therefore, its members understood that changes were bound to occur.

They considered themselves so progressive, and still imbued with the reformist spirit of their forebears, that they welcomed changes, but only insofar as they could control them. They were determined to direct the political and economic destinies of their town. They believed that with a long tradition of moral stewardship, they were also poised to direct its social destinies. It was incumbent upon them as the noble elite to influence the lower classes and stimulate them to adhere to Brahmin moral, social, and political values.[4]

But some changes, especially those they deemed a threat to their civilization, seemed to be beyond their control. Much of this perceived threat flowed from foreign immigration. The Irish were the first group of foreigners to seriously challenge the homogeneity of the population and the Anglo-Saxon Protestant hegemony. Other non-Anglo-Saxons followed—mostly eastern European Jews and Italians. Boston also changed racially in significant ways. The small Black population, whose beginning predated the Revolution, had done well under Brahmin stewardship. The Brahmin aristocracy was convinced that this group had imbibed its social, political, and moral values, and its members, the Boston-born Blacks, were fully integrated, albeit in their designated place in the society. Like the Whites, the indigenous Blacks, too, had developed their own hierarchical structure, which contained their own upper middle class of leading families—the Black Brahmins.[5] This established structure was also to be shaken by phenomenal demographic developments. With the Great Migration of southern Blacks to the north, Black migrants came to Boston in significant numbers, as they did in other northern cities.[6] The threat of the influx of Blacks who were "different" was compounded by the arrival at the same time of foreign Blacks. These Black foreigners were overwhelmingly from the British West Indies and are the subject of the present study.

If a cursory examination based on superficial observations had been done to determine the suitability of the West Indians for Boston society, it may have revealed that they would easily do well. Unlike the Irish, the West Indians were mostly Protestants, they embraced values that echoed the Puritan work ethic and civic responsibility, and, unlike the Jews and Italians, they as British subjects spoke and wrote English. But there was one big mitigating fact. In the socially constructed categorization of race, they were Black. What would their migration experience be in this destination, which at first glance exemplified their affiliations, standards, and values, yet in reality added them to the groups that may not really belong? In the following chapters, the present study will address this question by describing and analyzing the history of the West Indian community in Boston in the first half of the twentieth century.

Black foreigners have remained in the periphery of American immigration historiography, even though the study of ethnicity and immigration has witnessed remarkable progress since 1970.[7] Repeatedly, their historiographical marginalization is clearly reflected in general histories of "multicultural" or "ethnic" America which completely ignore or give only the scantiest attention to their experiences.[8]

The unsatisfactory state of Black immigration scholarship notwithstanding, British West Indians, composed of people from the English-speaking Caribbean and South America, have received relatively substantial attention.[9] Scholarly interest in this group started as early as the 1920s, when ethnic and immigration history was still very much in its infancy. Unfortunately, however, the research conducted from this time until the 1970s is skewed by its excessive concentration on the rivalry between West Indians and African Americans and its almost exclusive focus on New York City. West Indians were only attractive as subjects in downplaying the salience of race in socioeconomic mobility in the United States. For decades these immigrants were used to show that given the right group characteristics, Blacks did extremely well in America. Writers concluded that West Indians outperformed native Blacks in every sphere: they were more educated, more occupationally successful, more hard-working, more frugal, and more politically agile. An annotated bibliography of Black immigration and ethnicity in America, published in the 1980s, paints the picture. Over three-quarters of the entries on West Indians focus exclusively on the "West Indian versus African American" factor.[10] The main thrusts of the arguments of these studies are that West Indian Blacks were superior to American Blacks, that Black foreigners contributed immensely to the advancement of Blacks in America, and that the radical propensity and phenomenal success of the foreigners exacerbated the tensions between the two groups, resulting in deep animosity which made genuine intraracial cooperation impossible. Most of these studies went further to attribute the root of the disparity to a superior West Indian cultural heritage, including their earlier emancipation from slavery.[11]

Studying West Indians only in relation to their success vis-à-vis that of African Americans had gained a foothold as early as the 1920s. The main architects of this trend were West Indian political activists and intellectuals living in New York City who were anxious to establish their legitimacy as the brokers of Black advancement. Ironically, in their quest for this goal, the small West Indian elite became embroiled in various political rivalries with their American-born counterparts[12] and fought hard to vindicate their leadership roles. What better way to do this than to amplify the positive group characteristics? This situation, naturally, did not encourage a great deal of scholarly objectivity. At the forefront of the West Indian propaganda was Wilfredo A. Domingo, a prominent Jamaican activist and one of the first to expound on the role of historical cultural premigration values in the successful adaptation of West Indian immigrants. In his discourse, appropriately entitled "Gift of the Black Tropics," he attempted to explain how the homeland society helped cultivate persistence, ambition, frugality, and other traits found in West Indian immigrants.[13] Even earlier, in 1912, George Haynes' study *The Negro at Work* had drawn attention to West Indian entrepreneurial superiority.[14] Using such writers as Domingo and Haynes as their main sources, other researchers followed suit, constructing a body of literature which examined West Indians in America in light of their success and superiority over American Blacks.

Consequently, while the literature on this group of immigrants is impressive in terms of volume, especially when compared with that of other Black immigrant groups, there are some serious shortcomings. First, most of the literature is narrowly focused on a comparative study of two Black groups. Second, most of the conclusions were derived from biased, impressionistic accounts and not from well-grounded empirical investigation. Third, while most of the studies talk about "West Indians in the United States," their focus was often entirely on those who lived in New York City.[15]

As the twentieth century came to a close, a flurry of new studies addressed some of the shortcomings. Milton Vickerman's *Crosscurrents: West Indian Immigrants and Race* studied how ideas about and experiences with race, color, and class in the home society converged with the unique characteristics of race and racism in America to influence and shape West Indian identity and adaptation in America. Although Irma Watkins-Owens' *Blood Relations: Caribbean Immigrants and the Harlem Community* is about the much-researched New York West Indian community, unlike previous studies it brings to the fore the complex dynamics of work, ethnicity, gender, and class. Similarly, Ransford Palmer's *Pilgrim From the Sun: West Indian Migration to America* moves away from the myopic theme of the West Indian–African American rivalry to put the immigrants' experiences within a wider context of work, political economy, and social mobility. However, contrary to the title's suggestion of a national orientation, *Pilgrims From the Sun* is like previous works in its almost exclusive focus on New York. Historian Winston James also addressed some of the deficiencies in West Indian American historiography. In his study *Holding Aloft the Banner of Ethiopia: Caribbean Radicalism in Early Twentieth-Century America,* he tackles some of the pivotal questions on West Indians' contributions to Black radicalism in the United States. Importantly, James also searched for some of the answers beyond New York by looking at the Afro-Hispanic Caribbean radical tradition in Florida. These strengths notwithstanding, *Holding Aloft the Banner of Ethiopia* is still heavily focused on New York in its consideration of the activities and contributions of activists from the English-speaking Caribbean.

Sociologist Mary C. Waters also made her mark on the new scholarship on the West Indian American experience. Interestingly, her 1999 work *Black Identities: West Indian Immigrant Dreams and American Realities* revisits familiar terrain—New York, and the ubiquitous subject of West Indian success. But she breaks new ground in the way she analyzes familiar themes. She demonstrates clearly that the West Indian success story is not a simple one. Giving an unprecedented amount of attention to the second generation, she discusses how different levels of Americanization determined the socioeconomic achievements of the immigrants and their American-born children. Stressing her resolve not to follow the path of previous "conservative writers" who criticized African American culture and praised West Indian culture, Waters looks instead at the ways that racist structures and behaviors deny equal opportunities to people identified as Black in American society, whether they are native-born or foreign.

The revisionist trend continues in the twenty-first century. In *The West Indian Americans,* Holger Henke, looking at post-1965 Caribbean immigrants, breaks a significant path. For the first time clear distinctions are made between the diverse peoples of African, East Indian, and mixed ancestry who make up what has been traditionally simply dubbed "West Indian immigrants." But like Palmer and James, New York is still Henke's focus. Perhaps more path-breaking is Rachel Buff's *Immigration and the Political Economy of Home: West Indian Brooklyn and American Indian Minneapolis.* For the first time in a substantial study, West Indians are compared with Native Americans, a refreshing departure from the West Indian–Black American preoccupation. Finally, Percy C. Hintzen moved far away from New York to the West Coast to study post-1965 West Indians in California. In his book *West Indian in the West,* he demonstrates how the immigrants use performance, rituals, and symbols to define and represent their collective presence.[16]

Like Hintzen, the present work shifts focus from the traditional New York arena. It is an attempt to address the current historiographical imbalance and contribute to the ongoing revision of West Indian American history. Black radicalism and the phenomenal cultural production of the Harlem Renaissance brought a certain distinctiveness to New York, an appeal that lured researchers to study the West Indians of that city. The West Indians of Boston can evoke a similar appeal for the light they shed in analyzing that city's own traditions. From its inception, Boston was supposed to be like no other city. As two of Boston's foremost historians explain: "The history of Boston is unique because of the remarkable persistence of a theme first articulated in 1630 by its Puritan founders. Boston was intended to be a 'City on a Hill,' a shining example of how men and women motivated by a commitment to hard work and to personal, religious, and civic reform might change the course of history."[17] By the nineteenth century, Bostonians were celebrating the attainment of the founders' goals by pointing to Boston's lead in education, its cultured, genteel class of Brahmins, and its laudable abolitionist history, all qualities that made it the "Athens of America," "Freedom's Birthplace," and, simply, the "Hub of the Cosmos."

From Oscar Handlin's *Boston's Immigrants* to Thomas O'Connor's *The Boston Irish* to William DeMarco's *Boston's Italian North End* and Jonathan Sarna and Ellen Smith's *The Jews of Boston*, historians have evaluated these claims, showing how immigrant groups like the Irish, Italians, and Jews simultaneously reinforced and challenged the Yankee myth.[18] While such classics as *North of Slavery, In Freedom's Birthplace,* and *Black Migration and Poverty*[19] offer useful insights into how the American-born Black population fared within Boston's Yankee society, there is no comparable analysis on the foreign Black segment to serve the same purposes as do those on European groups cited above. Therefore, *The Other Black Bostonians: West Indians in Boston, 1900–1950* in some sense uses this non-European immigrant group to further understand the actual workings of Boston's traditions. While this objective is a crucial one which should contribute to the study of Boston's Yankee history, this work is not an exclusive study of a litmus test of Boston's democratic ideals. Rather, it is a work that attempts to describe and explain the West Indian experience fully, showing its many facets: the process of emigration, the dynamics of work, family life, community institutions, identity, ethnic consciousness, race consciousness, and social mobility.

The West Indian presence in Boston dates back to the late nineteenth century. Although information for this period is scant, from the observations of contemporaries, some facts are discernible. There were very few West Indians in Boston at the time, mostly mulatto men from privileged West Indian families, many of them professionals like doctors and lawyers.[20] Although John Daniels noted that some of the prominent West Indians were "well known in the Negro community," he admitted in the same study that the West Indian community by 1900 was so small that its existence was relatively unknown to the general public.[21] So it was not until around the eve of World War I that a permanent, more visible West Indian presence began to take shape. Moreover, it was now predominantly Black, working-class, and almost half female. Men, women, and children from some of the English-speaking Caribbean colonies continued to come to Boston from this period in varying volumes until the beginning of the 1950s. In 1952, U.S. immigration restrictions contained in the McCarran-Walter Act virtually cut off any substantial flow from that region for a decade, creating a watershed between the "old" and "new" West Indian immigrations.

The old immigration is what this book reviews. This wave occurred largely within the context of American commercial links with Latin America and the Caribbean. The United Fruit Company, headquartered in Boston, was most influential. The expansion of its operations to include passenger steam lines between terminals on the eastern seaboard and those areas in Latin America and the Caribbean where the company owned or managed plantations was to be one of the biggest facilitators of West Indian migration.[22] Entries in the *List of Alien Passengers* of the U.S. Immigration Services show that by 1920 close to sixty West Indians were arriving annually in Boston on United Fruit steam liners directly from the West Indies, mainly from Jamaica. Another twenty to thirty were "step migrants" relocating to Boston from Limon, Costa Rica, where Black West Indian United Fruit Company workers had created an English-speaking ethnic enclave.[23] While the majority of the West Indian passengers on the United Fruit vessels were ticket-holding passengers, stowage was a regular practice, common especially among laborers who loaded bananas and coconuts on the West Indian docks.[24] Exactly how many British West Indians immigrated to Boston in the first half of the twentieth century is difficult to ascertain, mainly because Boston was not the first port of arrival for many. Naturalization petitions and oral history help to retrace their journeys, showing that they eventually came to Boston from New York; Providence, Rhode Island; Hartford, Connecticut; Sydney, Nova Scotia; and St. John, New Brunswick.

It is instructive to point out that, conversely, Boston also served as a first stop in step migration. Some of the new arrivals clearly indicated, according to the *Passenger Lists,* that they intended to move to some other U.S. city, usually New York. From anecdotal evidence, some ended up staying while others moved, although in some cases after spending a fair amount of time in Boston. The most famous of such temporary Bostonians is W. A. Domingo, who had first come to Boston in 1910 to live with his sister, a boarding house operator. In 1912 he moved to Harlem where he was to carve out a remarkable political career.[25] The paucity of information on why a prominent historical subject like Domingo abandoned his plans to study medicine and moved out of Boston underscores the frustration in fully reconstructing the picture of the patterns of arrival, settlement, and movement of Boston's West Indians from 1900 to 1952.

Even though the number of annual arrivals was elusive, there were clear indications of the existence of a Black immigrant community, even if throughout the first half of the twentieth century it remained very small. According to census records, in 1910 West Indians numbered 566, which was five percent of the total Black population. In 1920, the number had risen to 2,877, and by 1952, when the "old" immigration ended, the West Indian population was estimated at 5,000, twelve percent of the total Black population.[26] Although there were immigrants from the British Virgin Islands, Trinidad, and Guyana, the majority of Boston's West Indians of this period had come from three islands—Barbados, Jamaica, and Montserrat.

The following chapters will look at this community of Boston West Indian pioneers. As a social history which uses a multithematic approach, this study intends to demonstrate the variety of facets that operated and interacted to shape one of Boston's oldest ethnic/immigrant groups.

Activism, the theme that has so captivated researchers, is indeed a crucial facet in the group's history and will be addressed fully in chapter 4. However, examination of this topic in this book will not revolve around the tensions between African Americans and West Indians. Instead, in addition to discussing the complex relationship that emerged between the two Black groups in their quest for Black advancement, this chapter will reveal and explain the dynamics that shaped intragroup relations within the immigrant community itself. Variables such as specific region of origin, socioeconomic standing (both in the West Indies and Boston), and gender and generational differences all worked to create diffusely focused, multi-ideological, and multitiered agitational styles within what has been generally dubbed "West Indian activism."

In spite of the differences in approach to and level of involvement in protest, one common experience was the recognition of the weighty implications of Blackness in America. Residential and occupational "choices," which to a large extent were dictated by structural forces that sharply divided Boston racially, ethnically, and culturally, clearly hammered home this reality. Chapter 2 describes and discusses the evolving economic and demographic determinants which effectively positioned the arriving Black foreigners within Black Boston.

Demographically situated within the Black community and lacking a physically distinct ethnic enclave, the West Indian community was not easily identifiable. Nevertheless, a vibrant subculture, defined by family, church, and associations, existed. Chapter 3 illuminates the workings of those components which defined this apparently invisible West Indian community.

Chapter 5 looks at a theme that is central not only to West Indian immigration history but immigration histories in general—social mobility. This section assesses Boston's West Indians' success from two main perspectives—theirs and others'. The analysis will identify and explain what the immigrants saw as success, how they arrived at their perceptions, and their yardsticks for measuring mobility. For a balanced assessment, this chapter also looks at the immigrants' accomplishments outside the definitions of the immigrant community (and the Black community for that matter) within the larger Boston society, which included American-born whites as well as European ethnics.

Chapter 1 in many senses is the prop of the entire study. Therefore, bringing it up last in this introduction is by no means an oversight. That chapter is an analytical overview of the premigration background, which contained the elements that propelled West Indians out, inspired their goals and aspirations, provided some of the facilitators for emigration, informed the immigrants' notions of life in America, and dictated the yardsticks for measuring success there. Chapter 1, then, for the framework it provides, is key to fully understanding most of the developments discussed in subsequent chapters. Although Boston's West Indians confronted and grasped the challenges emanating from the specific structures of that New England community, they continued to use their homeland as a central point of reference in responding to these situations and, in the process, in carving out a community which is the subject of this book.

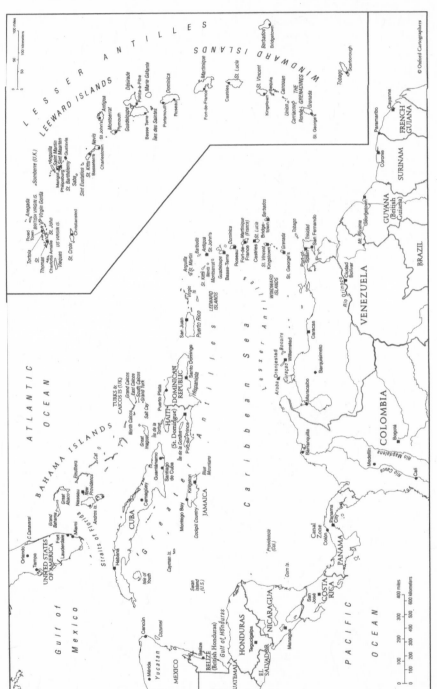

The Caribbean. *Courtesy of Winston James.*

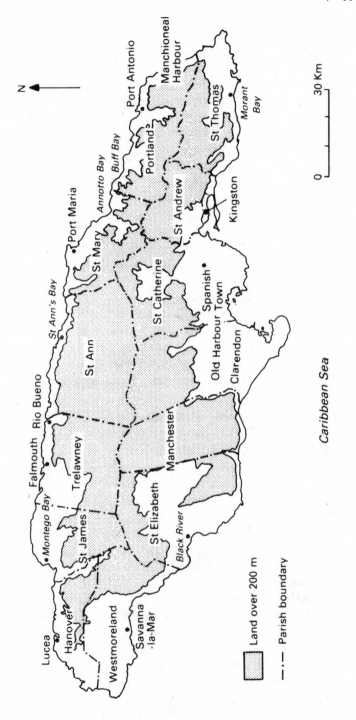

Jamaica and its parishes. *Courtesy of Winston James.*

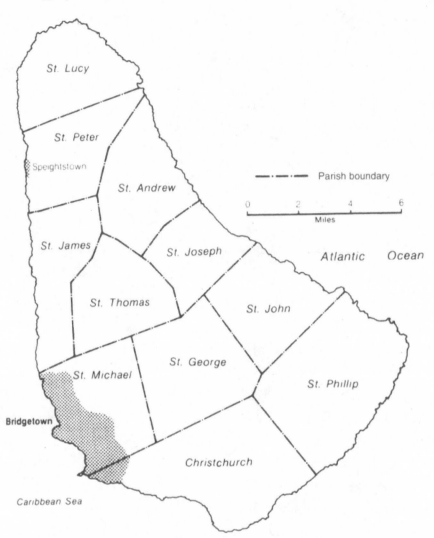

Barbados and its parishes. *Courtesy of Winston James.*

1

Origins of Migration: British West Indian Economy, Society, and the Lure of Emigration

On the living room wall of a woman who emigrated to Boston from Barbados in 1932 hangs a framed map of the island. Within this map are inscribed the words: "Even if you do not know where you are going, you know where you came from. So, Bridgetown [capital of Barbados], you will stay with me forever."[1] This statement sums up the necessity and purpose of this chapter, which reviews the premigration setting from which the immigrants came. This analysis is not a full history of the West Indies in the first half of the twentieth century. It merely seeks to identify and discuss those facets within the homeland society that are most germane for understanding the context within which migration occurred.

The British West Indies of the early twentieth century was a society of paradoxes. It contained impoverished colonies with severely malfunctioning economies, yet its economic potentials were in full view. With clearly defined indices of what it meant to be upper, middle, or lower class, it was a society with sharp distinctions between the classes, yet it contained tantalizing avenues for social mobility, foremost of which were education and emigration. It was a society in which race and color were strong determinants of social interaction, yet it was often touted as a plural society with parallel groups, which for the most part coexisted peacefully.

In this complex context of conflicting forces evolved one of the most fundamental characteristics of the society, encapsulated in the continuous and varied patterns of movements of its peoples within and outside the region. It is this mark, evident since the second half of the nineteenth century, that earned the West Indies the often-quoted reputation of "migration-oriented" society. No scholar investigates the West Indies without bringing up the migration tradition.[2] Furthermore, none explores that phenomenon without pointing to the centrality of economic forces in its creation and longevity. By 1900 almost all the British-controlled islands, already tied to a world economy, were plagued by a legion of problems: mono-cash-crop culture, outmoded agricultural systems, rudimentary manufacturing frameworks, exploitative foreign commercial activities which contributed little to local development, export of West Indian labor, and natural disasters in the forms of periodic hurricanes and a variety of crop diseases. The perennial structural malaise of the West Indian economic systems has been substantially researched by scholars from a variety of disciplines.[3] This analysis, therefore, will not rehash the arguments already advanced by existing studies about what was really wrong with the various island economies at specific periods. Instead, it is more useful to relate some of the experiences lived by the inhabitants affected by the economic woes, for these experiences were to shape in great measure the people's notions about class, status, emigration, and the image of living abroad.

No other symptoms of the economic malaise touched the lower classes as much as unemployment and low wages. Throughout the first four decades of the twentieth century, most of the British West Indian countries witnessed the continuous movement of people from the rural areas to fledgling urban, industrial areas in search of work, a trend clearly revealed by the censuses of 1911, 1921, and 1946. For example, the 1946 census showed that the population of Kingston had nearly doubled since the 1921 census, even though the general population of Jamaica only increased by half. Similarly in Barbados, the main urban centers of Bridgetown and St. Michael were reported to contain 39.65 percent of the population, an increase of more than 40 percent since the previous census of 1921. Georgetown, British Guiana, also reported an astounding urban population increase of 94 percent.[4]

While continuous waves of hopeful migrants continued to flow into the urban centers, industry and manufacturing remained rudimentary and too small to absorb the job seekers.[5] Although the majority were unskilled, there was a reasonable number of graduates of the industrial schools, where the men learned carpentry, mechanics, masonry, tailoring, cabinetmaking, shoemaking, and painting. The women were trained mostly as dressmakers or seamstresses.[6] But in the context of insufficient job opportunities, exploitative economic policies, and a negligible manufacturing sector, the acquisition of occupational skills was not the real issue. Skilled or unskilled, wages were generally low. For example, the average weekly earning of field workers between 1920 and 1935 was 17 shillings and 7 pence (17s.7d) for men and 14 shillings and 6 pence (14s.6d) for women. Domestic workers, the overwhelming majority of whom were women, earned between 2 shillings and 6 pence (2s.6d) and 5 shillings (5s) per week for anywhere from a ten- to thirteen-hour work day, usually six days a week.[7] In 1938, for nine to twelve hours a day, six days a week, male laborers earned 16s.6d, while the females received a much lesser rate of 7s.6d.[8] These wages were even more horrifying when contrasted with the cost of living, which was prohibitively high throughout the period under review.[9]

Renowned Trinidadian economic historian Eric Williams provides illuminating narratives that give practical meaning to these statistics, which are based on the colonial currency of the period. In the chapter on the condition of the Negro wage earner in his 1942 book *The Negro in the Caribbean,* Williams uses the more familiar units of dollar and cent to substantiate his thesis that the Negro in the Caribbean worked for the most pitiful wages. He weaves much of his discussion around food, the most basic of necessities for human existence. The following excerpts from his analysis vividly portray the situation in the British Caribbean of the 1930s:

> The Negro in the Caribbean, we emphasise, is primarily an agricultural laborer, working for pitifully low wages. . . . How much does he eat? The Negro cannot be adequately fed on a 25-cent-a-day wage for three days a week. The weekly budget of the Barbadian laborer is less than two dollars; of this food costs him seven cents a day.
>
> The laborer in Barbados is fed worse than a gaolbird [*sic*]; he cannot afford milk in his tea; say the planters, he does not like milk!
>
> The daily consumption of fresh milk in Jamaica's capital, with its 30,000 children of school age, is one-fifteenth quart per head; the Jamaica politicians say that the Negro prefers condensed milk. The average monthly consumption of fresh meat per head of population in Kingston, Jamaica, is barely one pound, and even this does not represent the true position, for the eaters of fresh beef are almost entirely confined to the middle and upper classes. The diet of the average worker can be classed at the best only as a maintenance diet, and there is no reason to doubt that many households live on the borderline of extreme poverty.[10]

Mainstream publications like the *Jamaica Daily Gleaner* did deal with issues of unemployment and poverty. But in the main, such newspapers were partial to the interests of the planter and merchant elites. For some of the most poignant demonstrations of the plight of the working class, one has to look at more radical publications like Marcus Garvey's *Blackman*[11] and *Plain Talk,* whose editor, Thaddeus Kitchener, was a return immigrant who had once lived in Boston. In 1935, a frustrated unemployed Kingston man wrote:

> Yes if a man can get nothing to do in his own island to buy his daily bread or to support his family, then I think him poverty [*sic*]. Take a man going out day by

day with his tool seeking work and getting none, coming back home to a home where his landlord is ready to give him notice if his rent is not paid. (*Plain Talk*, December 14, 1935)

What seemed like perpetual vassalage to the planter class in a post-emancipation West Indies was one of the most perplexing realities for those who still lived on plantations. One such person described the deplorable living conditions on the estates in the September 21, 1935, issue of *Plain Talk*: "the man, children and wife live in one room. During harvesting, as many as two men join them, while the planter still lives in his luxurious abode."

Although suffering was widespread among the working class in general, women were hit the hardest. Many of the contemporary observers from that class may not have known of the official statistics which revealed that unemployment was higher among women or that they were paid much less than men; yet they grasped the gender disparities nonetheless. A man, commenting on the predicament of working women in Spanish Town, Jamaica, wrote:

> It is a disgrace to see advantages taken of poor people. During crop time the poor women after working from Monday till Friday are compelled to work on Saturday. If they refuse they are told by those in authority that they can get no pay until next pay day. In the name of king and country what kind of health can our women keep when they have to wear one dress for two weeks, because they have no time to wash their own clothes. (*Plain Talk*, October 2, 1937)

Women in urban areas did not fare any better. Unemployment was so rife that women with at least an elementary school education and training in dressmaking visibly roamed the streets in search of work. This reality was so daunting to Adina Spence, a *Plain Talk* reader, that she wrote, "our accomplished women should all be transported to Africa, where it is said Queens and Princes shall come" (August 21, 1935).

The particular disadvantages faced by single women did not miss the attention of commentators, as shown by the following statement:

> As women we are facing hardship to the extreme; we who have children and absent fathers, we have to feed them and send them to school and pay weekly rents. How can we stand the strain, when for over four weeks or more, no work to get to carry on these routine expenditures ... Women needs [*sic*] help, especially those who are not carefully married. (*Plain Talk*, December 28, 1935)

Even children felt the enormity of the economic crisis. Not only were they deprived of some of the basics like sufficient food and adequate clothing, they were compelled to begin to contribute to the household income much too early and often at the expense of their education. Again, contemporaries recognized the adverse effects on the children, including the psychological ramifications. It was concern over such impact that prompted a woman to write to the paper drawing attention to the damaging effects of debt collection on children. They were routinely witnesses to encounters between their parents and irate landlords and storekeepers demanding payment. Moreover, many of the children were actively included in the devices of their parents and other adults to elude the collectors. The reader who wrote to the paper on the children's plight worried about the long-term consequences on the children's self-esteem and integrity (*Plain Talk*, April 24, 1937).

While papers like *Plain Talk* publicized the social and economic difficulties that plagued the working class, they were not the only conduits for venting frustration and disappointments. In fact, it was more common for people to write letters to relatives and friends living outside the Caribbean. Their letters revealed not only their desperation but also their ability to grasp and articulate the workings of the firmly entrenched socioeconomic power structures within which they lived. For example, Gladys Lewis of Christ Church, Barbados, lamenting the deplorable condition of her house, in 1939 wrote to her brother, Clairmont Lewis of Boston: "We are suffering here; it is perish time!"[12] Decades later, another relative was to write a similar letter, this time to Clairmont Lewis's daughter Elma Lewis. Olga Lewis emphasized continuity in their situation, maintaining that the social structures in Barbados had basically remained the same. "The only thing I got against Barbados," she declared, "is it is a place for the rich and the middle class, but as a poor man there is no or little survival. The only outlet for the poor man is to travel abroad."[13]

For the most part, the upper class either ignored the plight of the poor or failed to grasp the gravity of their predicament. Historical geographer Bonham Richardson, commenting on some historical documents on the white planter elite of early-twentieth-century Barbados, noted that the reports "reveal the arrogance, indifference, and superficiality with which many, probably most, of the white elite observed the lower classes of the island as people when they noticed them at all."[14] Indeed, when they did notice, a few of these nonchalant observers were compelled to remark on the hardship endured by the Black working class. For example, the daughter of a white planter wrote in a school essay in 1903:

> The Negroes who work on the estates live in little wooden huts along the roadsides, which consist of two rooms only . . . They eat wonderfully little, and will work from 7 in the morning till 12, without eating anything, and then they will eat a little rice or a biscuit, and work on till 5 in the evening, and they either have another frugal meal or sometimes go without.[15]

Thus, clearly, even by the admission of some members of the privileged class, the picture was bleak, horrendous, appalling, and desperate. But in the paradox that was the West Indian society, such a reality did not completely dampen spirits. Instead, if anything, it sharpened the resolve of the people to succeed along the lines drawn by the colonial system under which they lived. From their positions in the social fringes they grasped the indices which defined the middle and upper classes and aspired to the same markers—land, stable and salaried government employment, and even the opportunity to fully participate in such status-ascribing forms of recreation like cricket.[16] The optimism and ambition from the periphery almost matched the oppression and exploitation from the core. In fact, this fierce ambition was one of the hallmarks of the society. Malcolm J. Proudfoot, assessing the incessant movements of people in the Caribbean in the first half of the twentieth century, pointed out that "the West Indian peoples as a whole seem to have envisaged for themselves a much higher standard than has ever been contemplated, much less achieved by other tropical populations dependent on resources of a comparable kind."[17] Realistic or not, many West Indians of the early twentieth century saw upward social mobility attainable mainly through two avenues—education and emigration.

No one denied the importance of education for the development of the West Indian colonies; the debate was over the type of education most relevant for the economy and the people. The planter class, though weakened by the abolition of slavery, still clung to the vestiges of a plantation economy and therefore advocated a system of education for the Black West Indians that would ensure their competence as good agricultural workers. Often backed by the colonial government, the planter-merchant elite promoted such a system using euphemisms like "practical education," "respectable labour," and "honest toil." These terms, however, did not mask their real intention of creating a subservient, reliable labor force, suited for agriculture and related sectors. Actually, these proponents of agricultural education were unabashed about fostering their interests. In 1900 a West Indian agricultural conference was held in Barbados, with labor as one of the main themes. The participants, who included the heads of colonial education departments and school superintendents, were informed of the resolve of the archbishop of the West Indies that "peasant boys should be trained in an atmosphere favourable to agriculture . . . they should learn that tilling the soil and caring for crops is worthy of being studied by intelligent minds."[18] The Jamaica Imperial Association, founded in 1917 to "consider, discuss and deal with all matters which may affect the economic, social and commercial welfare and development of the colony," made no secret of the fact that one of its top priorities was educating an agricultural labor force.[19] In Barbados, a similar organization, the Barbados General Agricultural Society, sponsored contests and programs designed to create "excitement and a love for honest toil among agricultural laborers." Acknowledging that World War I hammered home the importance of the tropical colonies as potential providers of indispensable produce, in 1921 the colonial administration established the Imperial College of Tropical Agriculture in Trinidad to ensure the supply of well-trained agricultural workers.[20]

Additionally, outside of this kind of institutional advocacy, individuals from the elite continued to attempt to influence the molding of education. The *Gleaner,* for example, provided a comfortable forum for such planners by regularly publishing editorials and other pieces advancing the "planter style" education. A two-page contribution by one such advocate in the January 2, 1925, edition exemplified the practice. The author complained, "prima facie, one might have imagined that, from the economic point of view, Jamaica would have aimed at basing her educational system upon her economic requirements. But we have to admit that education has not between the years 1898 and 1924 had a very beneficial effect upon agricultural production." Lamenting the fact that most "Jamaican lads did not know how to plant bananas," he advanced a solution calling for the use of one of the parishes (districts) as an experimental center. There, only limited hours would be devoted to the three Rs (writing, reading, and arithmetic). Students would be exposed only to an elementary knowledge of geography and history, leaving the biggest portion of learning for "practical instruction in agriculture and allied trades." The girls, slated to be "suitable helpmates for the cultivators," would be instructed in the care of livestock, cooking, and dressmaking. Only a small percentage, this author concluded, should be allowed to pass on to office desks.

It was precisely this philosophy that guided the creation of the dual educational system which emerged in the West Indies after emancipation. The grammar school, accessible to the white upper class, mulattoes, the small emerging Black middle class, and the handful of working-class children awarded scholarships, operated a curriculum of academic subjects designed to prepare the students for leadership and careers in the professions. The much inferior elementary schooling, on the other hand, limited academic subjects and emphasized vocational training, aimed at producing, as a 1909 commission report declared, the "intelligent and industrious labourer and the mechanic or artisan."[21] As illustrated by its objectives and operation, this binary system was designed to produce leaders and subordinates along racial, color, and class lines already defined by the existing status quo, which itself was a legacy of slavery and colonialism.[22]

Though clearly largely driven by racial and class biases, the gendered ramifications of the educational system were discernible. Young women were encouraged to acquire vocational training in dressmaking, cooking, and housekeeping, and access to academic, secondary school education was severely limited.[23]

Even as it curtailed access to academic grammar schooling, the colonial administration, though not by design, confirmed the necessity of that kind of education for individual upward mobility. Elma Lewis recognized this conviction in her Barbadian immigrant mother: "My mother was very academically-oriented. She was not an educated woman, but that's what was most important to her."[24] Most West Indians envisaged opportunities for sound grammar schooling that would eventually lead to teaching, law, medicine, accountancy, public administration, and fulfilling careers in the civil service. While some seemed resigned to their exclusion from academic, professional paths, their resignation did not prevent them from envisioning their children in those arenas. This was why many looked upon their jobs as domestics, washerwomen, and laborers as springboards for the future of their children in fields completely different from and certainly far more elevated than their own. Their restlessness was glaring, often eliciting anger and panic from the elite, as the following observation demonstrates:

> Many boys even then [in spite of their vocational training] are manifestly unfitted for land work; and the girls would not be suitable helpmates for cultivators of the soil in the coming years. The inevitable result must be that both boys and girls would eventually think of the few larger towns or city of Kingston as the only places that might offer them suitable employment and failing this, the logical step would, of course, be emigration. (*Gleaner,* January 2, 1925)

By the beginning of the twentieth century, emigration as a prerequisite for success and social mobility had become an integral part of the West Indian psyche.[25] The practice of searching for higher wages beyond one's island, both within and outside the British West Indies, began to gain momentum as far back as the 1830s, right after emancipation. This search, deemed a temporary venture, assumed the return of the migrant with enough resources to vastly improve his or her standard of living and ultimately attain social mobility. This process, which Bonham Richardson calls "livelihood migration," continued for generations, becoming a tradition fully embedded in the economic and social tapestry of British West Indian societies.[26] While hardship and disappointment were realities faced by many migrants, most of the outcomes of livelihood migration fulfilled its objectives. The financial gains manifested themselves across the region. Remittances from kin and friends abroad were so important that for some they constituted the main source of income.[27] Many earners and recipients of migration money were able to take the biggest step toward prosperity in the colonial West Indian context—property ownership. They purchased land, much of which was former plantation estates now being parceled out and sold in two- to three-acre lots.[28] Another important marker of prosperity that the beneficiaries of migration anxiously sought was education, especially for their children. Even symbolic pointers of success in the form of clothing, house decorations, and newly derived speech accents made significant statements about the efficacy of livelihood migration.[29]

So, to use the common sociological model, the push and pull factors operated in tangible ways to stimulate emigration. The facilitators were also discernible, chief among which was the family. Financially, family members pooled resources to make the emigration of individuals possible. Many tickets were paid for with remittances sent by family members abroad. Renowned second-generation Barbadian writer Paule Marshall, for example, recalled how her late uncle's earnings in Panama paid for her mother's ticket to New York: "'Panama Money'—it was always spoken of with great reverence when I was a little girl."[30] By the 1920s, Panama was such a vital source of income that remittance from abroad, be it from Cuba, Costa Rica, or Venezuela, was simply dubbed "Panama Money."

Family support also came in non-monetary form. Perhaps the most valued non-monetary help, especially for women, was the caring for children of migrants by kin and friends. Child fostering, as this practice was known, was fully embedded in the workings of West Indian migration by 1920. The majority of West Indians who went to Boston, like migrants to other destinations, did not initially move with children. The children were left in the care of relatives—grandmothers, aunts, and cousins—and friends. This transfer of children upon emigration was usually not abrupt. As Douglas Midgett, who studied the system extensively, emphasizes, most of the children were likely to have grown up as part of a number of households, their interaction with adults extending to various categories of kin and non-kin. Sometimes it was the dissolution of conjugal unions that resulted in children being placed in new households. So the socialization of children was often undertaken by many people with whom they were in regular contact.[31] Of course, when fostering was used during emigration, the arrangement was always made with the understanding that the children and their parents would be reunited after a period of time, usually determined by the pace of the migrants' attainment of the objectives of migration. Although male family members may have expressed interest in the children's welfare and even rendered financial support, very seldom were men the principal "foster" caregivers. As anthropologist Isa Maria Soto emphasizes, when it came to this aspect of migration, women and children were the protagonists.[32]

Increased opportunities for transportation to desirable destinations also facilitated emigration. Since the late nineteenth century, ships carrying goods and mail, like the Royal Mail Steam Packet Company, had been transporting migrants within the Caribbean and to places like Panama and Costa Rica. By the twentieth century there were several such steamship companies, including the Atlantic Fruit Company, Caneo Company, Lanassa Company, and United Fruit Company. The United Fruit Company, by the outbreak of World War I, was undoubtedly the biggest connector of the Caribbean islands to the eastern seaboard of the United States and Canada. When the company introduced its passenger services it envisioned significant repercussions. This development, it believed, would help "publicize bananas, the production and sale of which was its main source of revenue."[33] But what it did not anticipate was how extension of its operations would directly enable the flow of Caribbean-born persons to North America. The American tourists who traveled to the West Indies on United Fruit ships not only contributed to a "wider awareness of banana as an important food item," as anticipated, they also flaunted what was interpreted as unlimited prospects in the United States. Additionally, prospective emigrants began to see real possibilities of finding their way to America. Of course, the passage was not cheap. Yet they reckoned that once they came up with the fare for steerage, there would eventually be a place for them in the United Fruit Company ships, which made the most frequent trips to the various West Indian ports like Kingston and Port Antonio, Jamaica. Even some who could not come up with the passage still entertained hopes of successfully stowing away at some point, while loading bananas and coconuts or working on the ships in other capacities.

As the foregoing overview of the British West Indies shows, in the first few decades of the twentieth century all the classic ingredients for migration seemed to be in place. There were economic problems, glaring demonstrations of the benefits of migration, vital family and community support, and the means to move out. These ingredients were clear to many, even those who eventually ended up not emigrating. What was not so clear was the challenges of adapting to new destinations that lay ahead. The emigrants lived in a milieu that enabled them to recognize the impetus and means to move out. What this move, especially to the United States, would involve in its entirety would be beyond their grasp. America's uniqueness, notably in terms of negotiating race, ethnicity, and immigration, would make the Caribbean American experience nothing less than a catharsis. As literary scholar Heather Hathaway points out, the act of migration "can leave one forever distanced and different from the land and people of one's origin, if also from the land of one's adoption."[34]

The next chapters reveal what eluded the migrants at the time of emigration: complex consequences of separation from homeland, family, and other community institutions (dislocation); reshaping of old identities, dealing with new, imposed ones, adjusting to new terms of work and status ascription (relocation); and the triumph, as it were, over displacement through the establishment of viable identities and institutions that enabled many of the immigrants and their children, as Hathaway would put it, to live within two worlds and not between these worlds (dislocation to dual location).[35] These processes, encapsulated in the "immigrant experience," were as profound as the forces that impelled the emigrants to move, but far less clear. The statement in Ms. Clara Williams' Barbados map seem to allude to a reality—the immigrants knew where they were coming from, but did they know where they were going?

2

Work and Housing in "Freedom's Birthplace"

In 1928, Amy Maud King, a dressmaker in Kingston, Jamaica, wrote to her sister in Boston expressing her strong desire to join her in America. She wrote: "I cannot wait to come to that good town, where I can get a good job, work hard, live well and give the children all the things I did not have."[1] This perception of vast, almost unlimited opportunities suggested by this letter was neither unique to its author nor to Black immigrants. Chinese immigrants who came to the West Coast in the 1840s envisioned it as Gam Saan, "Gold Mountain." Polish immigrants were convinced that by coming to America they would get their "bread with butter." Japanese immigrants of the last quarter of the nineteenth century and the early twentieth century imagined that in America "money grew on trees." And Russian Jews of the same period pictured America, a land much touted in their homeland, as a "Garden of Eden, the Golden land."[2]

Some prospective immigrants like the Italian man who declared "I didn't choose America, I chose New York"[3] had well-formulated ideas about specific destinations in the United States. In fact, according to immigration historian John Bodnar, "immigrants seldom left their homelands without knowing exactly where they wanted to go and how to get there."[4] Mrs. King, quoted in the opening of this chapter, was one of the West Indians who fell into that category. While her expectations were geared more toward Boston's economic possibilities, many of the prospective West Indian emigrants who expressly chose Boston were impelled by its educational and cultural climate. During the early twentieth century many of the young people of the British Caribbean aspired to go to Oxford or Cambridge, but only a select few actually had the opportunity to study and live in Britain before the 1940s. Therefore, from reports which filtered into the West Indies about Boston's genteel character, conferred by long Yankee traditions, many concluded that that New England city was in fact the next best thing to England.

As the Athens of America, it provided vast opportunities for education. This assessment may have contributed to W. A. Domingo's decision to make Boston his first destination in the United States, projecting that it would fit into his plans to study medicine. The cultural potential of that city was definitely instrumental in luring Clairmont Lewis from Barbados. He admitted that given his goals and aspirations related to high culture, Boston was the "right American city." In several speeches and letters, he proudly highlighted the fact that he took his wife and children to concerts and lecture halls. His stepson, Darnley Corbin, confirmed this as he later recalled that "every Sunday afternoon they [his parents] took me to Symphony Hall."[5] However, from the caveat reaching the West Indies that it was enough to "merely breathe the Yankee air,"[6] some of the emigrants may have anticipated the difficulty of gaining full access to the coveted Yankee institutions.

So there is no doubt that some West Indians had prior information about Boston and consciously chose to move there in the early decades of the twentieth century. However, it is also true that many knew little or nothing about the city prior to their arrival in the United States. They merely followed the routes of the passenger steamers, especially those of the United Fruit Company, headquartered in Boston. The *Passenger Lists* of the United States Immigration Services show that more than two-thirds of the English-speaking West Indians who disembarked in Boston from Port Antonio and Kingston, Jamaica; Bridgetown, Barbados; and Limon, Costa Rica, gave some other city, particularly New York, as their intended final destination. Many changed their plans, usually after either landing employment or hooking up with family (however distant) and fellow townsfolk. Furthermore, as already noted in the introduction to this study, substantial numbers came to Boston as step migrants from their first American homes in New York, Connecticut, Rhode Island, New Jersey, and even Nova Scotia and New Brunswick, Canada. These migrants most probably did not initially choose Boston—they chose North America.

The extent of specificity on destination aside, the West Indians who settled in Boston invariably came to formulate ideas about the possibilities for economic advancement and overall success. They envisioned plentiful jobs, good wages, occupational advancement, and decent housing,[7] all reasonable expectations. For one thing, like most immigrants, they constituted a select group of highly motivated, physically vigorous, and psychologically aggressive individuals. As many as 80 percent of the West Indians arriving in Boston between 1910 and 1950 were working-age adults between twenty and forty-five. At least 40 percent of these were skilled. More than 80 percent of the skilled women reported their occupation as dressmaking; 15 percent were hairdressers and 5 percent said they were cooks. The unskilled women put down domestic or housewife as their occupation. Some 60 percent of the men reported premigration occupations in carpentry, tailoring, painting, shoemaking, bricklaying, and masonry.[8] The fact that the majority had at least an elementary school education and could read and write English further convinced them of their readiness to function well in the American labor market.[9]

So, most of the immigrants could and did calculate the advantages of their premigration backgrounds. How the structural forces within the Boston and American societies would interplay with their own agency was more elusive. Even with their skills, resolve, and ambition, they had to operate within a society shaped by certain forces beyond their control. Two of the most potent of these that were to prove crucial in the economic and social development of West Indians in Boston were race and ethnicity. Focusing on work and housing, two prerequisite arenas for understanding immigrant adaptation, this chapter will provide insights into how these two forces worked to position the West Indian foreigners squarely within Black Boston.

Before attempting to evaluate how the Black immigrants fared, it is necessary to first have some insights into what Boston had to offer. Although not as big as the more familiar New York City, by the time West Indians began to arrive, Boston already had a long history as one of America's major cities and was expanding. The population was 561,000 in 1900 and rose to 781,000 by the close of the 1920s. Foreign-born people and people of foreign-born parentage constituted at least 70 percent of the total population. The Black population was, however, relatively small. In 1910, the city had only a little over 11,000 Blacks, a mere 2 percent of the total population. Growth was still slow by the 1940s, when their number stood at 23,000. The most rapid growth of the first half of the century came in the last decade, when the Black population mushroomed to 40,000 by 1950.[10] As already noted in the introduction, West Indians were always a small segment of Boston's Blacks, constituting only 5 percent of the Black population in 1910 and never rising above 12 percent in the first half of the twentieth century.

Like the expanding population, the economy was robust. One of the busiest ports in the nation, Boston prospered in maritime trade and manufacturing. The waterfront, one of the first sights taken in by the disembarking West Indian migrants, provided a vivid imagery of the city's prosperity. The bustling Boston harbor was divided into four major shipping districts: East Boston, the largest, with fifty-one piers; Atlantic Avenue, the oldest, with several wharves dating back to the Revolutionary era; South Boston, with eleven wharves; and Charlestown, which had twenty-three wharves, including those of the United States Navy Yard. All these docks were well-served by efficient railroad connections: the Boston-Maine, connecting New England and some parts of eastern Canada; the New York–New Haven–Hartford line; and the Boston–Albany.[11]

Endowed with this kind of infrastructure for transporting both raw materials and finished products, manufacturing thrived for much of the first half of the twentieth century. The leather and footwear industry was one of the most lucrative sectors. There were shoe factories and unfinished leather warehouses around the city, and a tannery in Roxbury.[12] Small candy factories in the North End and the larger chocolate manufacturing establishments of Lower Mills and the banks of the Neponset River in Dorchester underscored the vitality of the confectionery industry. Although dwindling by the 1940s, the textile industry was for a long period one of the city's significant manufacturing sectors. Several textile mills were located in East Boston, a strategic location for shipping. The garment industry, though not nearly as expansive as that of New York in the same period, was also one of the vibrant sectors of the economy. Factories, which made both men's and women's clothing, dotting Kneeland Street in the business district, bore testimony to this fact.[13]

Although Boston did not fully shift from a manufacturing to a service economy until the second half of the twentieth century, the latter was already a major employment arena by the early 1900s. Hotels, restaurants, schools, and hospitals provided various job opportunities; so did department stores and construction projects in the expanding city. The affluent neighborhoods of Brookline, Newton, Wellesley, and sections of Roxbury and Dorchester also contained opportunities for a variety of household occupations. Undoubtedly, therefore, before the Depression, Boston was among the most prosperous U.S. cities. As Wilfred W. Lufkin, collector of the port, proudly announced, "Maritime life was good. Imports doubled. Boston was second only to New York in imports and second only to New York in tourist trade."[14]

From this overview, it is clear that Boston had the kind of economy that was attractive to immigrants in search of progress. And, indeed, it was an important immigrant-receiving center during the first decades of the twentieth century. The newspapers, from the *Boston Globe* to the *Boston Guardian* and the *Boston Chronicle,* frequently reported on the arrival of immigrants and their eagerness to enter the labor force. The mere existence of plentiful jobs, especially before and after the Great Depression, however, does not tell the whole story. The criteria used to determine access to and remuneration for work are crucial for understanding how the society worked and how the immigrants were affected. Some of the same newspapers which publicized the numerous job opportunities also exposed, willfully or inadvertently, the realities of occupational closure. The classified section of the *Boston Globe*, the leading mainstream newspaper, for example, overtly displayed stratification in employment. These are samples of how advertisements were typically coined. "Colored man needed to work in tailor store as porter" (January 6, 1910). "Able-bodied Hungarian-speaking man wanted to act as assistant to foreman." "Supervisor needed, white man only." "Polish, non-Hebrew worker needed" (January 8, 1918). "Colored woman wanted for shining shoes" (October 4, 1918). "Catholic Collector Wanted" (January 7, 1940). "Girl Elevator Operator. Will train, neat, well-mannered white girl, age 18 to 28, size 12 to 16 . . ." (January 3, 1945).

These examples clearly underscore the variables at play: race, ethnicity, religion, gender, and, not to be ignored, physical stature. The racial and ethnic occupational niches carved by these categorizations were to define the society just as much as its Puritan and abolitionist traditions. For Blacks, their occupational niche, as the advertisements begin to suggest, contained the lowest rungs. These were mostly unskilled, menial positions like janitor, domestic, laborer, jobs which by 1930 were known as the traditional Negro jobs.[15] Occupational marginalization was blatant, constituting one of the most formidable obstacles for the city's Blacks. It was a struggle to move from menial jobs to visible, respectable positions, so much so that any advancement in employment was big news. For example, in 1933 the Black community reacted attentively to the news that the First National Stores chain was embarking on an "experiment of preparing Negro managers." Similarly, in 1935 the leaders of the community called for a show of support for the Tremont Street branch of Boston Electric and the First National Stores, both of which appointed their first African American managers. And in December 1936, the community livened up again to the news that five African American women had been hired as part-time clerks at F. W. Woolworth 5 and 10 Cents Store at the Washington Street, Roxbury branch.[16]

As well received as these strides were, they were qualified successes. The basic structure of marginalization and closure continued. In 1939 the *Boston Guardian* declared: "To encourage colored people to come here for employment is wrong . . . Thousands of colored people come to New England with hopes of settling here; but very few are able to stay and develop into the typical new England family."[17] The *Chronicle* joined the *Guardian* in expressing the Black community's dismay that First National Stores was caving in to pressure and seemed to be less committed to its earlier promise to create more access for Blacks in managerial positions. Black men in particular constantly registered their frustration over occupational closure. For example, in July and August 1943, they protested their treatment by the city's transit system. The occasion was the hiring of, according to them, "eight inexperienced, pretty white girls" to serve as subway and street conductors on the Boston El. The *Guardian* of August 7, 1943, reporting on the men's crusade, lamented that "the women were hired in spite of the knowledge that strong, able colored men have been engulfed in broompushing, manual labor obscurity, serving the company through hard years of loyalty with hopes for just such a reward as this." The account concluded, "It is undoubtedly easier for these young white girls to push a longhandled broom than to wrestle with heavy car doors and unruly passengers." Although the sexist undertones of this pronouncement cannot be missed, the feeling of relegation and near invisibility of the Black males is also conveyed.

Race and racism were, thus, clearly potent in employment. The two Black publications are replete with accounts of the various manifestations of racial discrimination. Investigations conducted by the journalists and letters written to the editors revealed that White supervisors and foremen, from American-born to Canadian, Irish, Polish, and Italian, frequently refused to work with Black workers, resulting in the creation of lower-paid, all-Black work shifts or the blatant rejection of Black applicants. This was especially the case during the Great Depression.[18] In April 1933, the Inter-Racial Conference, led by George W. Goodman, executive secretary of the Boston branch of the Urban League, reported that approximately 11,000 Negroes were gainfully employed, of which more than 60 percent were in domestic and personal service, the lowest-paid occupations.[19] Responding to this report, some White employers countered that Blacks found themselves in that predicament because of the extreme economic challenges of the era.[20] But even before the Depression, Boston's African American leaders had been articulating their interpretation of the causes of the occupational degradation of members of their race. They saw one underlying reason from which all the others flowed—the belief by Whites of the innate inferiority of Black people. In 1910 they were presented with an opportunity that buttressed their argument. Mayoral candidate James J. Storrow, a Boston Brahmin, had commented that he would not appoint a colored teacher, no matter how well qualified, in a public school with more than fifty White children. When asked why, he simply said, "the time has not yet come for it." At a mass meeting of Black citizens at St. Paul's Baptist Church, the leaders used this incident to analyze the root of some of the occupational disparity afflicting their community.[21]

Thus far, this analysis has been discussing the plight of Blacks in a general sense by focusing on the Black community at large. For the purposes of this chapter, it must now turn more specifically to West Indian immigrants, the subject of this study. How did this general context affect them? Simply put, though foreigners, as Blacks in America they could not dodge the obstacles. By their own admission, most of them who arrived with skills were unable to get jobs in their trades because of the racist barriers.[22] Most of the men found work as janitors and laborers in various establishments, especially on the docks, where they hauled cargo to and from the very sugar and banana boats which had transported them to Boston. Along with American-born Black men they also worked as doormen and porters, messengers and waiters in downtown hotels like Bellevue and Parker House and for the Pullman Company, which at the time was known nationally as the largest employer of Blacks.[23]

The second generation recounted the disappointment that met their parents upon beginning their new lives in Boston. Mel King, whose parents emigrated from Barbados and Guyana, recalled the frustration of his father and other skilled West Indian men forced to settle for menial tasks as laborers on the docks. Elma Lewis, whose parents emigrated from Barbados, recalled that her father was turned into a "bitter, angry and frustrated man" because he was "far more capable than what he was doing." Similarly, her mother, who always considered herself a lady, was crushed because as a domestic in Boston she had to clean someone else's house. Clairmont Lewis had some training in general contracting when he moved to Boston from Christ Church, Barbados, in 1916. From this time until he retired in 1972, he found work mostly only as a janitor and laborer for a number of Boston companies.[24] His wife, Edwardine Jordan Corbin Lewis, moved to Boston in 1915 soon after some upheaval in her life. Her first husband, Athelston Corbin, described as a "scion" from a prominent Barbadian family doing business in Trinidad, had just died. She moved back to Barbados from Trinidad briefly before she emigrated with a cousin to Boston.[25] In her new home, the change was drastic. Almost overnight, she was transformed from a housewife with her own maid to a full-time domestic servant. David Nelson, whose parents emigrated from Jamaica, acknowledged that his father was one of the few exceptions. He was able to get a job as a tailor at the Charlestown Navy Yard only because prior to emigrating he had done the same job in one of the U.S. Army bases in the Caribbean. Previous contacts saw him through the door to skilled work in his new home. Very few had such premigration contacts.[26]

While Black workers were described in general terms merely as Negroes, making it difficult to identify precisely the number of Black immigrants who acquired skilled jobs, it seems safe to conclude that securing such jobs was rare. This sentiment was expressed by an anonymous Jamaican reader who wrote a letter to the *Chronicle* published on April 29, 1933, describing Black access to skilled jobs largely as a "Chance affair." The most propitious period seemed to have been the war years when, in addition to increased production stimulated by war demands, the departure of White workers to the military created openings for Blacks. The *Guardian* and the *Chronicle* testified to this occupational entry. Various issues of 1943 and 1944 contain constant reminders and appeals to the Black community to seize the advantage of the newly created access to jobs, both skilled and unskilled, in the defense industry. From anecdotal evidence, it is clear that the West Indians, like other Blacks, heeded the call and acknowledged the advancement conferred by such opportunities. For example, a Montserratian man, recalling his father's immense pride at working at the navy yard, noted: "My father and the other few who worked in the yard used to hold their heads high. They knew they were more progressive than the load carriers and janitors. After all, as tailors they sewed the uniforms that the soldiers fought in."[27]

The Great Depression years, on the other hand, further reduced the limited opportunities open to Blacks. The Black foreigners were not exempt from the distinct hardships encountered by Blacks and other racial minorities throughout the country. "Last to be hired and first to be fired" applied to Black workers originally from the West Indies and those from Georgia, Tennessee, and Boston. For example, in 1933, the manager of Waldorf System, Inc., wrote a testimonial letter for Clairmont Lewis in which he touted Lewis, who had worked at his establishment for eight years as a janitor and fireman: " ... he has always been punctual and dependable and never lost a day ... We have dismissed him as a matter of necessary economics, his work now being done by one of our mechanics who under existing conditions has time to spare."[28] Although the letter does not allude to race, given the prevailing occupational structure, in which skilled positions in such companies were closed to Blacks, the mechanic mentioned in the letter was most likely a White man.

Like their male counterparts, West Indian women felt the insidious effects of occupational closure. Throughout the first half of the century they could not find employment as sales clerks in retail stores. They could not infiltrate the European-dominated candy, textile, and shoe factories. Even those that came as accomplished seamstresses could not get work in dressmaking shops and other areas of the garment industry. Domestic employment was where they found their niche. The overwhelming majority of West Indian women worked as maids, cooks, child care givers, and general housekeepers in private homes throughout the greater Boston area, but particularly in White Jewish neighborhoods in Roxbury, Dorchester, Mattapan, and Newton.

Although at the turn of the nineteenth century and early 1900s, Irish women had made significant inroads in domestic work,[29] Boston's Black female population presented stiff competition. By the period of significant West Indian migration to Boston, domestic service was recognized as one of the so-called traditional Black occupations. Little wonder, then, that entry into that sphere was relatively easy for the Black foreign women. Additionally, coming from English-speaking colonies, they understood and spoke English. Most were not fluent, for their English was in reality broken, pidgin English or patois. Whatever the name and deficiencies, their variant of English was understandable enough that they could easily communicate with the families that they worked for, which was usually a problem for non-English-speaking European female immigrants.

By the 1940s, West Indian women had gained a reputation as efficient, reliable domestics. This accomplishment was emphasized by many of the West Indian leaders, including Mrs. Hilda Wiltshire, president of the Boston branch of Marcus Garvey's Universal Negro Improvement Association, and Mrs. Gertrude Chandler, secretary of the Jamaica Associates and regional vice president of the Northeast Federation of Colored Women's Clubs.[30] As news spread back home of the need for West Indian domestics, prospective emigrants prepared themselves to enter the field.[31] Soon a chain developed, as women already in Boston recommended their family and friends to prospective employers. Many anecdotal accounts substantiate this development. For example, Victor Bynoe, who emigrated to Boston in 1928 from Barbados at age fourteen, recounted how his mother, Edna Bynoe, who was a hairdresser prior to emigrating, adapted to her new career as a domestic. Not only was she excellent in her domestic service job, which she did in addition to styling hair at home, she also served as a kind of employment broker. Bynoe remembers that she assisted countless newly arrived hometown women in securing domestic jobs.[32] Many of these women came to embrace the conviction that although American-born Black women were prominently represented in that occupational sphere, the employers manifested a preference for their service. There is evidence that White employers sometimes assured them of their edge over American-born Black domestics. This Montserratian woman's account was not uncommon: "The white family that I worked for actually pestered me to arrange for women from the islands to work for their family and friends, because they realized that we work better."[33] Some African American women complained that they were let go and West Indian women hired in their place. For example, Gertrude Warner, who came to Boston from South Carolina in 1932, alleged that she was a victim of this trend. She claimed that she had five friends, also from the South, who lost their jobs when their employers found West Indian help.[34] Although there is no record of an explosive, well-publicized conflict, this situation caused some intragroup rivalry. As the native-born African American women explained it, some White employers tried to plant seeds of discord in the Black female population by pitting West Indian women against their American-born counterparts, especially the southerners. White employers, they claimed, described them as lazy, dishonest, unreliable, and unwilling to work as domestics.[35] It was precisely this kind of notion that Samuel W. Warren, director of the Boston Employment Bureau, and Everett L. Hanna, director of the State Employment Bureau, echoed in 1936 when they declared that "American-born girls were too proud to work at domestic employment." However, not considering Black immigrant women, Warren and Hanna resolved that if the situation continued, they would find it necessary to bring girls from England and Ireland to fill the positions.[36] Contrary to their charge, however, many Black American women were willing to do domestic work, especially because they realized that that occupation was the one most accessible to them. Pronouncements such as this one contributed to African American women's resentment of foreign workers, regardless of race or nationality, because they believed they took their jobs.[37]

Although the negative pronouncements against American-born Black women were seldom substantiated, preference for foreign domestic workers was sometimes openly professed by the White employers. The following account is illustrative of this trend:

> For a long time, kids would proudly announce that their help was from another country—Ireland, Jamaica. Not that they [the foreign workers] were not good, they were the best. But there was also the status thing. We liked the idea that our help was imported. In fact, my mother once told me that there was actually a competition among the many families on my street [Humbolt Avenue, Roxbury] over where their help came from.[38]

Undoubtedly, then, there was some preference for foreign help, which worked to the advantage of West Indian women but also contributed to intragroup friction. Nevertheless, despite the successes West Indian women registered within this sphere, the fact remained that occupational closure was very much a reality for them as it was for the men.

Occupational closure, due to language barriers or discrimination, in some cases has been known to stimulate what sociologist M. S. Stuart termed an "economic detour."[39] This involves the shift of members of a group from the wage-labor sector to self-employment. This was the case with the Chinese, who entered and thrived in the laundry and restaurant businesses by the early twentieth century, or more recently with the Koreans in retail business. Adalberto Aguirre, Jr. and Jonathan H. Turner expound further on some of the dynamics of economic detour. They explain that members of such marginalized groups consciously seek enterprises that are least appealing to the majority group and discover economic niches within which they prosper. According to these sociologists, this phenomenon, which they call "marginal adaptation," tends to be successful when the minority population is small and does not enter areas dominated by the majority.[40]

So did Boston's West Indians qualify as a small minority that made an economic detour into self-employment? Interestingly, as early as the 1920s, West Indians in America were being touted for their entrepreneurship. Drawing parallels with Jewish entrepreneurs, some New Yorkers even labeled them "Black Jews" and "Jewmaicans." There was also a saying in Harlem that "when a West Indian got ten cents above a beggar he opened a business." By 1950 the propensity of West Indians to operate small businesses had come to be identified as one of the main positive characteristics of that group that gave it an edge over American-born Blacks.[41] But almost all the references to support this contention came from New York. There was virtually nothing about West Indian businesses in Boston. More recent scholarship on West Indians in New York has questioned the accuracy of the early-twentieth-century depiction of West Indian participation in businesses. For example, Irma Watkins-Owens urges that "black ethnic entrepreneurship in Harlem must be framed in the larger context of the control of Harlem's businesses by white, often ethnic, entrepreneurs."[42] But while the picture of New York was distorted in those early interpretations, the absence of Boston in those accounts more accurately portrayed a reality. During that time Black entrepreneurship in that city was generally dismal. Up to the 1920s Black leaders directed much of their attention on pressuring White establishments to hire Blacks in more respectable positions. But by the mid-1930s they had changed their tune, campaigning for the development of Black entrepreneurship. This campaign culminated in the formation of the Greater Boston Negro Trade Association in May 1938. Its main objectives were to enhance existing Black businesses and assist in the launching of new ones. The efforts of this organization seemed to have borne fruits because by 1940 the city's Black businesses apparently had increased appreciably.[43] In 1940, of the thirty Black businesses surveyed by the *Chronicle*, only two were owned by West Indians. The overwhelming majority were owned by Black Americans who had migrated mainly from North and South Carolina, Virginia, Georgia, Ohio, Pennsylvania, Illinois, and Michigan. These businesses were mostly service enterprises designed to cater to the needs of a Black clientele. There were three main Black-owned grocery stores in the South End—Bennett Cooperative Grocery on Camden Street and Columbus Avenue, owned by Charles Bennett, a migrant from North Carolina; B. J. Benn Grocery on Shawmut Avenue, owned by B. J. Benn, also from the South; and the largest Black-owned grocery store, owned by Jesse Goode, originally from North Carolina. The big Black-owned real estate companies were Roberson Real Estate, whose proprietor, Charles Roberson, was from Louisiana, and E. Z. Roundtree Real Estate Company, owned by South Carolina native Eugene Roundtree. Geneva Arrington from Philadelphia owned and managed Arrington Hairdressing Salon and Beauty School. Napoleon Chisolm, originally from Rock Hill, South Carolina, established Chisolm's Funeral Chapel. And Thomas Photographic Studio was owned by a husband and wife team from South Carolina. This sample of Black business in Boston in the first half of the twentieth century provides sufficient insights into the types of businesses and the origin of their founders and operators, who were clearly mostly American-born Blacks. It is thus safe to conclude that only a small number of West Indians were self-employed. Included in this were West Indian women who operated boarding houses, especially on Tremont Street in the South End. In the 1920s and 1930s the most prominent West Indian businessman was Benjamin S. Abbot from Jamaica, who operated a home and window cleaning company in Newton.

Why this weak presence of West Indians in entrepreneurship? Aguirre and Turner, who point out that minority groups can find lucrative economic niches in the margins, also postulate that African Americans and Chicanos have been unable to find specialized niches because "their numbers are simply too great."[44] As this chapter has already shown, although West Indians were foreigners, as Blacks they operated largely within the economic parameters of African Americans. It is thus reasonable to consider the possibility that their absorption into the larger Black group stifled their self-employment opportunities. But while this may be partially responsible for the low rate of entrepreneurship, much of the explanation lay in the immigrants' premigration background.

As the previous chapter explained, by 1900 West Indians had been socialized to recognize certain indices of success and mobility, such as education, stable and salaried civil service jobs, and land/home ownership. The Black majority aspired to these markers, which some had begun to acquire by the 1920s. Interestingly, the phenomena of economic detour and marginal adaptation were exemplified in the colonial West Indian societies by the so-called intermediary groups of Chinese, Indians, Jews, and Lebanese.

As "middleman minorities,"[45] these immigrant groups moved into and controlled niches which the powerful, dominant White planter class did not occupy and from which the native Black majority was discouraged.

As social scientist Carl Stone explains in his study "Race and Economic Power in Jamaica," by 1938 a hierarchical economic structure was discernible in Jamaica and other West Indian societies. Moreover, this structure displayed some clearly defined racial, color, and ethnic lines. The White population, though declining in status, was still the dominant group and still controlled much of the land and large-scale plantation agriculture. The intermediary ethnic groups—mulattoes, Chinese, Lebanese, and Jews—controlled the commercial sector. Lebanese and Jewish merchants virtually monopolized import and export commerce, while the Chinese became well-known for their visibility in the small retail grocery trade.[46] Blacks, the numerical majority according to Stone, were discouraged from entering commerce and instead were limited largely to small peasant farming, unskilled wage work, and limited artisan occupations. Occupational mobility, however, was not non-existent for this group, because, as Stone himself acknowledges, by 1938 a few Blacks had succeeded in making inroads into professional occupations such as teaching, nursing and drug dispensing, and non-manual positions such as clerks and policemen.[47]

Such, then, was the socioeconomic context from which Boston's West Indians came in the first half of the twentieth century. So in Boston, self-employment was not particularly high on their list of migration goals. Traditionally, in the homeland they did not look to that avenue for individual or group progress. After all, small business was for the Chinese and the Indians, whose non-English, non-Christian backgrounds forced them into that realm. Still using familiar yardsticks from home, the Black immigrants hoped to acquire success and middle-class status through wage employment and education of their children. The negligible involvement in small business in Boston, therefore, should not be seen as an anomaly or an aberration.

Like employment, housing was crucial to the immigrants' adaptation. Similar structural forces within the Boston society were to interplay with their premigration experiences, aspirations, and agency to shape their residential patterns. When the West Indians arrived they met a city of neighborhoods. Each major ethnic/immigrant group by the early 1900s was establishing itself in specific areas of the city and basically claiming these as their turf. Previously, in the nineteenth century, the North End and West End were areas where diverse groups of new European arrivals congregated. By 1920, however, the North End had begun to be more exclusively Italian. Other Italian enclaves were also created in East Boston. The Irish also carved neighborhoods in South Boston, Charlestown, sections of Roxbury, and north Dorchester. Jews, like the Irish, had also moved from the North End and West End to Roxbury, Dorchester, and Mattapan.[48] The Black population, though extremely small (only 2 percent in 1910), exhibited similar features. Like the Caucasian majority, more than three-quarters of Boston's Blacks were not native to the city. In the first three decades of the twentieth century, two Black migrations occurred simultaneously—the bigger, more noticeable migration of American Blacks from the South[49] and the less visible arrival of those West Indians who are the subject of this study. Also, like the White ethnic groups, the Black population changed residence. For much of the nineteenth century Blacks clustered along the northwestern slope of Beacon Hill down to Cambridge Street in the West End. At the turn of the century, overwhelmed by the influx of European immigrants, they began to move to the South End.

Between 1900 and 1950 the "Black section" of the city evolved into three main subsections. First, there was the South End, with its center at the intersection of Massachusetts Avenue and Columbus Avenue. Also known as Crosstown, this was where most of the Black entertainment concerns—ballrooms, lounges, and night clubs—were located. The Intown section of Black Boston was an area which included Lower Roxbury and the outer South End. Blacks dominated whole side streets like Hammond, Flagg, Kendall, Ball, and Davenport. Located on the major thoroughfares like Columbus Avenue and Tremont Street were Black service businesses such as doctors' and lawyers' offices, undertakers, barbers and hairdressing salons, and the two most renowned restaurants among the Black population during this period—Slades' Barbecue and Estelle's. The third subsection did not emerge until around the close of the 1930s. This area, sometimes called the Hill, was Humboldt Avenue, Walnut Avenue, and side streets. This area had been a staunch Jewish neighborhood until the 1930s when Blacks began to move into the big Victorian houses they had just purchased from the vacating Jews. To move to this neighborhood from the South End and Lower Roxbury, these Blacks actually had to bypass an Irish community, or as Anthony Lukas puts it, they "leapfrogged over a resistant Irish community."[50]

This racial/ethnic demographic structure was a viable one that in some ways predetermined some of the contours of West Indian history in Boston. So how did the Black immigrants fit into this city of ethnic neighborhoods? First, an important fact worth noting is that the West Indians never forged a visible, clearly defined enclave. For one thing, their relatively small numbers precluded such a development. Nevertheless, although they were dispersed throughout Massachusetts in places like Plymouth, New Bedford, and Worcester, they were clearly concentrated in Greater Boston. One of the earliest areas of West Indian settlement was across the Charles River in Cambridge. Attracted by the availability of menial jobs in the early 1900s, many West Indians rented apartments in houses around Central Square on Massachusetts Avenue, Western Avenue, and side streets. In 1920 it was estimated that 5 percent of the Blacks living in Cambridge were West Indians.[51]

Even more popular as an area for West Indian settlement was the South End, which by 1930 had the highest concentration of the Black foreigners. The reasons for the attraction to this neighborhood were clear. Up until the 1940s that section of Boston was not a Black neighborhood per se, but more of an immigrant haven. Second-generation West Indian Mel King described it in that period as a multiracial and multiethnic neighborhood with more than thirty-six racial, ethnic, and cultural groups.[52] King's observation is buttressed by William Leahy in his essay on the population of Boston in the first few decades of the twentieth century. He points out that the South End, mainly because of its proximity to the business district, was very attractive to all groups of immigrants. Consequently the population was heterogenous, "holding Greeks, Syrians, Poles, Lithuanians, Portuguese and Negroes."[53] Still, within this maze of multiple ethnicities, West Indians found their favorite pockets. They clustered along Massachusetts Avenue (starting roughly from Huntington Avenue, southward to Harrison Avenue), Columbus Avenue, and Tremont Street. They also lived on the side streets of these main streets, on streets like Northampton Avenue, Shawmut Avenue, Windsor Street, Worcester Street, Yarmouth Street, and Dartmouth Street.[54]

By the late 1930s West Indians were expanding with the general Black population beyond the South End into Roxbury proper. They rented and bought houses on Humboldt and Walnut Avenues and side streets, areas that were previously Jewish neighborhoods.[55] By 1950, the period when this study ends, the Black population had expanded into Dorchester and was poised for the penetration and eventual takeover of the very Jewish Blue Hill Avenue.[56]

As with almost every immigrant group, for West Indians, proximity to the workplace was a compelling factor which determined residence. The South End was conveniently located for the men, most of whom worked as laborers in the nearby docks and as janitors, messengers, and haulers in commercial establishments downtown. The women, too, found the neighborhood suitable for their employment needs. Some worked as cleaners and elevator operators downtown. The majority, who worked as domestics, still found that Brookline, Roxbury, Dorchester, and Mattapan, where most of the private homes where they worked were located, were easily accessible from where they lived. An important attraction of the area was its effective transportation network. The subway, under Tremont Street, had been in operation since 1898 and was one of the lifelines of the neighborhood.

The availability of attainable occupations, reliable transportation networks, and relatively cheap housing drew West Indians to the areas of the city which, for the same reasons, were clearly evolving as the "Black belt" of Boston. Therefore, in addition to the general immigrant adaptation issues that dictated choice of residence, Boston's West Indians had to face the insidious interplay between race and spatial organization. Demographic restrictions on Blacks largely because of their race were recognizable. The *Boston Guardian* declared in an editorial on July 27 1942, "Colored people cannot live where they please. The different white populations push us away and decide where we can stay." As some racist White realtors devised various tactics to prevent Whites from renting or selling to Blacks, some Black realtors made it their crusade to thwart their efforts. For example, renowned real estate entrepreneur Eugene Roundtree, owner of E. Z. Roundtree Real Estate Company, boasted in 1942: "Being well thought of by many influential whites, I capitalized on their friendship for the benefit of my people. I had them at heart and induced the whites to sell to them."[57] Little wonder, then, that Roundtree became a familiar name in the West Indian community. A regular reference in the West Indian *Chronicle* publication, Roundtree, as Barbadian American Victor Bynoe explained, came to be the man to see if one wanted to rent or buy a house. The immigrants were advised against wasting their time with White agents or racist owners.[58]

It was not only the adult first-generation immigrants, who dealt directly with agents and landlords, who grasped the reality of the workings of race and space. Some of the children who were privy to some of the negotiations and reactions got some insights as well. For example, David Nelson poignantly described his recollections:

> All my life growing up, I remember our landlords were all Jewish. Maybe because they were also isolated they were willing to rent and sell to Blacks. Because of their actions, anyway, Blacks were able to break into some all White areas; but not without a lot of rejection. I remember when my parents bought our house on Humboldt Avenue. The White people on the other side [it was a duplex] moved out. They did not even take all their belongings, that was how fast they wanted to flee . . . The Jews opened areas for Blacks to move in, but they moved out too. The Italians and Irish just will not sell.[59]

This chapter has attempted to reconstruct some of the most crucial facets of the West Indian migration experience. The facts and the stories related by the immigrants and their children discussed here lead to some unavoidable conclusions: West Indian immigrants, in spite of making some headway, encountered formidable obstacles in employment and housing; these obstacles were largely the result of the Black foreigners' fate being inextricably intertwined with that of the native Black population. So in significant ways, the West Indians were absorbed into a Black Boston. But membership in this racially defined category was not potent enough to stifle the resolve for distinctiveness, which manifested itself in a viable West Indian subculture.

Bananas bound for Boston. Some of the men and women who eventually found their way to Boston and other parts of the United States had labored as porters, carrying bananas and coconuts to boats bound for the eastern seaboard. *Photograph by A. Duperly & Sons (early twentieth century). Courtesy of the Boston Public Library, Print Department.*

Jubilee in Market Square, Kingston, Jamaica. Many of the immigrants to Boston had moved to and lived in vibrant urban centers like Kingston before emigrating. Boston Herald *(1926). Courtesy of the Boston Public Library, Print Department. Reprinted with permission of the* Boston Herald.

In Trafalgar Square, Bridgetown, Barbados. *Photo by Underwood & Underwood. Courtesy of the Boston Public Library, Print Division.*

Jubilee Market, Kingston, Jamaica. *Photograph by A. Duperly & Sons (1907). Courtesy of the Boston Public Library, Print Department.*

Harbor in Bridgetown, Barbados, showing custom house and quay. *Boston Photo News Co. (1913). Courtesy of the Boston Public Library, Print Department.*

Hat weaving in Jamaica. This and dressmaking were common household occupations for women. Boston Herald *(1934). Courtesy of the Boston Public Library, Print Department. Reprinted with permission of the* Boston Herald.

Head office of the United Fruit Company, Kingston, Jamaica, where many emigrants purchased their steamer tickets (early twentieth century). *NLJ Photo. Courtesy of the National Library of Jamaica.*

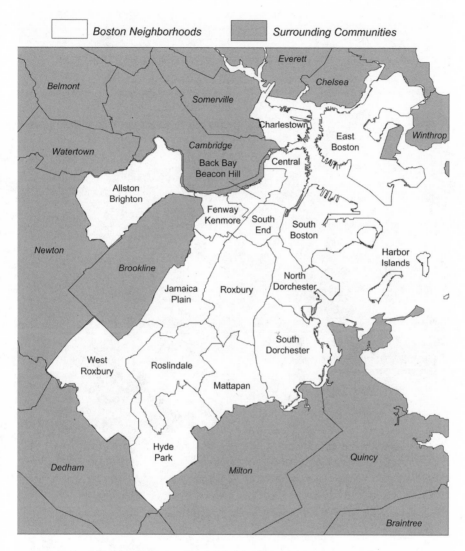

Boston neighborhoods. *Reproduced from the 2002 Boston Indicators Report of the Boston Foundation. Courtesy of the Boston Foundation and the Boston Redevelopment Authority.*

Washington Street El on its way through the South End. The highest concentration of the West Indian population was in the South End, and the El provided vital links to places of employment in South Boston, downtown, Brookline, and suburbs like Newton. *Photograph by Leslie Jones (1929). Courtesy of the Boston Public Library, Print Department.*

Black and White workers unloading bananas at the United Fruit Company dock at Boston's Long Wharf. Many West Indian men worked as laborers unloading bananas from some of the very boats that brought them to Boston. Photograph undated. *Courtesy of the Boston Public Library, Print Department.*

3

Identity, Culture,
and Community

In 1934 the West Indian community of New York presented a memorial
pledging their loyalty to the British crown to Gerald Campbell, the British
consul general. Touched by this gesture, the British ambassador in Washington, D.C., R. L. Lindsay, sent a circular to all the consular officers instructing
them to gather information on the West Indian communities in their respective jurisdictions, in an attempt to better "foster the loyalty to and pride
in their [the West Indians'] British nationality." The consul generals of
Chicago, San Francisco, and Philadelphia submitted reports to the British
embassy describing the occupations, residential patterns, and mutual benefit organizations and sports clubs in their respective West Indian communities. The "Summary of Consular Reports" described the results from Boston
in this way:

> His Majesty's Consul General at Boston states that, while there must be a
> certain number of British West Indians in that city, they form no cohesive
> group, nor do they register at the Consulate General. Probably for this reason
> no contact has been maintained by his Majesty's Consulate General with British
> West Indians in the district, and Mr. Ford [the British consul], while liking West
> Indians and being desirous of showing them that they are not officially ignored,
> is inclined to doubt whether, in view of the different conditions obtaining in
> Boston, it is feasible for him to follow the example set by His Majesty's Consul
> General in New York.[1]

In essence, then, the consul general was saying that there was really no
West Indian community in Boston on which to report. Ironically, however,
by that time West Indians had established a church, a newspaper, a mutual
benefit association, and sports clubs. There was, indeed, a West Indian community. What was it composed of? What were the functions of the various
community institutions? How did West Indians perceive and deal with their

identities based on their membership and experiences in this community? These are the main questions this chapter seeks to answer as it attempts to rescue the West Indian community from the obscurity that belied its viability in the first half of the twentieth century.

An examination of Boston's West Indian community must start with the family, for as immigration historian Judith Smith rightly observed, "whether they [immigrants] traveled alone or in groups, their uprooting was given meaning by their identities as family members."[2] A cursory glance at early-twentieth-century West Indian society and West Indian migration patterns might not capture the centrality of the family in the maintenance of a foreign Black subculture. During that period, West Indian family life and community organization were under assault. A 1938 Royal Commission appointed by the British parliament to survey the social and economic conditions in the West Indies reported acute disorganization in family life and community. Jolted by the commission's findings, many scholars, using Western standards, attempted to illustrate the chaos in the society, caused by the effects of slavery, colonialism, unsanctioned conjugal unions, a high rate of illegitimacy, and endemic migration.[3] The high rate of illegitimacy found by the British commission belied the stability which underlay the average West Indian family. True, officially sanctioned conjugal unions were few and, true, the rate of illegitimacy was high, but the Black British colonials still displayed a keen sense of family and kin. Scholars, especially sociologists and anthropologists, have proposed that in the West Indian setting more appropriate terms than "family" would be "domestic unit" or "the household." What such researchers uncovered were close-knit, well-organized units of immediate and distant biological relatives and non-biological kindred living within recognizable households.[4]

The extended family or household was thus already an established institution in the society that the West Indian migrants left. They did not come to Boston from a vacuum as far as household organization was concerned. Nevertheless, their migration patterns at first glance would seem to have militated against the effectiveness of this premigration experience. As the *Passenger Lists* clearly show, unlike most European immigrants arriving in the same period, West Indians seldom entered Boston in family units. Adult men and women more commonly came neither with their partners nor with their children, a fact which may seem to endorse the concern of the Royal Commission, and other critical investigations, over the adverse effects of migration on the West Indian family. While the possible disruptive effects were undeniable, the family was so central in the migration venture that even that institution was molded to accommodate the demands of emigration. As chapter 1 of this study discussed, the family was, in fact, one of the facilitators of migration. Importantly, reunification more often than not was also worked into the plan. The majority of West Indian children and young teenagers admitted into Boston in the early twentieth century told the examining immigration officers that they were coming to join one or both parents. A few others mentioned other biological relatives like aunts and uncles.[5] The anecdotal data collected for this study paints the same picture. Several men and women recalled reuniting with family members after being left in the care of family and family friends in the homeland for anywhere from one to ten years. Often, even children born in the United States were sent to relatives in the homeland, reuniting with their parents in Boston when they were old enough not to pose a serious obstacle to their parents' employment and other economic pursuits.[6]

Reflective of the West Indian society they were coming from, most of the immigrants were either single or in common-law long-term relationships prior to moving. In Boston, a few reunited with their previous partners, but more commonly, they began new relationships, which, unlike in the homeland, mostly ended in officially sanctioned unions. The rate of endogamy among the first generation seemed to have been high.[7] Endogamy in this case is not applied strictly only to marriage between people from the same island. Many of the marriages were between people from different islands within the British West Indies. These endogamic unions were mostly made possible by the subculture within which they were shaped. Stories like David Nelson's about how his parents met were typical. Nelson recalled that his mother, who was from St. Elizabeth Parish, and his father, who was from Kingston in St. Andrew, did not know each other in Jamaica prior to moving. In Boston they were, according to Nelson, "literally matched" by another West Indian immigrant, a mutual friend who later became Nelson's godfather.[8] Similarly, Clairmont Lewis of Christchurch and Edwardine Corbin of St. Lucy met each other in Boston through some Barbadian friends. Such connections and networking were made possible by and conducted within specific community institutions like the church and associations, which will be discussed later in this chapter.

It is important to keep in mind that family in this case included not only immediate family, but also kin—cousins, uncles, aunts—and even close friends, some of which were neighbors and acquaintances in the homeland. Additionally, many close relationships were forged in Boston, as Glenis Williams, who migrated from Jamaica in 1946, explained:

> All my children knew Elfreda as aunt. We are from the same parish in Jamaica, but I did not know her there. I met her here when she worked for the family next to the one I worked for. Over the years we became such good friends that we became family.[9]

Reminiscent of the homeland, Boston's West Indian families had permeable boundaries which turned non-biological fellow country folk, friends, and neighbors into kin. It is clear, then, that the creation of extended families in Boston was not a reactive process, stimulated simply by the challenges of migration, but rather a projection and utilization of a premigration social resource.

Perhaps nowhere was the resourcefulness of the family more appreciated than in its role in the attainment of economic stability. Scholars have emphasized the centrality of the family in the immigrant work experience through what they have variously called a family work culture, family economy, and household economy.[10] While the overwhelming majority of the studies on the subject are on European immigrants, West Indian immigrants have displayed strikingly similar patterns of a family economy.[11] Like so many cultural patterns they exhibited in Boston, a family work culture was not newly introduced in their new home, even if it was modified. In premigration, the financial welfare of the family was always a concerted effort. Children were raised to understand that they had to do their own share of gardening, tending livestock, general housework, and helping out in the fields. Extended family members also helped in farming the family plot. Child care, always a major concern for working mothers, was a family matter. Relatives developed reciprocal patterns of caring for each other's children in order to enable mothers to work in gardening, plantation agriculture, dressmaking, domestic service, or higglering.[12] As chapter 1 of this study explained, the family was instrumental in making livelihood migration possible.

Therefore, when Boston's West Indians nurtured a family work culture it was a transference of an old tradition and not the development of a new one. So what were the indicators of this family work culture in Boston? Acquiring employment was very often a family endeavor. As this study has shown already in the case of the West Indian domestics, family members were known, actually expected, to help new migrants learn the ropes about finding employment and preparing for certain occupations. The anecdotal data demonstrate the numerous ways the immigrants carved niches in their places of employment and paved the way for family members and friends. George Commissiong, for example, explained his experience in this way:

> I was in such good standing with my boss that he would always hire anyone I brought in. If he did not have any vacancies, he would even call and visit other people in order to get jobs for my people. It was in this way that I secured jobs for my wife, my sister and two brothers.[13]

It is interesting, mainly for the purposes of comparison, to mention here that a system of family cooperation in job acquisition also operated among the native-born Black.[14] It is also true, however, that Blacks were generally less effective in carving a formidable kinship network to help newly arrived family members get jobs.[15] As chapter 1 explained, Boston's Blacks had to contend with occupational closure and White solidarity. In spite of these blockades, West Indians, as well as southern Black migrants, were still able to pull some strings in assisting family members get jobs and adjust to them.

West Indian women, who had always worked, constituted a vital arm of the family economy. In the homeland, although some were officially labeled "housewives," they worked seasonally in the fields as distributors of fertilizers and transporters of harvested crops to loading areas. Almost all the women worked on the family plot, cultivating vegetables and raising livestock. In addition to these chores, those women in urban centers like Kingston, Jamaica; Bridgetown, Barbados; and Plymouth, Montserrat, also worked as washerwomen, housekeepers, and dressmakers.[16]

In the new setting in Boston, some aspects of women's work were modified, but the main contours remained. For one thing, there was no question about whether the women should seek employment, even though the majority had children by the time they emigrated. For many European ethnic groups, motherhood constrained women from working outside the home. They had to evolve strategies for earning an income by doing paid work at home.[17] West Indian women with young children sometimes resorted to the same solution. Those who had acquired skills in hairdressing or dressmaking pursued their occupations at home. But these were not very fulfilling as full-time jobs because patronage was limited. Their clients were almost all West Indians, an extremely small segment of the city's population. Moreover, many of the alternative strategies, like industrial homework, were not readily accessible to Black women. With European managers and foremen firmly entrenched in the factories, piecework was blatantly given to women from their own ethnic groups. So, in the circumstances, most West Indian women had to work outside the home as domestics in private homes and as housekeepers in public establishments.

How the immigrant generation juggled work and raising children is one of the features that provide insights into the dynamics of a family economy within an immigrant subculture. One common trend, as already mentioned, was to leave the children in the West Indies or send them there from the United States. For those children in Boston, the immigrants tapped into familiar premigration experiences to develop family and community-based patterns. The men, fathers and uncles, helped out when they were not at work. Older children, many of whom were born in the West Indies, helped to take care of younger children. Some families had two or three teenage children. Relatives and other immigrants who lived close by would bring younger children to such households, while the mothers and fathers went to work. A Jamaican woman who came to Boston at age sixteen testified to this: "As older children, we helped our mothers, aunts and close family friends to take care of the small ones when the women went to work, usually to take care of other people's children."[18] Boston lawyer Victor Bynoe illustrated this contribution and the children's commitment to the family economy:

> My parents worked very hard. My mother got up at six o'clock in the morning, went to work in a Jewish family's kitchen, scrubbed floors, washed the laundry and came back home at five o'clock in the evening. By that time I had supper ready for them [the family, which included six children]. She would go upstairs to a hairdressing room and work on people's hair till 10, 11 o'clock at night. I made sure my siblings were alright and everything in the house was taken care of. I did all these with much pleasure because I knew that my parents were not working just for themselves, but for the common good of the whole family.[19]

The contributions of young adults to the family economy went beyond child care and housework. They also brought wages of their own. By the age of sixteen many of them worked out of the home after school and on weekends. Cooper House, a community center in the South End, was instrumental in situating Black children in jobs in both Black and White establishments. The neighborhood grocery stores were favorite employers of West Indian children. Elma Lewis, a second-generation Barbadian, described, through her own experiences, this viable contribution of children: "To the children in the Lewis family, working outside the home was as important as working inside it. Money was needed for everyday things as well as for future schooling."[20]

While the earnings of children contributed to the family income and parents welcomed their input, they were equally determined that the children's role in the economy did not clash with their educational pursuits. It has been frequently documented how among some European immigrant groups, children's education suffered because of the emphasis on their contribution to the family economy. Although John Bodnar, for example, was careful to consider that religious values which taught that public schools threatened the moral fiber of the immigrant community were a significant factor that kept the children from school, he emphatically acknowledged the significant role of child labor in the low statistics of schoolgoing children of immigrant working-class families: "The claims of the family economy were so strong and economic need sufficiently high that immigrant children in nearly every group [he focused almost exclusively on European groups] and in every city throughout the United States chose work when it was available over extended schooling."[21] This definitely was not true for Boston's West Indian immigrant community. Proper education of the children was for most of the immigrants the pivotal stimulus for emigrating. Therefore, not even work for increased family income took precedence over that objective. This subject will be discussed in greater length in a subsequent chapter on social mobility. It will suffice now to merely emphasize that while the contribution of children to the family economy was far from negligible, work did not interfere with their schooling.

The family income was used for a variety of expenditures, first and foremost for the basic necessities—rent, food, and clothing. The family coffers also paid other expenses like sending remittances to relatives still living in the West Indies, paying passages for family members to emigrate to Boston or some other destination, and footing the initial costs of helping the new arrivals adjust. A collective purpose was, thus, the basis of the family economy. It did not matter if family members did not share the same workspace or even have the same occupations. It did not matter how each member contributed to the income-generating potential of the household. It did not matter the specific expenses that the earnings of each member covered. What mattered was that all the earnings were pooled together and used for concentric ventures which ultimately ensured the family's survival and advancement.

In many ways the family stood as the broker between the immigrants and the larger Boston American society. Much of the information new immigrants got about their new home came from the family. Mr. Robert Campbell, who admitted he stowed away from Port Antonio, Jamaica, to Boston in a United Fruit vessel in 1937, described this phenomenon:

> If not for my relatives and some other people from my parish [region/district in the island], I would have gone crazy in this aloof society. I lived with them, I talked with them. They showed me the ropes . . . where the jobs were, where to shop, the areas to go to, and the people who liked and respected us and the people who didn't.[22]

At the same time the family attempted to regulate exposure to American society, it also oversaw the retention and practice of homeland cultures. Like most immigrant groups, West Indians believed that some aspects of the American society threatened the moral and social fabric of their cultures.[23] Therefore, again, like most first-generation immigrants, West Indian parents clung to the idea of retaining their cultural identity and instilling "homeland values" in their American-born children. A second-generation Barbadian recalled this aspect of the West Indian American community in Roxbury where he was raised:

To this day I will hear my mother, my father and my two aunts saying "back home we respect older people; back home we were taught to work hard for money, but we still cherished human life and good relations over material things." It was always back home, back home. You know what they were trying to do? They wanted me to see what Barbados had which America lacked. And thank God they did, because it is the balancing of the two that made me what I am today.[24]

Similar sentiments about the role of the West Indian family in Boston were echoed in a statement about the role of Edwardine Lewis as a wife and mother: "The children were taught to observe ideals of the highest tradition: honor, extreme industry, dedication to service of God, professional excellence and respect for cultural heritage."[25]

The West Indian family in Boston was undeniably one of the formidable structures of the community. As a unit the family negotiated and regulated the dynamics of making a living. It was a broker or a mediator between the immigrants and their children and the larger society. And it provided some form of equilibrium for the immigrants as they encountered a range of perplexing social departures from what they were familiar with in premigration.

Another bulwark of the Boston West Indian subculture was the church. This is not surprising because the early-twentieth-century immigrants were coming from societies where Christianity was firmly entrenched in several facets of life and community.[26] Although in certain islands Roman Catholicism was a strong force, as a region, the British West Indies was generally more Protestant, with Anglicans predominating in Jamaica, Barbados, and Montserrat, the three British West Indian societies from which the overwhelming majority of the immigrants to Boston came. In fact, Barbados, then often referred to as the "England of the West Indies," was so staunchly Anglican that for much of the first half of the twentieth century all the other denominations combined constituted no more than 10 percent of the Christian population.[27] The Methodists and the Baptists were also fairly well-represented, according to the censuses. In addition to the well-established orthodox Christian denominations, independent Black and Pentecostal churches had begun to spring up by the beginning of the twentieth century. Not to be ignored is also the belief in African folk religious traditions like obeah and myalism, which can be traced back to the period of slavery. It is important to consider the influence of the African-derived religious practices, for, as scholars have pointed out, some of the outwardly professed Christians also subscribed in varying degrees to the non-Christian, Black beliefs.[28]

Whatever the Christian denomination or the extent of contact with African folk religions, by 1900 the church occupied a significant place in the life of West Indian people. In addition to the spiritual and emotional support that churchgoers got from the teaching of "the word," going to church had its social values. The elite and middle class, especially, saw church attendance and other related church activities as a means of affirming their social status in the society. The working class, too, saw the church as a means of social elevation. It was an integral part of Western, European culture. In church they met "cultured" people—the schoolteacher, headmaster, civil servants, a new graduate from a British university, a vacationing successful emigrant from the states, etc.[29]

The Jamaicans, Barbadians, and Montserratians who came to Boston in the first decades of the twentieth century thus had a strong sense of the role of religion, especially the spiritual and material value of the church. It is therefore understandable why in Boston attempts were made to transplant that facet of their premigration community experience. Although from the anecdotal evidence from oral history, it seems that most of the immigrants first attempted to seek denominations with which they were already affiliated, practical decisions based on their residential location in the South End and Roxbury became paramount in the final analysis. According to Gerald Vincent, a Harvard graduate student studying Blacks and the church, in 1940 Black Catholics, most of them Jamaicans and a few Montserratians (approximately 115 altogether) attended St. Augustine–St. Martin Church on Lenox Street, off Shawmut Avenue in the South End. St. Marks Congregational Church on Townsend Street, Roxbury, drew a large number of Anglicans and Methodists (between 300 and 450). The Baptists attended the Twelfth Baptist Church on Warren Street in Roxbury.[30] Some West Indians also attended the non-denominational Church of All Nations on the corner of Tremont Street in the South End. This church was one that attracted immigrants of various national origins and ethnic groups.[31]

All these churches were essentially "American," and more specifically "African American," churches, and the Black immigrants felt comfortable in them. But while these churches played significant functions in the lives of the immigrants, St. Cyprian's Church is the one to highlight in an assessment of the church in the West Indian subculture. Inarguably one of the indices of the existence of the Black foreign enclave, St. Cyprian's Episcopal Church on the corner of Tremont and Walpole streets in lower Roxbury was, throughout the first half of the twentieth century, *the* "West Indian" church. It had its beginnings in May 1910, when a group of mostly Jamaicans and Barbadians, feeling unwelcome in the White Episcopalian churches, began to meet in the home of Miss Ida Gross, a Jamaican immigrant, at 218 Northampton Street. Starting with just a handful of attendees, by 1920 the congregation had grown to more than fifty on some Sundays, rendering it too large for a house church. The foreign, Black Episcopalians were invited to use the facilities of the predominantly White Church of the Ascension on Washington Street, Boston, for their services on Sunday afternoons. But after the members of this church flagrantly displayed racism, bigotry, and contempt by fumigating the church after the Black foreigners left, the latter decided it was time to begin to work toward owning their own building.[32] St. Cyprian's,[33] opened in 1924, was in many respects representative of a reactive process against racism, a deep American malaise with which the immigrants were inevitably confronted.

By its location alone, in the heart of the Black community, St. Cyprian's from the outset was poised for its place in the West Indian community. Almost immediately, it became the concentric point of West Indian socioreligious activities. According to church records, from 1921 to 1940, 793 people were confirmed, 831 were baptized, and 305 marriages were performed. The registered members, or in strictly ecclesiastical terms the communicants of the church, were predominantly Barbadians who, as pointed out earlier, were staunch Anglicans, the Anglo–West Indian equivalent of Episcopalians. Jamaicans accounted for roughly 35 percent of the membership.[34] In 1925 there were 410 communicants, a Sunday school of 125 pupils, and 12 school officers and teachers. By 1937 the congregation had grown to 627 communicants, 390 Sunday school pupils, 18 Sunday school officers and teachers, and 27 young adults in the confirmation class.[35] The officially registered membership, however, does not reflect the extent of the West Indian presence in the church, for the "non-communicant" West Indians, while continuing their membership in St. Mark's, St. Martin, the Twelfth Baptist, etc., forged strong links with St. Cyprian's. Many unofficial members came for the practical assistance they received from this church, which, emerging as it did within the context of the immigrants' adaptation, geared several of its endeavors to the welfare of the foreigners. In the late 1920s, for example, the church established what Barbadian American Victor Bynoe emphasized should be seen as an "immigration agency." This "agency" was made up of influential church members—two lawyers and three journalists—who arranged contacts between prospective employers and immigrants, provided letters of recommendation, and helped with passage and accommodation when necessary.[36] The church assisted parishioners and affiliates in securing jobs, and skilled members volunteered to train new arrivals. One of the most instrumental bodies in this endeavor was the Agnes Guild, one of the church's women's organizations. Its members volunteered to teach new immigrant women to sew, read, and learn the art of housekeeping.[37] The Agnes Guild seemed to have emphasized skills necessary for successful inroads into domestic employment, which, as the preceding chapter discussed, was at that time the main occupational arena for Black women.

Arrangements were also made sometimes through the church for members to attend the Everett Evening School on Northampton Street in Roxbury to take courses in sewing, cooking, and citizenship (for naturalization).[38]

St. Cyprian's was also a common venue for the activities of the secular associations, which organized a variety of functions—from recitals to concerts to lectures and tea parties. These associations, perhaps the most tangible icons of the West Indian subculture, will be described and analyzed in depth. But before going on to that, this chapter will wrap up this direct focus on St. Cyprian's as a community institution by commenting on the role of Leroy Fergusson, the pastor from 1921 to 1951, much of the period covered by this study.

Reverend Fergusson was a native of Raleigh, North Carolina. Prior to moving to Boston, Fergusson had served in many ministries in the South, mostly in North Carolina. His last position before coming to Boston in 1920 was head of the Colored City Mission in Louisville, Kentucky. He began to serve the budding St. Cyprian's congregation before the move to the church's permanent location. He oversaw the building and dedication of the church in 1924. Fergusson, though as an African American was technically an outsider, is ubiquitous in the history of the Boston West Indian community. He is mentioned in association records, his sermons were cited in the community newspaper, and he is recalled in the oral history. He was well-known and respected in the community, especially for his campaign for self-help. His premier vehicle for transmitting his message was his sermons, which were replete with admonitions on the efficacy of self-help, hard work, and cooperation. His address at the Thanksgiving service to celebrate the second anniversary of the Barbados Union, Inc. in 1939 was "The heights of economic progress can be attained by the application of cooperation in corporation."[39] Through such messages, Fergusson appealed to what was already a familiar phenomenon among African Americans, especially those of the South. By the end of the nineteenth century, "to seek for ourselves" had become a motto in several African American communities. The rationale of this concept dictated that in the face of racial discrimination, so endemic in American society, Blacks had to fend for themselves through formal and informal community institutions. Reverend Fergusson had been trained and had served in this Black southern tradition. Therefore, when this southern Black came to Boston and was promoting self-help among a predominantly

West Indian congregation, he was passing on a tradition that was rightfully his and theirs. In this capacity, Fergusson was in a real sense what immigration historian Victor Green calls an "ethnic broker." While Green and John Higham, among others, have examined how leaders from an ethnic group serve as intermediaries between their particular ethnic, immigrant community and the American society,[40] Fergusson offers an example of a leader from a different group playing the same role within an immigrant community. This is significant and worth highlighting, especially given that early assessments often created the impression that it was always the Black foreigners influencing and assisting American Blacks to be more resourceful in combating racial and economic barriers.[41] But in this case, Fergusson and his work and stature in St. Cyprian's and the Boston West Indian community give insights into how an American Black, steeped in his tradition of self-help, tapped into the similar self-help proclivity of a Black immigrant group to make a mark in their subculture.

Irma Watkins-Owens describes strikingly similar trends in her study of the Caribbean and African American communities in New York in 1900–1930. John H. Johnson, Sr., a native of Virginia, played a role similar to Fergusson's as pastor of the heavily Caribbean congregation of St. Cyprian in San Juan Hill. In 1928, his son, John H. Johnson, Jr., founded St. Martin's, which Watkins-Owens says later became the "bastion of the Caribbean middle class in Harlem."[42] But as strikingly remarkable as this similarity in the pattern of American-born Blacks ministering to predominantly Caribbean congregations is, there is no evidence of actual links between the Boston and New York Episcopalian communities, and certainly no indication that this leadership pattern was dictated or desired.

St. Cyprian's was a vibrant institution. Undeniably, its strong affiliation with the community's secular organizations gave it much of this vibrancy. As Elma Lewis vividly remembers: "It seemed like there was never a week that one Caribbean association was not doing something at the church."[43] The associations can be grouped roughly into three types: country/island associations, pan–West Indian associations, and sports clubs. Jamaica Associates, founded in 1934, was the first of the island associations. Barbados Union, Inc. followed in 1937, and the Montserratians formed the Montserratian Progressive League in 1939. Significantly, this foray into organization under clear island affiliation was not the immigrants' first venture into associational life. Organizing along pan–West Indian lines preceded the island organizing of the 1930s. As far back as 1915, when the community was still taking shape, the West India Aid Society was formed. As its name suggests, it was a mutual benefit society designed to help immigrants from various parts of the West Indies.

No consideration of pan–West Indian ethnicity in associational life is complete without cognizance of the Boston branch of the Universal Negro Improvement Association (UNIA). UNIA was an organization founded by Jamaican Marcus Garvey in his native land in 1914. Upon emigrating to New York in 1916, Garvey established the headquarters of his association in that city and oversaw the founding of branches throughout the United States, from Los Angeles and San Francisco on the West Coast to Atlanta and New Orleans in the South to Detroit and Cincinnati in the Midwest and Philadelphia and Boston in the Northeast. By 1920 the organization had more than thirty branches and the flamboyant Garvey boasted that his organization had at least 500,000 members, making it the first mass movement of Blacks in America. With the motto "Up You Mighty Race, You Can Accomplish What You Will," Garvey and his adherents worked toward their ultimate goal of Black nationalism in the West Indies, the U.S., Canada, Europe, and Africa through their message of Black pride, education, and economic independence.[44]

The Boston UNIA, established in 1919, was like other branches in its structure, with two presidents, one female and one male; and generation- and gender-based suborganizations, notably, the African Legion, the Black Cross Nurses, the Young People's Auxiliary, and the Ladies Unity Club. Although more generally in U.S. history Garveyism is remembered as an Afro-American movement, in many specific senses UNIA was a West Indian organization. The Boston branch demonstrated many of the same characteristics of the main New York body and regional branches which highlighted this fact. The membership was overwhelmingly West Indian. Importantly, as if to physically affirm the West Indian connection, the Boston UNIA was also housed in the building on the corner of Tremont and Walpole streets, right across from St. Cyprian's which, as explained earlier, was such a pivot of the West Indian community.[45] The next chapter, which deals with West Indians and activism, will return briefly to Garveyism in Boston. At this point it will suffice to merely identify the Boston UNIA branch as legitimately one of the pan–West Indian associations that defined the foreign Black subculture.

Recreational clubs were also very important in sustaining a sense of community. Literature on the experiences of immigrants focuses heavily on work, sometimes creating the impression that play was almost non-existent. But it is a historical fact that leisure has always been a vital part of the migration experience.[46] While the island and mutual benefit associations organized recreational events like banquets, balls, concerts, recitals, and tea parties, it was the sports clubs, more specifically, the cricket clubs, that were most symbolic of West Indian leisure. Cricket clubs began to emerge in Boston almost with the first trickles of West Indian immigrants in the early 1900s. By 1920, there were six such clubs—the Windsors, Windsor Minors, West India A, West India B, Standards, and Wanderers. These teams practiced and competed in Franklin Field, the huge Boston city recreational area that bordered Roxbury and Dorchester. Beyond Boston, sometimes some of the teams qualified for and competed in the American Cricket League with teams from New York, Rhode Island, and Connecticut.

This development of cricket in Boston is one more aspect that echoes the premigration background. The immigrants were attempting to transplant what by that time was a national pastime in their homeland. The transplantation, however, was not without significant modifications. In the British Caribbean colonies, this "national sport" was a sport of status, for a long time fully accessible only to the privileged Whites, mulattoes, and Blacks who attended prestigious West Indian secondary schools and British universities.[47] In Boston, where the distinctive color- and class-based proscriptions did not operate, the complexion, as it were, of the sport was modified so that all shades of black and individuals of diverse occupations and socioeconomic strata participated fully.

Some of these modifications were also reflected in gendered ways. Women became increasingly more active in the development of cricket than they had ever been. The girls and women were involved in several processes that supported the sport and the American Cricket League. Both written and oral sources describe their efforts in organizing entertainment, food, and fundraising for purchase of uniforms and sports equipment.[48] The tea breaks, a *sine qua non* for any cricket match, were catered and supervised by the women. True, the sport did not change so drastically as to enable the girls and women to be batters and bowlers, and their roles were still within the periphery and in the traditional domestic arena of food and entertainment, but their now more visible presence contributed to the transplantation of the sport and stands as an example of one way that a British West Indian cultural trait was nuanced in a new setting.

The Boston West Indian subculture, which for many during that period had to be ferreted out from a more visible Black community, was rightfully an ethnic enclave with the classic components of family, religious center, and associations. As scholars often point out, one of the biggest indicators of the existence of such entities is the ethnic press.[49] There also, the West Indian community met the qualifications, for no list of the community institutions would be complete without the *Boston Chronicle*. Remarkably, that publication is more commonly known in Boston's history not as a West Indian immigrant institution but simply as "the other Black newspaper." The first acclaimed Boston Black paper of the twentieth century was William Monroe

Trotter's *Boston Guardian,* founded in 1901. By 1920, through such highly publicized developments like the feud between its editor and Booker T. Washington, its crusade against the showing of the movie *Birth of a Nation,* and its denouncement of America's entry into the First World War, the *Guardian* was nationally recognized as one of the nation's radical Black publications. While the *Chronicle* never did gain such a national reputation, in Boston it was an icon in the Black community and actually cut into the readership of the *Guardian,* overtaking it to become "the leading Black newspaper" in Boston in the 1930s.[50]

While there is no denying the significant place of the *Chronicle* in Black Boston in a general sense, its specific origins and orientation lay in the Boston West Indian subculture. Its founders were West Indians. In 1915, when the West Indian population in Boston was still only a few hundred strong, a group of Jamaicans formed the Square Deal Publishing Company. They were Thaddeus Kitchener, Alfred Haughton, L. George Murray, Eleanor Trent Wallace, Chas Brown, Elisha Jackson, and John Wallace, all immigrants in Boston, and Uriah N. and Rose Murray of Jamaica. The weekly (every Saturday) newspaper launched by this company in the same year was named the *Boston Chronicle,* with the motto "Fearless and Uncompromising—Advocate of Justice, Rights and Opportunities." As this motto rightly suggests, the *Chronicle* was an instrument of Black protest in the city, a very important facet that will be dealt with in more depth in the next chapter. The main point for now is that not only was the *Boston Chronicle* an indicator of the existence of a foreign Black ethnic press, it was a conduit for projecting, affirming, acclaiming the very subculture within which it operated.

As already mentioned, the *Chronicle* was the "other African American paper," not an unreasonable label given its extensive and often passionate coverage of issues pertaining to Black America. Yet on more careful perusal, its unique characteristics as a foreign Black weekly emerge. In covering sports the paper frequently reported on boxing and baseball in the United States, but about three-quarters of its coverage went to cricket. It provided updates on cricket in Boston and the American League; it also profiled the star cricketers of the West Indies, the United Kingdom, and other parts of the British Empire, especially Africa and South Asia.

Because the various organizations regularly sent announcements of meetings and other activities, sometimes citing whole sections of minutes in the paper, the *Chronicle* today stands as one of the richest sources of the history of the West Indian associations. The society column unfailingly carried a wealth of information about individuals, families, and groups in the community. The reports gave detailed descriptions of weddings, christenings, and graduation receptions, and they also described vacations to the homeland, right down to details such as specific places and people visited and even the steamers on which the vacationers traveled. The consistent detailed reporting on conditions and developments in the West Indies underscored the paper's continued link to the homeland. The *Chronicle* is replete with homeland news, from hurricanes and political upheavals to updates on the construction of new churches and schools.

Finally, the *Chronicle* provided deep insights into European colonies beyond the West Indies. Specifically, it paid attention to the colonies in Africa and regularly reported on a variety of developments, from a locust invasion in Angola to resistance in Sierra Leone.[51] The *Chronicle*'s affiliation with a foreign Black subculture is further illuminated by this sense of belonging to a colonial union in what cultural historian Paul Gilroy would call a "Black Atlantic."[52]

The *Chronicle,* along with the other institutions which constituted the foreign Black enclave, performed a variety of functions. Like the church, the associations provided practical assistance to the members of the community. This assumed forms typical of immigrant communities: financial assistance to help with health care and funeral expenses; networking to help members of the community, especially new arrivals, procure employment and housing; and loans and scholarships for the education of the second generation. The West India Aid Society was formed primarily to carry out such functions. But the other associations, though not expressly mutual benefit or benevolent societies, performed the same role. Jamaica Associates, for example, had a benevolent committee with a standing fund for "Jamaicans in need." Sometimes, these Jamaicans in need were not even, strictly speaking, members of the local community, as was the case when the committee gave cash and clothes to nine stowaways who were being deported from Boston to Port Antonio.[53] Similar assistance was often given to communities in the homeland. In fact, an organization like the Jamaica Associates emerged out of the efforts of a group of Jamaicans who got together to collect money, clothing, and other items for those affected by the devastating hurricane which ravaged Jamaica and other Caribbean islands in 1934. The tradition of sending material assistance to homeland communities was firmly embraced and demonstrated by the Jamaica Associates and the other organizations.

Again, it must be noted that this practice of pooling resources to help unfortunate members of the community was not discovered in Boston. By the time West Indians began to arrive in Boston, lodges and mutual benefit associations had become formidable props of various communities in the homeland. In Jamaica, for example, the Jamaica Mutual Life Assurance Society and the Jamaica Burial Scheme Society had assumed such proportions that the *Daily Gleaner* was compelled to write about their efficacy.[54] Historian Walter Rodney arrived at the same conclusion in his study of how Barbadians introduced lodges and benefit societies to British Guiana in the late 1870s and 1880s. According to Rodney, benefit societies were a salient hallmark of Afro–West Indians, who, by fostering them, demonstrated "the inherited African pre-occupation with community organizations which would guarantee benefits in times of sickness and death."[55]

This keen sense of altruism notwithstanding, leisure and recreation were paramount to the associations' existence. They all organized parties, balls, and banquets to celebrate the anniversaries of their founding and to commemorate holidays whose significance lay not in their new home but in their premigration societies. Two such holidays were Emancipation Day (marking emancipation of slaves in the West Indies) and Empire Day. Here also, the now familiar element of transplantation is evident. These were holidays that the immigrants had been accustomed to celebrating in the West Indies where even the holidays that were specific to British imperial glory were marked with enthusiasm. While this fact seemed to apply to all— planter, merchant, civil servant, and ordinary folk—the pressure which came with colonialism clearly had an influence, especially on the ordinary folk. With the caption "The Meaning of the Empire Explained and the Duties of Citizens Emphasized," the *Daily Gleaner* of June 2, 1930, described how the various parishes "fulfilled expectations" by celebrating Empire Day. Empire Day, it reminded its readers, was about patriotism and loyalty to the British crown. In 1935 Lieutenant Colonel W. P. Drury, reporting on his trip to Barbados to the *Western Morning News* of Plymouth, England, described this loyalty of the colonized:

> Barbados is an intensely loyal island to England, and on Jubilee Day a lady, who is the owner of a plantation, invited the coloured population of the district to come to her house and hear the broadcast of the king's speech. The moment His Majesty's voice came on the air the whole crowd knelt.[56]

Why did Boston's West Indians insist on celebrating these imperialist-oriented holidays, even after their departure from the colonies? Could it have been nostalgia? Indeed, in some sense, yes, since longing for familiar patterns of the premigration setting is not unusual among immigrant groups. However, it is important to understand that the desire to cling to British West Indian holidays went beyond nostalgia. In significant ways open commemoration of such holidays was calculated. It was a tool to affirm the immigrants' foreign identity, a fact which reveals yet another function of the associations.

The associations, by their very existence, conferred and confirmed the foreignness of the West Indian subculture. The changing dynamics of individual and group identities are often a significant facet of migration experiences.[57] In the case of this group of immigrants, conceptualizing, reconceptualizing, and negotiating identities, whether they recognized it or not, came to hinge on their position as Blacks in America. This reality was vastly different from their initial expectations, like that of Betty Williams who when she first came to Boston believed that she was "Bajan [Barbadian], plain and simple Bajan." She had to rethink her identity; Bajan was not enough.[58] Indeed, initially, many of the immigrants identified mostly with their island of origin; therefore they were Jamaicans, Barbadians, and Montserratians. But the host society had collective identities for them. Most Whites simply saw them as Black people. Those who bothered to acknowledge their foreign status at best saw them as West Indians or, less perceptively, as Jamaicans, not caring whether they were from Jamaica or not.

What concerned the immigrants most was being lumped with the general U.S. Black population, a historically subjugated racial group. Being locked out of most occupations reinforced their awareness of the disadvantages of this mistaken affiliation and, to combat it, West Indians tried to preserve their island identities, upholding and projecting foreignness while building new identities based on their U.S. experiences. They eventually projected four main ethnic identities: their island identity; a pan–West Indian identity; a British identity; and, in many cases reluctantly, a Black American identity.

To project their foreign identities the Black immigrants had to employ certain strategies channeled through a combination of physical and vocal mannerisms, community institutions, church membership, associations, holiday celebrations, and recreational choices.

Many West Indians, especially in the first few years after migration, deliberately dressed "tropically," especially in the spring and summer months. The men wore flannel pants, silk shirts, white shoes, and straw hats. The women wore silk skirts and light-colored blouses.[59] The *Boston Chronicle* of March 17, 1945, described the distinctive dress of West Indian arrivals to New Bedford, Massachusetts: "Over two hundred Jamaican men were brought in to work in the Firestone Textiles. Although they were given winter clothing, supplied by the government, they prefer to wear their own. This way the residents of the city easily distinguished the Jamaicans by their straw hats, white duck trousers and brown or white shoes."

Sounding different was another way to distinguish themselves. Although Americans, especially Blacks, made fun of their patois, many West

Indians deliberately maintained their accent, claiming that they spoke "finer English," especially compared to that of the southern Blacks who at the time made up most of Boston's Black population. With pride, some first-genera- tion West Indians tell of times when their accent immediately set them apart from other Black people in a group.[60]

Glaring as such physical and vocal signs were, the more profound cre- ators and indicators of identity were the West Indian community institu- tions that both tied the immigrants together and set them apart. As the cor- nerstones of the West Indian subculture, the West Indian associations not only provided practical support, they also served as forums for articulating identities. Besides mirroring the immigrants' identities as Jamaican, Barba- dian, or Montserratian, the associations also reinforced West Indian and British identities. As mentioned earlier, parades and tea parties celebrated emancipation in the West Indies and British holidays like Empire Day and Coronation Day. A British identity was more than a match for the White American status quo, for they had been taught that everything British was superior.[61] The extent of the West Indians' tenacity was clearly demonstrated in 1943 when, even as the British West Indies was involved in a constitu- tional struggle with Britain, the *Boston Chronicle* of May 10 reported that a segment of Boston's West Indian community was extending an invitation to the Duke and Duchess of Windsor for a visit they were convinced would underscore their status as British subjects.

Perhaps no other element reflected this British identity more than cricket. Cricket sports clubs, most symbolic of West Indian leisure, were crucial to the community. The sport was one of the main indices of the im- migrants' foreign identity. A non-American British sport, it not only under- scored their identity as foreigners, but also importantly affirmed their Brit- ish affiliation.

How concrete was this British affiliation? Was the Black foreigners' Brit- ish identity a symbolic ethnicity? Technically, the immigrants, coming as they did from British colonies, were British subjects. Officially this identity was recognized, as illustrated in the *Passenger Lists* of the U.S. Immigration Services, which described them as "British Negro." The official designation aside, what kind of ongoing links did the immigrants forge with British diplomatic institutions in their host country? As the beginning of this chap- ter demonstrates, in 1934 the British consulate in Boston knew virtually nothing about the existence of this group of British subjects. In some sense this is hardly surprising because as numerous dispatches from the British embassy in Washington, D.C., to the Foreign Office in London continuously maintained, British citizens in America typically did not register at the Brit- ish consulates. Nevertheless, the consulates were able to learn about the existence of some of these citizens and interacted with their communities. For example, in 1922 the Boston consul general sent out an important circular about how to ensure the British citizenship of children born in the U.S. The Boston British organizations that the memo was sent to were the Victorian Club of Kenmore, Scotch Charitable Society, Welsh Associates, Order of Scottish Clans, and the Canadian Club.[62] But West Indian associations are absent from this list, even though the West India Aid Society and cricket clubs were then already existing.

British West Indians in the United States in the first half of the twentieth century were well-known for proclaiming their affiliation with the British crown. But very little is said about how representatives of the British crown responded. What did they think of this loyal Black segment of their empire? Unfortunately, the records are again silent about the specific case of Boston's West Indians, but some illuminating inferences can be gleaned from the better-known New York community. In 1934 in a dispatch to the Foreign Office, the British ambassador, referring to the "New York colony of British subjects," described West Indians in this way:

> They tend to consider themselves, not without reason, superior both socially and culturally to the rest of the coloured elements there; and for that reason they are rather a problem. Most of them bear British names and are intensely proud of their British nationality. . . . At the same time they suffer from acute and unconcealed inferiority complex, and mostly feel themselves caught hopelessly between two fires—the contempt of the white and the hostility of the inferior coloured elements with whom they have to associate. They are apt, moreover, to have an exalted idea of the nature of the help that a consular officer can render them vis-à-vis the local authorities and even the law courts.[63]

Oblivious of the sarcasm with which their allegiance to and faith in British sovereignty were viewed by the official representatives of the crown, Boston's West Indians confidently fostered and projected their British identity. Even the American-born children were included in this resolve. The first generation made concrete attempts to develop and sustain foreign identities in the second generation by involving them in the activities of the subculture. Sons and Daughters of the Associates, an offshoot of Jamaica Associates, for example, was an organization for the children of Jamaican immigrants and "other interested children of West Indian parentage," which had as one of its main objectives the development of a Jamaican/West Indian/British identity among the children.[64]

The realities of the Boston/American context within which the immigrants and their children operated militated against the full realization of such objectives. For all practical purposes, the "West Indian" children were treated as indistinguishable from African American children. Low expectations greeted them in school, as in 1924 when V. T. Graham, a psychologist sent by Ruggles Street Nursery to evaluate three-and-a-half-year-old Elma Lewis, described her as a "mentally alert, responsive, precocious little negro girl, whose mental development as measured by the 'I.Q.' is probably, as is usual with members of her race, at a higher peak now than it will be as she grows older."[65] David Nelson, a second-generation Jamaican from a staunchly Catholic family, could not attend parochial school in the 1940s because he was Black. As he explained: "The discrimination was *de facto*. Black Catholics were few to start with and the few parochial schools which existed then were full of Irish Catholic kids who hated blacks . . . no one said anything, but we knew we did not belong in those schools."[66] Mel King, whose parents came from Guyana and Barbados, also knew the torment and confusion of grappling with multiple identities:

> I grew up on the one hand feeling positive about being West Indian and Black; but on the other hand, I had to grapple with the negative imagery of being a Black child in the United States, not wanting to identify with people who were and who behaved in a Steppin Fetchit Rochester model. Every time one of those movies was shown, we had to fight the next day in school because someone would come up and mock you. As far as white teachers and white students were concerned, people who were Black were considered Negro or colored, but White people were of American or Italian or Irish descent. We resisted that by insisting that we were West Indians.[67]

Thus, the reality was that despite the efforts of the family and the immigrant church and associations, the children of West Indian immigrants lived within the larger American society, specifically, the Black American society. They attended the same public schools as children of American-born Blacks and forged strong friendship ties with them. Amanda Houston, whose parents were American-born, recalled those ties:

> Too much has been made of the rift between West Indians and native-born Blacks. Of course, we all had our peculiar identities, but one thing that bound us was the fact that we were all Black children with lofty aspirations, struggling in a society which thwarted our every move.[68]

The Hattie B. Cooper Community Center on Shawmut Avenue in the South End was a physical symbol of this viable intersection of the two groups of Black children. A settlement house established in 1920 by the Women's Home Missionary Society of the Fourth Methodist Episcopal Church (an African American church), the Cooper House was, among other things, an after-school educational recreational center for neighborhood children. The center's programs fostered a certain cohesiveness that cut across family and cultural backgrounds:

> After school and during vacations we hung out there. I mean children whose parents were from Jamaica, Barbados, Cape Verde, Boston, North Carolina, Virginia, all over. At the center we forgot about our origins and just had a good time as Black Americans.[69]

Similarly, Elma Lewis alluded to this influence on the Caribbean, American-born children outside of the West Indian subculture. Emphasizing that "it was not just her church [St. Cyprian's]" that shaped her, she recalled the lasting experiences that she got from going to after-school programs while her mother worked.[70]

Therefore, at the same time that the children of immigrants were watching cricket matches and participating in the activities of the Sons and Daughters of the Associates and other such organizations which defined their identities as West Indians and British, they were also "hanging around" Cooper House, attending public schools, and interacting with neighborhood children, aspects which defined their Black American identity. The children, more integrated into the larger society, became race conscious and contributed in bringing about the same in their parents. Take the following example where a Barbadian woman recalled the day when she became, among other things, a Black American:

> My son, a well brought up boy, came home from school looking very rough. Some Irish kids had angered him by calling him a good for nothing nigger. This was not the first time, but this time it really got out of hand. I was furious with him. I said, "Why don't you just make it clear to these kids that you are not a Negro? You are Bajan, a West Indian, a British." With tears running down his cheeks he replied: "But Ma, I am not completely those things. I am an American, a Black American. And you too, ma, when most people around here see you, they see a NEGRO [my emphasis]."[71]

Race consciousness and cooperation with American Blacks were often promoted by some of the leaders of the immigrant community, some of whom were the founders of their distinctive immigrant community institutions. In 1936, for example, Jamaica Associates invited Jamaican-born James S. Watson, a municipal court judge in New York City, to give the keynote speech at a ceremony commemorating the second anniversary of the group's founding. Weeks before his arrival, some Jamaicans had begun to brag to U.S. Blacks and other West Indians about this symbol of the success of Jamaicans in America. Under the headline "Boston Jamaicans Fete Judge Watson," a *Chronicle* article on February 15, 1936, described him as a "distinguished Jamaican, one of the most noteworthy colored men in America and one of the nation's ablest judges." But the judge's message, quoted in the February 22 *Chronicle,* was one of unity with U.S. Blacks: "You must spurn the specious arguments of those who would instill in you a sense of inferiority to those whose sojourn here in this land long antedated yours. Just as a fusion of Russian and Swede, Pole and Austrian, Irish and German made this great land an exemplary democracy, so must the admixture of Jamaican and North Carolinian, Barbadian and Pennsylvanian, Trinidadian and Georgian [work] to the common good of this buffeted race of ours."

This attempt to work for the common good of the race was demonstrated in some concrete ways. Cooperation in matters of self-help and mutual benefit was one such marker. The Progressive Credit Union, incorporated in December 1929, was emblematic. With its motto "Thrift Each Pay Day," the union encouraged Blacks of the South End and Roxbury to save with it. Starting with twenty members and assets of $281, by 1935 the membership had grown to 400 and in 1940 there were a thousand members and assets of $45,100.[72] Members benefited from loans for a host of needs—health care, taxes, school tuition, weddings, funerals, etc. In 1940, of the thousand members, about 150 were West Indians, underscoring the fact that the union was not a West Indian institution; more appropriately, it was a Black establishment. Moreover, it was clear that the impetus for its establishment came mostly from southern-born businessmen. North Carolina native Edward Cooper, manager of the South End branch of the First National Stores, hammered home this point:

> Coming from the South we were aware of the significance of self-help. So we did not waste any time initiating plans for the establishment of the union. This institution is proving indispensable under the circumstances. We are strangers here and in many cases when we die we want to be taken back to our homeland and buried there. To that end the Progressive Union has helped many families defray the costs of a worthy funeral. Besides this grim area, the institution has helped us adjust. We have to help ourselves because the established system will not.[73]

This immense role of southern Blacks notwithstanding, it does not seem like they monopolized the running of the organization. West Indians also held significant offices, like Barbadian American Victor Bynoe, who was treasurer for thirty years.[74]

Many years after the founding of the Progressive Credit Union, the process of collaboration for self-help was again concretely displayed in the founding of Co-op Way, Inc. This time the initiative came from the Black foreigners. In 1948, as some Barbadians were forming the Barbadian Mutual

Society for the purpose of sending assistance to the homeland, they decided to simultaneously work with American Blacks to establish the Co-op Way. Only a few months after the Co-op Way's launching, the West Indian and southern Black leaders organized lectures which focused on the usefulness of co-ops in Barbados and North Carolina.[75]

Cooperation between the two groups was also displayed in performance representation. Most symbolic of this was the St. Cyprian's Drum and Bugle Corps. This ensemble, made up of mostly second-generation West Indians and sponsored by the "West Indian" church, was, as the *Boston Guardian* emphasized, a fixture in Black Boston's civic and patriotic parades, including the annual celebration in March of Crispus Attucks Day.[76]

This interaction through community institutions provides clear examples of how the experiences of the two Black groups intersected. The striking similarities in the traditions, status, and aspirations of both southern migrants and the West Indian foreigners drew them together. The common interests and concerted efforts were manifested even more assertively in their encounter with and responses to racism, a theme that is developed fully in the next chapter.

For Boston's West Indians, race consciousness and cooperation in community organization never translated to an ossified Black American identity. Instead, while acknowledging their status and identity as Blacks in Boston, the immigrants continued to develop and project their inherited foreign identities and sustain those institutions which fostered and affirmed those identities. Nowhere was this dualism played out more vividly than in their quest to denounce injustice and advocate equality and progress both in Boston and in their homelands.

4

Militant Immigrants and Relentless Ex-colonials?

On Sunday, July 8, 1934, an African American man, J. Borden, was with his family at his Copeland Street home in Roxbury when police burst in to arrest him on a misdemeanor charge. They chased him and subsequently shot and wounded him, claiming that he resisted arrest and threatened them. Members of the community, angered by what they saw as yet another incident of police brutality against Blacks, rallied and attempted to mount a case against the city's police department.[1] Their efforts were largely unsuccessful, and soon it was rumored that some West Indian radicals were claiming that the American-born Negro lawyer handling the case was responsible for the stagnation. To "straighten things out," the *Chronicle* sent a West Indian–born reporter to interview Borden's lawyer and determine where the case was going. Irritated by what seemed like the reporter's insinuation that he was incompetent, the lawyer asked the reporter if he would have done things differently if he were in his shoes. When he replied in the affirmative, the lawyer said: "It does not surprise me. That is just the way a West Indian would act."[2] This statement suggests that by the 1930s Boston's West Indians may have carved a reputation for their aggressive confrontation of racial assaults.

It is impossible to fully cover Black activism in the first half of the twentieth century without considering the contributions of West Indian immigrants, and the 1920s and 1930s provide some of the best illustrations. Who could deny the prominence of Jamaican Claude McKay in the Black nationalism of the Harlem Renaissance or the fiery stepladder/soap box agitation of Virgin Islander Hubert Harrison and Barbadian Richard B. Moore? Absolutely impossible to ignore in the same epoch is the impact of Jamaican Marcus Garvey, who, espousing Black nationalism and pan-Africanism, successfully inspired the first mass Black movement in the United States. Citing these and other examples, some contemporary reviewers concluded that the West Indian role was not only crucial to the success of the Black American struggle, it was indispensable. West Indian leaders themselves contributed in great measure to this interpretation. For example, Jamaican Wilfredo Domingo, who was one of the best-known Black activists both in New York and Jamaica, declared in his essay entitled "Gift of the Black Tropics":

> The West Indian has thrown himself whole-heartedly into the fight against lynching, discrimination and other disabilities from which Negroes suffer. . . . The outstanding contributions of West Indians to American Negro life is the insistent assertion of their manhood in an environment that demands too much servility and unprotesting acquiescence from men of African blood. This unwillingness to conform and be standardized, to accept tamely an inferior status and abdicate their humanity, finds an open expression in the activities of the foreign-born Negro in America.[3]

Similar sentiments appeared in Jamaica in *Plain Talk,* former Jamaican Bostonian T. A. Kitchener's paper:

> You have produced no leaders who are worthy of the name. We have given you Marcus Garvey who in one breath has said more; who in one movement of his muscles has done more for racial advancement everywhere than all the so-called leaders of the Negroes produced in America have done since the first boat load of us were brought from West Africa.
> . . . The West Indian comes to the United States prepared.[4]

Pronouncements like those cited above were meant to underscore the initiative and tenacity of the Black foreigners in challenging an oppressive milieu, which they believed had created conformity among American-born Blacks. This was certainly the aim of those commentators who drew attention to the brazen acts of female West Indian garment workers in New York City in the 1930s, who, unlike their American-born counterparts, ignored the barriers designed to keep them out of the needle trades.[5]

The existing literature on West Indian dedication to and radicalism in the Black struggle for the most part presents "West Indian activism" as a monolithic phenomenon to which all the immigrants subscribed, even though the views and actions examined are often those of the small vocal elite. It places much emphasis on the ironic schism between African Americans and the Black foreigners and, finally, it focuses almost exclusively on New York. This chapter, the focus of which is on Boston, moves from the traditional arena. It approaches the topic with more attention to its complexity by showing that activism among Boston's West Indians was diffusely focused, multi-ideological and multitiered. Finally, it attempts to rescue the

masses of the Black immigrant community from historical obscurity by fer-
reting out the attitudes and actions of the so-called non-intellectual, non-
political, and inarticulate. A meaningful way, therefore, to examine West Indian activism in Boston is to look at this phenomenon as it targeted two
fronts—Boston and the homeland, for these two sites were central in shaping how the immigrants organized and agitated.

In Boston the problem hinged on racism, which constituted one of the
most formidable areas of culture shock for the foreigners. Boston's West Indians, like many Black immigrants, were often quoted as saying that they
never experienced racism until they came to America. This overstated declaration, unfortunately, is often taken literally. On the contrary, there is
ample evidence that race and color were pivotal features in the societies they
left behind. Consider the following description:

> If you were to go into all the offices throughout Jamaica you would not find one
> percent of black clerks employed. You will find nearly all white and coloured
> [mulatto] persons . . . for proof please go through our Post Office, Government
> Offices and stores in Kingston, and you will see only white and coloured men in
> positions of importance and trust and you will find the black men and women
> as store-men, messengers, attendants and common servants. In the country
> parts you will find the same order of things. On the Estates and Plantations you
> will find the black men and women as labourer, the coloured man as clerk and
> sometimes owner and the white man generally as master.[6]

As the passage clearly indicates, these scenarios were not Alabama,
Georgia, or Mississippi. They were not about a northeastern U.S. city, either,
although the description of job discrimination is similar to the situation in
Boston, described earlier in chapter 2. The quote is Marcus Garvey's description of a typical racial situation in the West Indies of the first half of the
twentieth century.[7]

The shock was therefore not about encountering racism for the first
time, but being exposed to the distinctive American brand of racism. For
some this exposure began during the journey to their new home. The
United Fruit Company, whose steamers provided the primary means of
transportation, was accused of the "worst kind of discrimination on the
basis of skin-color." In 1934 a group of investigative journalists, headed by
the Jamaican historian and *Chronicle* contributing writer J. A. Rogers,
looked into persistent allegations of Black passengers, the majority of whom
were West Indians. The team found that the worst cabins and eating areas
were given to Negroes. According to its report, published in the *Chronicle* of
May 13, 1934, racial slurs were even used by the white staff. The steamer experience was a harbinger of the racial affront that would inevitably face the

Black foreigners in their new home. For those who did not experience the racism on the high seas, as the Rogers report called it, and those who did but dismissed the incidents as isolated, blatant and persistent racist incidents and situations in Boston were to hammer home the point.

Long before a West Indian community emerged, Boston, and Massachusetts in general, had acquired national and international acclaim for political and social reform geared toward justice for all. As a twentieth-century scholar of nineteenth-century New England put it: "Massachusetts was not just any state, but arguably the home of antislavery and the capital of the culture of the North."[8] As a champion of Black freedom and progress, Massachusetts was, as expected, touted for the advancement of its Negro population since the eighteenth century. Granted that the glowing reports of White abolitionists and other Whites may have been exaggerated, the echo of similar sentiments by members of the Black community counted for much validation. They acknowledged the freedom of Negroes to speak their minds, the remarkably low rate of illiteracy among Boston's Blacks, and the distinction of a prosperous merchant and professional class of Black Brahmins.[9]

Even with this endorsement from the city's influential Blacks, Boston was not a "paradise for the Negro," as the *Boston Herald* of May 1904 had claimed. Discrimination and intergroup conflict stemming from racism became even more evident with the arrival of American-born Blacks from the South. John Daniels, a White social worker in Boston during the Progressive Era, discussed these trends in his seminal work on Black Boston, *In Freedom's Birthplace*. Writing much later, historian Stephan Thernstrom offers persuasive statistics to support his arguments that for much of the first half of the twentieth century, Boston's African Americans were relegated to the bottom rungs of a racially and ethnically defined hierarchy. African Americans, who Thernstrom says as a group could be considered a truly permanent proletariat, were still outranked by White immigrant groups whose first generation initially encountered handicaps similar to those of the largely unskilled Blacks.[10] In the final analysis, not even the established history of a celebrated Black Brahmin class could surmount the potency of race.

If, in spite of the accomplishments of the Puritan founders, Boston's Black community was disadvantaged in serious ways, it was not for the inertia of the native Black Bostonians. Since the abolitionist era, protest had been one of the hallmarks of the community. Black leaders like David Walker, Susan Paul, Charles Lenox Remond, and Sarah Remond rallied people together for a variety of causes—freedom, equal educational opportunities, fair employment practices, better housing, suffrage, etc. Firm demands for civil rights for Blacks girded their actions, as was the case when they protested the showing of D. W. Griffith's *Birth of a Nation*. In 1915, led by *Guardian* editor William Monroe Trotter, Boston's Blacks mounted some of the most vehement opposition to that movie, which depicted Blacks as barbaric and a threat to Euro-American civilization. For this and many other causes, Faneuil Hall, that bastion of Yankee tradition, reverberated with the Black activists' cries of protest. This venue was very often where they went, as the *Guardian* of February 27, 1904, put it, "to rock the cradle of liberty." Evidently, then, Boston's Blacks did challenge the status quo. Historian Mark Schneider, who studied the opposition to the encroachment of Jim Crow in Boston, maintains that Boston had "a proud history of resistance to oppression," one of the factors which made that city a hotbed of African American militancy.[11]

These facts are relevant here because they clearly demonstrate that Boston's native Black population was not a passive one, jolted only by the arrival of a group of militant foreign Blacks. Rather, by the time the English-speaking West Indians arrived, a Black protest tradition had been established, from which the immigrants would draw and to which they would also contribute.

The most tangible apparatus for agitation by the Black foreigners was the *Boston Chronicle,* with its ominous motto of "Fearless and Uncompromising—Advocate of Justice, Rights and Opportunities." Admittedly, the owners, editors, and reporters were mostly middle-class men, like barristers Thaddeus Kitchener and Alfred Haughton, medical doctor Uriah Murray, and Harvard graduate William Harrison. Despite this genteel provenance, the paper appealed to a broad section of the Black population, which included a significant working-class audience. An icon in the Black immigrant community, this West Indian institution was also a formidable force in the larger Black community. It was an organ of incessant crusading for economic, political, and social rights. Less than a decade after the launching of the paper, its editors and reporters had gained a reputation for their fiery contributions, which exposed the many patterns of racism and advocated a tough, no-nonsense stand against the status quo.

The *Chronicle* revealed some of its strongest qualities as an advocate for Black advancement in the economic sphere, an arena of unending struggle. It routinely carried exposés which demonstrated blatant racial discrimination in employment. This was particularly so during the Great Depression, when in Boston, like elsewhere, Blacks were often the last to be hired and the first to be fired.[12] The paper went beyond the mere reporting of injustice and attempted to translate awareness into action. Throughout the 1930s and early 1940s, it ran the following front-page declaration:

NEGROES ARE REALLY WAKING UP!

THINKING Negroes around Roxbury are now spending their money only in stores owned and operated by Negroes and in other stores where they can find colored help.

Very few Negroes are now spending their hard-earned dollars in places where they haven't a chance to secure jobs for themselves or their children.

This approach was typical of the don't-buy-where-you-can't-work boycott strategy which defined Black economic nationalism in the Depression era.[13]

One of the emphases of Uplift Ideology, so emblematic of African American middle-class protest, is economic progress through self-employment.[14] The West Indian journalist agitators, like many of their American-born counterparts, incorporated this strategy in their activism. The June 8, 1935, editorial declared: "In a prejudiced white world the Negro is not associated with successful business, consequently every Negro business enterprise drives a wedge a little farther towards breaking down any opposition that confronts the colored man in the commercial field." Convinced of this role of Black entrepreneurship, the *Chronicle* promoted self-employment. One way it sought to do this was to ferret out and give publicity to Black-owned businesses in Greater Boston. Between 1935 and 1948 it profiled Black entrepreneurs and their establishments.

The hairdressing industry, which the *Chronicle* acknowledged was "an important lifeline among our group and means much to our girls in particular," was one area that received particular attention. To underscore its significance, the paper ran several pieces about the hairdressing business both in Boston and in the nation in general. It helped its readers understand Black women's creative role in this sphere, especially in their formulation of hair care systems. During that time the Apex and Poro systems were the two most popular ones in Boston. In June 1932, the paper published a detailed interview with the founder of the Apex System and Apex Hair College, Mrs. Sara Spencer Washington. In 1935 a similar piece was done on the founder of the Poro System, Mrs. Annie M. Turnbo-Malone of Chicago. While demonstrating the significant strides made in the industry, the *Chronicle* continued to alert Black women to the ever-present threat posed by White competition. It urged the Board of Black Hairdressers to be more assertive about staving off what the paper saw as blatant attempts by Whites to encroach on a Black economic niche. The brazen assault was explained in the editorial of December 7, 1935, entitled "The Handwriting on the Wall": "Right in our midst two white establishments have been catering to colored patronage, and it is likely that others will follow. Some are sending white girls to have their hair done in colored shops and so learn how it is done; others are hiring colored girls to work in their shops, and will see to it that they teach white girls who will eventually supplant them."

The need for the organized promotion of Black business was one of the major concerns of the Black leadership. In 1932, when Phi Beta Sigma adopted a national resolution to work for "Bigger and Better Business for Negroes," the *Chronicle* devoted space to explaining the efficacy of that "noble experiment." It covered that organization's activities, which were geared toward educating Blacks about available opportunities. It identified useful networks like the "Negro-loving" banks and Black credit unions and cooperatives. Through these gestures, the West Indian–owned *Chronicle* contributed to a strategy of defiance already embraced by American-born Blacks for the uplifting of their race.

Physical assaults on Blacks were also a concern that drew the attention of the West Indian leaders. Conducting its own investigations and urging its readers to send in reports of assaults, the *Chronicle* made it a duty to expose subtle and direct violent racist assaults. The following from the August 27, 1935, issue is an example of the kind of "lists of assaults" that frequently appeared in the paper:

1. A group of white men chased, caught, and beat up two Negro men.
2. Negro longshoremen beaten by white strikers and abused by white police. No arrests.
3. Negro women kicked in the stomach on Tremont Street by white gangsters in broad daylight. No arrests.
4. Aged and infirm Negro beaten by white hoodlums.
5. Two Negroes have their skulls split by axe and nightstick when policemen went on a rampage. Negroes were unfairly charged with drunkenness and arrested.

Evidence was never hard to come by. Boston was a city of neighborhoods that were defined by race, ethnicity, and class. By the 1930s, invisible yet palpable boundaries had emerged, and explosive encounters still occurred. Nat Hentoff, who grew up in that tumultuous milieu, vividly recounts how Blacks, Jews, Irish, Italians, Protestants, and Catholics collided in the Puritans' "beacon on the hill."[15] *Chronicle* and *Guardian* documentation showing that attacks on Blacks and Jews were frequent in the 1930s and 1940s is supported by oral history and the compilations of the Boston NAACP and the Jewish Anti-Defamation League of B'nai B'rith.[16] Members of these racial and ethnic groups were frequently ambushed and seriously beaten by gangs of Whites, particularly Irish Catholic youths from South Boston and some areas of Dorchester. While most of the Black victims were ordinary working-class people, successful, middle-class, prominent Blacks were not immune. An example is the attack on internationally renowned tenor Roland Hayes in 1935, when his home in Brookline Village was vandalized by a group of White youths in what Hayes and many believed was a racially motivated attack.[17] Another headline-making attack was on the *Chronicle*'s own editor, second-generation West Indian William B. Harrison. Harrison's parents had emigrated to Boston from Jamaica around the period of World War I. He was a Harvard graduate and a respectable leader of the Black community who lived in the Humbolt Avenue middle-class area of Roxbury. Moreover, it was even rumored that he sometimes wrote speeches for Boston mayor James Michael Curley.[18] Yet in April 1947, a group of "black-hating youths" ambushed and beat him severely only a few blocks from his home.[19]

As the opening paragraph of this chapter began to reveal, in addition to these blatant criminal acts of racism by civilians, the Black community also contended with police brutality. The treatment of Blacks by an all-white Boston police force was a thorn in the side of the community throughout the first half of the twentieth century. When the West Indian Blacks arrived, they joined what was already an ongoing struggle between law enforcement and the city's Black population.[20] By the 1930s, West Indian leaders were among the foremost crusaders against an unfair justice system. The *Chronicle* editor, Jamaican T. A. Kitchener, emphasizing his qualifications as a barrister who had studied in the inns of England, put together a team and led an inquiry into court cases that involved Blacks. The investigation revealed, according to the *Chronicle* of September 17, 1932, that "[a] careful survey of all the cases tried before certain judges of the Roxbury District Court shows that there is the cancer of prejudice against Negroes that is wrecking the structure of the great institution of justice." This and other such findings demonstrated how vulnerable the Black residents were in the face of a racist police force and an unfair legal system. In that same year, Kitchener organized meetings to convince the residents of the predominantly Black neighborhood of Roxbury of the necessity of a civic league. The upshot, the Negro Defence Association for the "preservation of peace and safety in the black community," was largely the work of Kitchener and the *Chronicle* activists.

The shortcomings of the federal legal system and its failure to protect Blacks on a national level were also frequently tackled by the paper. It covered incidents of racism across the country, from police brutality in New York to lynchings in Indiana to continued enslavement of Blacks in Mississippi to the extension of Jim Crow into Hawaii. No other incident gave it the opportunity to analyze racism in a national context than the case of the Scottsboro Boys.[21] Like other Black publications across the country, the

Chronicle devoted extensive coverage to the case, which quickly became an international cause célèbre. Besides regular updates of the progress of the trials (including retrials and appeals), the paper printed the views of its readers as well as feature articles analyzing the implications of unfolding developments. Howard University Dean Kelly Miller, a regular columnist, contributed a series illustrating the insidious nature of Jim Crow in the South, its northern parallels, the struggle between the NAACP and the communists over control of the boys' defense, and the defiant reactions of African Americans across the country.

The actions of the *Chronicle* journalists did not particularly demonstrate a uniquely foreign, immigrant, West Indian propensity. Activism through journalism fit into the tradition of Black protest in the United States. This tradition dates back to 1827, when *Freedom's Journal,* the first African American newspaper, emerged, with its editors' pledge to "plead our own cause."[22] During the *Chronicle*'s heyday, across the country, Black publications like the *Amsterdam News, Pittsburgh Courier, Chicago Defender,* and *Crisis* were conducting similar crusades. In many respects the *Chronicle* itself was a collaborative venture of Black foreigners and American-born Blacks. Although most of the editors and reporters were West Indian immigrants (mostly Jamaicans), the regular contributors included nationally recognized African American intellectuals and activists like Carter G. Woodson, Kelly Miller, and Paul Robeson. Though based in places like New York and Washington, D.C., these activists contributed to numerous Black publications around the country.

The external support for the agitational quality of the *Chronicle* did not only come from non–West Indians. West Indian journalists-cum-activists, mostly based in New York, also left their fiery imprint. Two of the most prolific of these were Jamaicans Vere Johns and Joel A. Rogers. While the relationships with the "big guns" were very helpful in enabling the *Chronicle* to adhere to its motto, they did not transform the paper to a mere vassal of a more radical West Indian community in New York or elsewhere. The West Indian and African American journalists in Boston were agitators in their own right, who, in spite of outside contributions, were the ones most responsible for making the *Chronicle* such a vital instrument of Black activism.

While West Indian leaders recognized the effectiveness of protest groups and direct action, they were not oblivious to the necessity of change through the ballot. Here also the Black foreigners were to follow some set patterns. The West Indians began to arrive at a time when ward bossism was ascendant. This was a period when in many major U.S. cities, the political districts, known as wards, were controlled by powerful politicians, most of whom were American-born children of European immigrants. Boston's twenty-five wards were mostly controlled by Irish Americans. The highest concentrations of Boston's Blacks fell into two districts—wards 9 and 12— which by 1920 were controlled by Irish American politicians. For much of the first three decades of the twentieth century, Blacks of these districts followed a pattern where they tried to make the political process work for them through their support for and faith in the elected White ethnic politicians.[23]

Even though in the early 1900s Boston's Blacks, like African Americans elsewhere, still clung to Abraham Lincoln's Republican Party, significant changes were taking place. Overwhelming Black support for Democrat John F. Fitzgerald[24] in the 1905 mayoral race was portentous of the future Irish-Black relations in electoral politics. The newly formed Black organization, the Boston Suffrage League, launched an effective campaign against the Yankee Republican candidate Louis Frothingham. Many of the speakers at a forum described as "a memorable meeting in the annals of the Negroes' struggles for liberty in Massachusetts" reminded the audience of the contempt of Yankee Republicans and their failure to take a stand against the encroaching southern-style Jim Crowism.[25] Again in 1908, the largely Republican Black population endorsed Fitzgerald, this time to demonstrate their protest over Republican president Theodore Roosevelt's blatant racism in his response to the Brownsville affray.[26] The slogan among African American voters that year was "Remember Brownsville!"[27]

Yet another show of Black support for Fitzgerald came in 1910, when he made his comeback after his 1908 defeat. His Republican opponent, James Jackson Storrow, was the personification of Yankeedom if ever there was one. A Harvard blueblood, Storrow had gained a reputation for his contributions to the Brahmin-controlled Good Government Association, especially in the area of school reform. In fact, it was over this matter that he directly crossed Black Bostonians. As Black citizens were reminded by their leaders, Storrow had once remarked that he would not appoint a colored teacher in a public school with more than fifty White children.[28]

The zenith of the Black-Irish political alliance came with James Michael Curley. During the various Curley eras (he was mayor from 1915 to 1919, 1922 to 1926, 1930 to 1934, and 1946 to 1950), the needs of African Americans were worked into his Boston Tammany Club. The strongest link between this Curley political machine and the Black populace was an African American brother duo—Silas (Shag) and Balcom Taylor. From their drugstore, Lincoln Pharmacy on Tremont Street in the South End, they rendered a variety of services to the Black residents of Wards 9 and 12 in the true spirit of ward bossism. Black Bostonians sang their praises:

Shag [Taylor] would do anything for anybody . . . He was the Black closest to James Michael Curley . . . Shag did a lot of little favors for people, the same way Curley did a lot of favors for the Irish people. Michael Curley and Shag Taylor worked together to do what they could in those days with the segregation what it was . . . [29]

The Black community stuck with this their closest Irish American ward boss, even when he ran afoul of the law and went to prison. The *Boston Guardian* reaffirmed this loyalty in 1942: "We congratulate Mr. Curley for the magnificent come back. . . . The race can feel confident that we still have an advocate . . . in the person of Mr. Curley who has proved his interest and friendship by a long list of helpful acts."[30]

The Black foreigners, too, grasped the viability of the patronage system. Even though their leaders possessed qualities often said to derive from their West Indian background, they were willing to join in an already unfolding political trend. Sometimes they revealed their reservations about the established African American brokers, as can be gleaned from Kitchener's sarcastic remarks: "The plum daddies and mammies, those men and women who go between the masses of voters and the political aspirants, are all crawling and trying to woo our newspapers to assess their candidates in favorable light."[31] And Bynoe once said about Shag Taylor:

Taylor was no person, in my opinion, to be a leader of the colored people . . . they [blacks] knew him for what he was, and you didn't have to give him too much . . . They would give him liquor; they'd give him anything. And he was the dispenser of goodies.[32]

Yet the West Indians did not aggressively attempt to replace these brokers and a political trend with their own West Indian–inspired alternatives. If anything, the evidence shows that for the most part they worked with the established brokers and within the established political milieu. Ward bossism was brought into the Black immigrant community mainly by the *Chronicle* journalists and other leaders, who were instrumental in the founding and running of the West Indian institutions. Their positioning in both the immigrant and American worlds enabled them to perform this role: they were founders of and officeholders in West Indian associations; they were affiliated with the *Chronicle,* an instrument of Black activism; and they worked closely with both Republican and Democratic political groups/clubs in wards 9 and 12. These intermediaries effectively brought political agendas to the floor of the West Indian community institutions. Most of the members became aware of ongoing discourses on the state of Black Boston through their participation in the activities of the various organizations.

David Nelson recalled his parents' "political education" through their participation in Jamaica Associates:

> My parents got an earful about how to make the Constitution work for Blacks
> from the activities of the Associates. You didn't just go to those meetings and
> functions for tea parties, music and dance. You went there to find out about the
> problems, how to approach them and which politicians are best suited for the
> job.[33]

Indeed, less than a year after its founding, Jamaica Associates began to acquaint its members with the insidious aspects of Boston politics. In 1934 local African American brokers along with some of the West Indian leaders of the *Chronicle* came to speak to members of the association about the necessity of voting out the incumbent attorney general of Massachusetts. Joseph E. Warner was accused of discrimination and ingratitude to loyal Negroes of the Republican Party who had helped get him elected. Once in office, according to the political critics, he acknowledged Jews, Irish, and Italians by giving them good and respectable offices, while the only position he offered the Negro was messenger.[34] In that same year, as Mrs. Betty Williams of the Barbados Union recalled, the Curley factor was raised in several meetings of the various island associations. Members were encouraged not only to vote for James Michael Curley but also to make use of the services of his Boston Tammany Club. West Indian leaders like T. A. Kitchener and Alfred Haughton of Jamaica Associates, Ernest Headley of West India Aid, and African American doctor and staunch Taylor (Balcom and Shag) ally William Worthy addressed audiences at West Indian associations' functions, admonishing them to disregard allegations of Curley's reputation as "dishonest and foremost bankrupter of the city." They reminded them that it was "always simple" for Black people to "get an audience with James Michael."[35] When Kitchener launched a campaign against the Republican leaders of Ward 9, whom he accused of attempting to sabotage Negro enterprise, he first publicly indicted them at a West India Aid Association meeting.[36]

The associations and their members were not passive consumers of information about the political stakes. They built fundraising for "desirable candidates" into their annual activities. And they issued clear statements of support for actions deemed conducive to Black progress, as when Barbados Union endorsed a request to the governor to appoint African American attorney Irwin T. Dorch as judge.[37]

Patronage from benevolent White politicians was not an immovable facet of the electoral arena. The political marriage between the Black voters and brokers and White politicians was not completely smooth sailing. From the onset the support of Irish politicians by the Black leadership was never monolithic. Convinced that most of the Irish politicians were opportunists, skeptical Black leaders did not feel that the Irish experience in Yankee Boston, however bitter,[38] created any kind of genuine empathy for Blacks. Such critics raised specific flaws. For example, in 1915, in spite of Black protest, both Mayor Curley and first Irish American Catholic governor, David Walsh, did nothing to stop the showing of *Birth of a Nation*.[39]

While the *Birth of a Nation* fiasco lasted a short time, mostly during the showing, the disappointment over minimal economic gains remained constant. The very Black politicians and publications who commended the "friends of the race," also challenged these "friends" to commit more to providing employment and other economic opportunities for Blacks comparable to what they offered their White supporters. From Fitzgerald to Curley, no Irish American boss came out excellently in an assessment of how their friendships translated to tangible material gains. As Bynoe later freely admitted, some West Indian and African American leaders, in spite of the formidable lobbying of the Taylor brothers, actively worked to replace Curley.[40]

So far, the protagonists have been the elite. What was the relationship beyond this vocal group? It is quite easy to feel the frustration of historian Noel Ignatiev, who noted that in his research he found not a single diary or letter or anything of that sort where an ordinary Irish man or woman recorded in any detail the texture of daily life and relations with the Black people who were often his or her closest neighbors.[41] Newspaper reports, church records, and oral history seem to suggest that the majority of interracial unions in Boston in the first half of the twentieth century were between Black men and first-generation Irish women. But many questions still remain to be explored in this social history. Why were the unions between Irish men and Black women not nearly as common as those between Black men and Irish women? How did the Irishmen and other members of the Irish American community react to these unions? What were the experiences of the children of these unions? And, most pertinently, what was the rate of interaction between ordinary West Indians and Irish Americans?

Far less blurry are the relations between Black and Irish American workers. While Fitzgerald was visiting the African Meeting House to denounce Jim Crow or James Michael Curley was having audiences with Black individuals referred to him by Shag Taylor, White workers, mostly of Irish descent, were vehemently opposing the entry of Black workers into their spheres of livelihood. Constantly under fire in the Black press was the Irish-dominated Boston Central Labor Union, which was accused of being one of the foremost Jim Crow institutions in that northern city.

Longshore and domestic services were the two major occupations where the two ethnic groups collided. Bridget, the reliable Irish maid, was a fixture by the twentieth century; so was the image of the dependable African American domestic. Although historians of Irish American women's history such as Hasia Diner[42] have pointed out that the Irish women had an advantage because they spoke English, there is evidence that Black women in Boston, including the southern migrants and West Indian immigrants, posed fierce competition. These women, who also spoke English, may have been preferred by some Yankee employers because, unlike the Irish Catholic women, they were more often Protestants and would have been deemed a more suitable influence on the children of Puritan descent. Economic rivalry contributed in preventing a unified Irish-Black front, even as the leaders of both groups carried on a viable, though flawed, political alliance.

Although none of the West Indian leaders ever acquired the political stature of the American-born Taylor brothers, they were influential mouthpieces of the Black electorate; Kitchener, the ever-energetic *Chronicle* editor and community leader, exemplified this fact. For example, in 1932 he defiantly declared: "No other group, Italian, French or Greek would listen to the plea of any man who insulted them."[43] Using conduits like the *Chronicle,* the leaders tried to enforce this conviction, as illustrated by the following editorial of October 20, 1934:

THE BOSTON CHRONICLE appeals to every Negro voter in Boston and the Commonwealth to present to the leaders of both major political parties the following program as a fair and impartial consideration for the bulk of their votes in the November elections and their continued party support:

1. That a Negro be appointed as a probation officer in the Roxbury court at once.
2. That D. Z. Foley place a Negro on his staff immediately.
3. That Attorney General Warner drop the bars and add a Negro lawyer to his office staff.
4. That both a Negro physician and dentist be placed in the Whittier Street Health Unit at once.
5. That Negro men and women be given fairer consideration for general employment in city and state departments.
6. That a Negro lawyer of repute be placed on the Massachusetts bench.

This program and this alone should be the principal basis upon which every Negro voter should base his conclusions. Throw your vote to the major party that acts first and most extensively in these matters.

This editorial also clearly illustrates the prevalent pattern of Black political activism into which the foreign activists entered. Access activism, as political scientist James Jennings calls it, sought a "piece of the pie," which often meant merely replacing White incumbents with Blacks. According to Jennings, it referred to "goals, preferences, and behavior aimed at economic accommodation with existing structures and distribution of wealth . . . the rules of the game or the position of interests with significant economic power are not challenged."[44]

Nevertheless, by the mid-1930s it was important for Blacks to elect their own Black representatives and not just their White ethnic benefactors. In fact it was deemed obligatory for them to support fellow Black office seekers. This was why those Blacks who in 1935 did not vote for Ernest D. Cooke, the only African American out of six candidates for city council from ward 9, were branded "Black Judases."[45]

West Indian leaders were actively involved, along with their African American counterparts, in this office-seeking aspect of the electoral process. Again, the *Chronicle* provided the cadre for this role. All the editors in the period from 1935 to 1948—Kitchener, Haughton, and Harrison—ran for various offices in wards 9 and 12. Kitchener even established his own small political machine. The Kitchener Group for Ward Nine was made up of West Indians Kitchener, C. Hilton Greene, David Chambers, Haten Maloof, William Cogbill, and African Americans Henry Bryant, Rose Bryant, Luke Holmes, Frank Mitchell, and Jessie Shaw. Although for the most part they ran as Democrats, in the 1940s, some West Indians and West Indian Americans flirted with communism, foremost of whom was William Harrison, who ran unsuccessfully for state representative for ward 12 in 1946. Their political affiliation aside, the West Indian leaders adopted slogans and platforms which echoed a radical rhetoric of an unrelenting Black crusade within the political status quo. It is thus important to recognize that when the West Indians participated in the electoral process they did so mostly as Black Bostonians and not as some distinctive constituency of foreign origin.

A consideration of West Indian activism within African American/American contexts must involve an examination of the immigrants' relationship with the National Association for the Advancement of Colored People (NAACP). That organization, though never unanimously wholeheartedly embraced by Blacks, was largely viewed as one of the significant twentieth-century organs for attaining civil rights, justice, and equality.[46] Before the 1930s, the Boston branch of the NAACP did not appeal to Black Bostonians, even though it had assumed a public stand in its support of William Monroe Trotter's 1915 protest against *Birth of a Nation*. In the first few decades of the twentieth century, there were signs that the issue of leadership in the Boston NAACP was a divisive factor. Some Blacks were convinced that real power was in the hands of the White members, even though

Butler Wilson, an African American, was president for two decades, from 1916 to 1936. In fact, some critics cited this as evidence of the machinations of Whites, who ensured such a long tenure. The disputable issue of the extent of White influence aside, it appears that in those first decades, the Boston NAACP did not take a decisive enough stand against increasing discrimination and de facto segregation.[47] It is not surprising, then, that West Indians, like American-born Blacks, were not eager to be paying members. Nevertheless, the West Indian leadership did see some viability in the NAACP as an instrument of Black advancement. *Chronicle* reports show that prominent members of the West Indian community attended meetings and publicized NAACP objectives and activities. However, firm West Indian interest in that civil rights organization seems to have only come with the overhauling of the NAACP in the late 1930s. Increased visible Black representation in the leadership and the transfer of the organization's activities from detached, upscale White areas to the heart of the Black neighborhoods loudly echoed the branch's new trajectory. Furthermore, direct and pointedly worded assaults on specific forms of racism and inequality defined its new militant tone.[48]

No other individual epitomized the West Indian connection to a refurbished Boston NAACP more than Victor Bynoe. Born in Barbados and raised within the West Indian immigrant community of St. Cyprian's Church, the Barbados Union, cricket, and tea parties, Bynoe was still connected to the reality of living in Black America. While he acknowledged the necessity and viability of West Indian immigrant institutions, he never wavered in his conviction that the most effective strategy for Black advancement was activism within American Black organizations, which more accurately reflected the country's collective Black population.[49] Therefore, Bynoe, a central figure in the Boston NAACP membership drives of the late 1930s and early 1940s, became an intermediary between that African American institution and the Black immigrant community. While his efforts and those of some of the other West Indian leaders succeeded in raising the level of West Indian membership and participation, the Boston NAACP never seemed to have occupied a central position in the group's activist agenda.

Much more central to that immigrant community was Jamaican Marcus Garvey's Universal Negro Improvement Association (UNIA). In typical Garveyite fashion, the orientation of the Boston branch was pan-African Black nationalism, which espoused Black pride, self-improvement, the development of Black enterprises, and the separation of the races. The exact extent of the operations and accomplishments of the Boston UNIA is difficult to ascertain because vital records perished when the Boston UNIA building burned to the ground. Local newspaper reports, oral history, and, very importantly, pertinent reports in the "News from Branches" section of the *Negro World* (the UNIA publication) help reconstruct that history. The Boston UNIA activities were similar to those of the other West Indian associations. It sponsored talks and debates on Black America, like the debate on the "Progress of Negro Women" (September 15, 1935). It organized forums for discussion of pan-African interests, like the Symposium on the Fate of Ethiopia and Negroes Around the World (December 8, 1935). Along with the Jamaica Associates and the Barbados Union, it sponsored annual Christmas tree parties, where it distributed baskets and money to children and their families. And, as the second generation still fondly recalls, the organization put up some of the most spectacular parades to commemorate Black pride.

While the Boston branch of the UNIA never achieved the notoriety that the main UNIA division had in New York, there were strong ties between the two. Boston frequently sent representatives to the flamboyant UNIA activities in New York and endeavored to keep its organizational structure, ideology, objectives, and activities close to the core spirit of the national UNIA.[50] Undoubtedly, with such a resolve, the agenda of the Boston UNIA seemed radical on the surface. Yet the evidence gleaned from the sources identified earlier seems to suggest that Garveyism in Boston was more rhetorical than practical in its orientation and accomplishments.

This assessment should, however, not detract from the effectiveness of that organization in instilling pride and a sense of Black nationalism in those who participated in its activities. Victor Bynoe recalls:

> The first Sunday of my arrival here, my father and my mother took me to the meeting. They had meetings on Sundays, Sunday evening at 4 o'clock. And there was the first time I got my introduction to the Garvey movement. . . . I was 14 years old. . . . They had formed a group of young men, who were cadets. The women were in uniform, and they had a men's corps . . . that was an every-Sunday proposition. You had to go because your parents took you. And, of course, it was the fundamentalist concept of nationalism—and Black this and Black that. And, of course, as you grew up, you got to understand what it was—a means of trying to inoculate the people into some sense of who they are and what they should be doing.[51]

Elma Lewis had similar reminiscences of family involvement in Garveyism:

> I was raised to be a pan-African. He [Lewis's father] was a follower of Marcus Garvey, and we belonged all our lives to the Universal Negro Improvement Association. Mother was a Black Cross nurse . . . he [her father] belonged to the African Legion. My brothers sold the *Negro World* . . . and I was a Girl Guide. The motto of Garvey was "Up you mighty race, up you mighty people; you can what you will . . ."[52]

But even these active participants recognized the limitations. Much later, in the 1980s, Bynoe lamented Garveyism's failure to involve itself assertively in politics:

> The Garvey movement did not take part in politics. Individuals in the Garvey movement might have, but the Garvey movement as a whole never subscribed or attempted to get involved in politics. It was not a large group. They were strictly West Indians and they were usually Barbadians and Jamaicans and a few others . . . there were no outstanding leaders as far as the Garvey movement was concerned among the local group . . . the intellectuals did not get involved in the Garvey movement. They were aloof . . . because I think they were concerned about the political opposition to the Garvey movement that was rampant . . . so they didn't have enough strength to become a political entity . . . if they had a hundred people at a meeting, it was plenty.[53]

Garveyism in Boston, according to Bynoe, indeed helped to uplift the spirits of some members of a racially oppressed segment of the population, but it did not really go beyond "the converted." The policy makers, the police, prejudiced employers, workers, and unionists, who made life unbearable for Blacks, were basically untouched by the movement.[54] This observation is supported by the silence from mainstream circles. Publications like the *Globe* and the *Herald* provide no hint that the Garvey movement was threatening enough to force action and possibly change in targeted institutions. The White-controlled publications may deliberately not have acknowledged the efficacy of the Black movement, but the Black publications, too, provide no insights into Garveyism as a formidable assailant of racism against Blacks. Therefore, while Garveyism undoubtedly influenced its adherents in the Black community in general and the Black immigrant community in particular, its impact in prompting change through activism was definitely not substantial.

While through the UNIA, the NAACP, and the *Chronicle,* West Indians were able to point out the flaws in Boston/American society and demand reforms, this focus was only one side to their protest tradition. On another side they appeared to be relentless ex-colonials who, though physically removed from the colonial setting, would not stop invoking their colonial affiliation, which they used not only to oppose injustice in Boston but also to attack the colonial system in the homeland. Agitation as ex-colonials, or perhaps more accurately as transnationals, occurred largely within the parameters of the immigrant community. The immigrant institutions served as conduits for creating and articulating political agendas, in addition to their more tangible social and cultural roles. As this chapter has already demonstrated, the West Indian associations were used to involve the immigrants in American political life. But the Black struggle in America was only one orientation of these institutions and a secondary one for many of their members. The immigrants (specifically the leaders) appeared relentless and militant, always protesting or demanding something, but much of their energy was also directed at the flawed colonial structure at home and what seemed like the increasing disintegration of British rule. A barometric review of the associations' activities clearly mirrors this inclination. Their political activities reached a zenith twice: in 1938, during the labor riots which engulfed the whole British West Indies, and 1942 and 1943, when demands for constitutional reforms overtook the region.[55] In February 1938 the Barbados Union organized meetings and demonstrations to address the ongoing unrest in the island. Efforts were targeted particularly at freeing jailed activists. These culminated in a strongly worded resolution to the governor demanding a fair trial and proper legal representation for the defendants. In the same month the Jamaica Associates invited nationally renowned Jamaican Claude McKay to speak on the situation. And in June of the same year, that organization formed a committee to investigate and report on the labor unrest in Jamaica. The mandate to the committee included the charge to take assertive actions, which should include "protest to the highest British officials and a commendatory letter to Bustamante [Alexander Bustamante, Jamaican trade union pioneer], leader of the strike and a pledge to him that the large Jamaican population of Boston is solidly behind their Jamaican fellows."[56] And, finally, 1943 saw what was arguably the biggest event ever launched through the combined efforts of the West Indian associations. With the Jamaica Associates in the lead, the associations (including the Barbados Union, Montserrat Progressive League, and the newly formed Bermudian Associates) sponsored a two-day symposium—May 30–31—on the theme "The Four Freedoms of the Island of Jamaica, British West Indies." Dignitaries, including the members of the high-profile New York West Indian elite, the British ambassador, renowned African American leaders, and West Indian nationalist leaders, were invited. The sponsors even invited and hoped that the Duke and Duchess of Windsor, who were visiting the United States at the time, would attend.[57]

Even without the presence of the estranged members of British royalty, the event was still pronounced a success. Admonishing the attendees that "the West Indian abroad is the hope for those in the islands," one of the keynote speakers, Dr. Eric E. Williams (later to be prime minister of independent Trinidad and Tobago) identified and discussed crucial economic and constitutional matters that needed to be addressed, with a view to working toward self-government.[58]

These examples help illustrate the intensity of Caribbean/West Indian nationalism which underscored much of West Indian activism during that period. It is instructive to note that Boston's West Indians were not unique in this pattern. In fact, this Caribbean nationalism abroad was understandably more visibly manifested in New York, which was headquarters to many of the individuals and pan-Caribbean organizations which were directing some of the nationalist efforts both in the West Indies and abroad.[59]

Many of the immigrants made a conscious choice of placing agitation for better conditions in the West Indies ahead of the Black struggle in Boston. The rationale for this can be found in the immigrants' premigration experiences and their understanding of the migration venture itself. The majority clung to the conviction that their stay in Boston was temporary. The migration plan was to work hard, educate their children, and return to the homeland with enough savings to live middle-class lives, West Indian style. No wonder, then, that many saw active participation in some coalitionist, collective American Black activism as time-consuming and likely to hinder the attainment of their objectives. So they devised subtle, individualized ways of dealing with the problems. From many examples, the reaction of West Indian women to the Housewives League will suffice to illustrate this point. The Housewives League, a branch of the Boston Trade Association, was formed in 1939 to address the problems facing Black women, especially those in domestic service, which had come to be seen as a guaranteed economic niche for Black women. Apprehension over heightened competition from Irish women and increasing complaints of mistreatment of Black domestic workers by their White employers triggered this concern.[60] A few months after its formation, many West Indian domestic workers wrote to the *Chronicle* expressing their ambivalence about the league. While they acknowledged the necessity of having a Black domestic workers' advocacy organization, they feared that expending time and energy on its functioning would be inimical to their plans. Part of one of the letters in the *Chronicle* of September 9, 1939, read:

> If I spend all that time going to Housewives League meetings, I will miss work, get into trouble and lose money. If that happens, how will I send my children to school, send money to my mother in Kingston and save money to go back? What I need to do, instead, is do my job properly so that my family [employer] will know that I am the best worker and treat me well. If they don't, I will leave them and go to one who does.

The views expressed here not only illustrate reservations about collective activism but also provide an example of the kind of individualized actions taken to register protest.

Continued belief in the impermanence of their stay in Boston contributed greatly to the nurturing of foreign identities, which among other

things framed how the immigrants viewed protest. Many saw a British colonial identity as an efficacious strategy. Upholding and projecting this foreign
identity by itself defied a system that tried to lump them with a historically
disadvantaged group. But more importantly, the continual clamor for the
intervention of the British government (through the consulate in Boston
and the embassy in Washington, D.C.) on their behalf is ample indication of
their conviction of the viability of that identity in ensuring their rights as
British subjects in America. Appealing to the British government was not a
new practice that emerged in the immigrants' new home. On the contrary,
direct appeal to the highest British official was the norm in the West Indies
by the 1930s. According to one of the governors of Jamaica: "The first thing
that black people want to do when they think they are oppressed is to go to
the Governor."[61] Even the seemingly militant leaders of the *Chronicle,* who
advocated coalitionist protest, often orchestrated the demands for British
intervention. A woman who wrote to the *Chronicle* may have expressed the
conviction of many in the West Indian community when, commenting on
reports about Jim Crowism in the South, she remarked that "they had better
not bring that here to the West Indians because if they do, they would have
to contend with the wrath of His Majesty, the King of England."[62]

This confidence in British support was evident throughout the first half
of the twentieth century, even when the immigrants were agitating against
the British colonial administration of the homeland. British support, however, did not seem to go beyond intervention on behalf of detained stowaways and the appearance of the ambassador's representative at a few social
events. Why this minimal British support? Was the Black British expatriate
community simply insignificant? While contempt for a Black British community is a tantalizing explanation, the neglect could be also due to practical constraints from inadequate staffing of the consulate. In his report to the
Foreign Office in 1943, Ambassador R. E. Barclay admitted that the consular
offices had not been able to honor the numerous requests for speakers and
other roles relating to public relations. Importantly, he emphasized that the
consulates in seaport towns, where "the shipping and other routine duties
are a heavy burden," were the most affected.[63] Boston was one such consulate. The possibility of consular wives filling in as substitute speakers, "instead of spending a large amount of their shopping time queuing up for
liquor,"[64] was not pursued seriously. Whatever the real reasons, a lukewarm
British official presence, grossly incongruous to the degree of the immigrants' invocation of British support, cannot be denied. Nevertheless, the
projected British identity was not negligible in protest. The assessment of
one immigrant adequately explains its potential: "We all knew that many of
our resolutions and petitions were never acted upon. But we continued to

scream loudly about our affiliation and the powerful avenues for seeking action, and our tormentors backed away and gave us what we wanted."[65]

While, as mentioned above, the leaders invoked the colonial connection, it is clear that they also fully grasped the inevitability of the encounter with American racism and the necessity of also agitating within broader Black organizational movements. True, they manipulated the colonial connection periodically, but their immense race consciousness was evident in the causes and strategies that they espoused. In the 1930s, Thaddeus Kitchener and Alfred Haughton, editors of the *Chronicle* and executive members of Jamaica Associates, spearheaded campaigns to encourage the members of St. Cyprian's and the West Indian associations to participate in the Black labor movement. These two leaders also participated in the activities of the Race Relations Committee of the Boston Federation of Churches, conveying to other West Indians the significance of not only solidarity among Blacks but interracial cooperation as well. William Harrison, another editor, carried this approach to a height when he orchestrated a Jewish-Black coalition to combat discrimination against the two groups in Roxbury. Importantly, the few West Indian women leaders made similar strides, a fact underscored by their involvement in the Women's Club Movement, which itself was a defining element of Black women's activism in the United States during that period. The extent of their involvement is reflected in the election in 1947 of Jamaican Gertrude Chandler, secretary of Jamaica Associates, as regional vice president of the Northeast Federation of Colored Women's Clubs.[66]

Although these leaders did succeed in eliciting some support for their coalitionist approach, most of the immigrants continued to offer, at best, only lukewarm support for collective protest outside the parameters of the West Indian community. This attitude was frustrating to the leaders, some of whom could not fully understand its rationale. For example, Victor Bynoe, who worked tirelessly to increase West Indian interest in the work of the NAACP recalled: "At association [West Indian associations] meetings, we spent time explaining the importance of supporting the NAACP and the Urban League. We thought we were pretty clear about how advancement for all Blacks can only come through united efforts. Most of them [the West Indian members] did not say anything, they just didn't come [to activities of the African American organizations mentioned]."[67]

But some did explain their attitudes, if not to Bynoe. During a rally organized by *Chronicle* editor William Harrison to promote his Jewish-Black alliance, at least two members of the audience explained their reluctance to support such a movement. One woman, a domestic worker from Barbados, said she did not see how she could join forces with her Jewish employers who, because they paid her salary, "ordered her around for ten to twelve hours of the day." Such a pronouncement reveals the extent to which considerations of class differentiation influenced the trajectories of activism. Another person in that same audience, a Jamaican man convinced that he was expressing the sentiments of many, reminded Harrison that the Jews were Whites, who at that very time were fleeing from their old neighborhoods because they did not want to live with Blacks who were now streaming in.[68] Therefore, their choices were not often as irrational as Bynoe and some other leaders may have thought. They were aware of some of the hurdles of collective activism, and unlike the middle-class leaders, who developed ideological convergence which called for a more universalistic agenda, the rank and file could mostly only see their own projected goals and the possible obstacles to attaining them.

It is clear that though far less talked about than the New York West Indian community, the West Indian community of Boston was no doubt quite vibrant in activism. The many events, activities, and personalities of the first half of the twentieth century bear testimony to this fact. They also sufficiently demonstrate that the protest activities of members of that community cannot simply be tied to one militant movement whose role in Black activism in that city was indispensable. Similarly, they cannot be described solely in terms of an anti-colonial crusade against a homeland the migrants despised for the deplorable conditions that impelled them to leave in the first place. These caveats against oversimplification point to the multiplicity and complexity of what is simply dubbed "West Indian activism." Because of this recognition, the focus of this chapter was guided by a crucial question. When assessed as a group, were Boston's West Indians relentless ex-colonials and militant immigrants, or were they pragmatic transnationals who, in spite of the rhetoric and commitment of their leadership, attempted to construct and follow the safest path to a materially rewarding immigrant life and a reformed homeland society to embrace them on their return?

PROGRAM

𝔐eeting 𝔈xtraordinary

under the auspices of

BOSTON DIVISION, Inc.
UNIVERSAL NEGRO
IMPROVEMENT
ASSOCIATION

Sunday. October 5, 1930
3:30 and 8:00 P. M.

L'OUVERTURE AUDITORIUM

1065 Tremont Street, Boston, Mass.

PRINCIPAL SPEAKER

LADY HENRIETTA VINTON DAVIS

PROGRAM 25 CENTS

Cover of a 1930 program of the meeting of the Universal Negro Improvement Association, Boston Branch. *From the Elma Ina Lewis Collection, Courtesy of the Archives and Special Collections Department, Northeastern University.*

Victor Bynoe (in military uniform) receiving gift as outgoing president of the Alumni Association of Northeastern University from President Asa Knowles. Victor Bynoe, a renowned alumnus of Northeastern, emigrated to Boston from Barbados at age fourteen. As a leader of the community, he tried to bridge the relationship between African Americans and West Indians, mainly through his work in the NAACP. *Courtesy of the Archives and Special Collections Department, Northeastern University.*

(*at right*) Undated photograph of David Nelson (fourth from right) being sworn in as assistant attorney general in charge of consumer protection at Norwood Hospital. His father, Maston (sitting on wheelchair), was recovering from an auto accident in the same hospital. His mother, Enid, and brothers Raphael and J. D. Nelson also look on. Boston Herald. *Courtesy of the Boston Public Library, Print Department. Reprinted with permission of the* Boston Herald.

Young attorney David S. Nelson confers with Mayor John F. Collins after being named chairman of the Boston Youth Activities Commission. These men represent two "non-Yankee," "non-Brahmin" groups, which had come of age in a new Boston. Nelson's parents had emigrated from Jamaica, and Collins was the son of Irish-American Catholics. Boston Herald *(November 6, 1966). Courtesy of the Boston Public Library, Print Department. Reprinted with permission of the* Boston Herald.

Elma Lewis speaking at the Boston Museum School commencement. Lewis, whose parents emigrated from Barbados, was one of the most renowned African American leaders of late-twentieth-century Boston. Boston Herald, *photograph by James K. O'Callahan (June 6, 1969). Courtesy of the Boston Public Library, Print Department. Reprinted with permission of the* Boston Herald.

Politician and activist Mel King, whose parents emigrated to Boston from Guyana and Barbados (via Nova Scotia), was born in Boston and became the first African American to run for mayor of that city. *Courtesy of Mel King.*

5

"Making Good in America" and Living the West Indian Dream

On September 25, 1937, the *Boston Chronicle* carried a detailed report about a "noteworthy" Jamaican. Eustace D. Burton, who had just graduated from Northeastern University with a degree in engineering, was exemplary. He emigrated to Boston from Jamaica after his mother's death. He did a variety of odd jobs before ending up in an automobile shop where he worked by day and attended school at night. The article concluded that Burton's case was a good example of how West Indians "make good in America." It illustrated that "men with the will to do and the ability to achieve, eventually attain their desired ambitions." Indeed, socioeconomic mobility is an integral facet of the immigrant experience, so integral that every study of an immigrant group at some point addresses the question of how well individuals and the group as an entity have fared in their adopted home. For the present study, this chapter is that point.

The progress of Black immigrants from the Caribbean has interested scholars since the early 1900s. But the focus was mostly on the Black foreigners' success relative to that of American-born Blacks.[1] In this preoccupation with comparing West Indians with American Blacks, most researchers did not stop to ponder the important question of how the immigrants themselves rated their success. While many foreign-born Blacks quickly learned to revel in the favorable rating they got from such myopic comparison, the native-born Black was not always the overriding yardstick that they used to measure their success. As chapter 1 of this study pointed out, the immigrants came with preconceived notions about success. Although some of their ideas were inevitably modified given the realities of the society into which they entered, the main frame, as conceived in the homeland, seemed to endure. The West Indian society was continually used as the major yardstick for measuring success and mobility. It followed then, that the immigrant generation continued to aspire to the same elements encapsulated in middle-class status, as defined by the West Indian society of their time.[2]

Statistical information is vital in examining themes such as socioeconomic mobility. But sometimes it is problematic, as in this case where the statistical data are inadequate. For much of the first decades of the twentieth century, the official statistics only provide details for the bulk "Negro" population, without breaking it down to American- and foreign-born, something that was routinely done for the White population. In the rare instances when such a breakdown did occur, the designation was simply foreign-born Negro, which included English, French, and Spanish-speaking Caribbean natives, as well as the few Black immigrants from the African continent. The issue of paucity aside, even if the statistical data were abundant and reliable, sometimes they submerge the faces and voices of the human subjects whose experiences are being examined. In this chapter the immigrants' own perceptions and voices are crucial. This conviction and the shortcomings of the statistical sources shape the qualitative narrative which follows.

When John Leo Bynoe moved to Boston in 1919, he resolved that it did not matter if he died a "lowly carpenter." All he wanted was to work enough hours to earn enough money to "make his plans work."[3] Indeed, economic stability was a prerequisite for the attainment of the goals of migration. The most convincing indicator lay in the immigrants' ability to hold jobs and generate income, or as they put it, "make daalars."[4] Occupational mobility for the immigrant generation largely went in two directions—horizontal and downward. Seldom was there upward, vertical occupational mobility. Horizontal mobility seemed more prevalent, as many continued to do unskilled, menial jobs that were similar to the ones they had pursued in the colonies prior to emigrating. In Boston, the land of opportunity, where they had come to seek a better life, they had virtually no opportunities to develop skills and move out of a low-status occupational stratum. Moreover, of the few who had been skilled or semiskilled artisans in the homeland, many, especially the men, took a downward plunge to being common laborers, housekeepers, and janitors. Confinement to the lowest rungs of the blue-collar stratum resulted in low incomes not just for African American Bostonians but for foreign Blacks as well.[5] Importantly, however, this daunting reality was generally not seen by the immigrants as an obstacle to socioeconomic mobility. Unrealistic as this attitude appears on the surface, it makes perfect sense once an assessment of mobility is seen through the immigrants' own lenses. Even with the most menial and lowest-paying jobs, they had a degree of economic stability they never had back home, simply because in Boston they earned more. For example, men who earned

17 shillings and 7 pence or 17s.7d ($3.93) a week as laborers in the West Indies earned $8–$10 a week in Boston. Women domestics, who earned a miserly 2s.6d–5s (60 cents to $1.20) a week, by 1915 could earn $4–$8 in Boston.[6]

The main consideration for the immigrants, therefore, was not that one was a domestic, a porter, or a janitor, but rather the pay as compared with that of the homeland. A first-generation Barbadian illustrates these sentiments:

> I used to walk down Shawmut Avenue to go to my job as a laborer with my head held up high. As I thought of all those heavy things I was going to carry on the docks and the White bosses who would be yelling at me, one thing kept me going, kept me walking proudly down my street: I kept thinking that in Christ Church [in Barbados], as a mason I was earning what I think would convert to two dollars for a week's work, and I came here to Boston and was earning six to eight dollars, it depends, for a week's work as a laborer.[7]

Thus, although this man had technically experienced downward occupational mobility—from a skilled artisan to an unskilled laborer—he was more economically stable than he had been in Barbados. What he and many others did not allow to discourage them was the painful fact that if they had had more ready access to skilled jobs in their field, they could have earned far more—for the man quoted here, maybe something like $4.50 a day, with union backing. With the goals of migration uppermost in the immigrants' minds, economic stability, not necessarily economic prosperity, was what formed the foundation for socioeconomic progress. It was this economic stability that enabled them to accomplish their objectives. The accomplishments were in turn used as criteria for measuring success.

Arguably, first on the list of these criteria was the educational achievement of the children. Tertiary and professional schooling was a very important social marker, as was the case in the homeland. There, education was a big asset, actually the *sine qua non* for social mobility.[8] The immigrant generation, a product of that society, clung to the notion that education assured unlimited progress. David Nelson recalled his father's commitment to his (David's) education so that, according to his father, he would not encounter the struggles of a tailor but enjoy the rewards of a professional life. Elma Lewis's Barbadian mother envisaged for her daughter the genteel life that evaded her. "When I entered Emerson College," Lewis recalled, "my mother began to see the fruits of her labor." Mavis Sinclair remembered how much she admired her mother Rhoda Ingram, a dressmaker from St. Ann, Jamaica. Her mother was so talented, "she did not make dresses, she worked wonders." But Sinclair remembered vividly that her mother deliberately tried to quench her daughter's attraction to dressmaking. "Dressmaking does not take you anywhere in Jamaica or in Boston," she remembered her mother saying. "I will not rest until I use my seamstress money to help you get a profession." Mavis Sinclair became a teacher and her brother a doctor.[9]

By 1940 many of the immigrants who came in this first major wave, according to the *Chronicle* of August 23, 1947, had children who had acquired a college education. This development, the paper conceded, would have been virtually impossible for many of them in the islands from which the parents had originated. Education of the children was seen as such a huge success that it often overshadowed many problems, like racial prejudice, which, ironically, the educated children were more likely to encounter. In Boston, as in all other major U.S. cities, young, Black university graduates, including those of West Indian descent, were among the most frustrated of the general Black population. They experienced tremendous difficulty, certainly more than their White counterparts, in utilizing their education and skills, mainly because of the racial barriers they encountered.[10] This predicament was most evident in the Depression era, as a January 6, 1935, *Chronicle* editorial pointed out:

> Their [Black graduates'] professors did not tell them, no, neither did the smiling commencement speakers, "There just ain't no jobs." Its bad for the White student, it's worse for the colored. We would not discourage our Negro boys and girls. To them we say you have got brains and brawn, you have also a glorious tradition behind you; there's gold in these United States of yours; pitch in, find a niche and make it yours. It's the survival of the fittest.

It was with exactly this kind of optimism that West Indian parents viewed the educational accomplishments of their children. Families competed for space in the *Chronicle* and association and church notices to announce the educational progress of their children. The notices in the *Chronicle*, and sometimes the *Guardian* as well, were vivid. They told of how the parents had come from the British West Indies with a strong work ethic, saved diligently, and brought their children up with the highest values. The accounts usually ended with descriptions of the graduation ceremonies, how, for example, Mr. _____, laborer, mason, or tailor, and Mrs. _____, domestic or washerwoman, watched with pride as their son or daughter graduated with flying colors as a doctor, lawyer, engineer, or classical performer. The newspaper reports were written in such a way that the reader could visualize the rocky but steady path up the social ladder.[11] Clairmont Lewis's obituary, for example, emphasized that "[a]lthough he was self educated, he raised his three children to be professionals in the arts."

Home ownership was perhaps the second most important, although more tangible, indicator of social mobility. The immigrants transferred the high premium placed on home ownership in the homeland to their status in their new home. By the end of the 1930s, even as the Great Depression unfolded, West Indians of all social strata had begun to buy their own homes, mostly in the South End. As Victor Bynoe explained, "almost everyone we knew from the islands were buying their own property."[12] Then in the 1940s it became even more fashionable and indicative of upward mobility (for Boston's Blacks in general) to purchase homes in the Roxbury neighborhood of the Hill—Humboldt Avenue, Walnut Avenue, Seaver Street, and side streets. Most of the houses these Black new homeowners were buying were houses that were being vacated by Whites, mostly Jews, who were fleeing to the suburbs.[13] Many West Indians and their children, like the Nelson family mentioned in chapter 2, did not fail to notice the hasty departure of the White families that followed the increasing Black presence. So there is no question that by the time the Black foreigners began to buy property, they had begun to grasp the reality of de facto residential segregation along racial and ethnic lines. But for the most part, it did not matter that the only place they could fairly easily buy homes was in an increasingly segregated, depreciating Black neighborhood. What really mattered was that now they owned a house, or as many of them would say in patois, a "yard" to call their own.

In and from their yards they lived a lifestyle which, in their view, conferred a middle-class status on them. This lifestyle was reflected largely in cultural activities, which, in the homeland, were mostly socially out of bounds. As chapter 3 explained, a great proportion of the associations' activities were elitist, especially by West Indian standards—tea parties, lectures, debates, balls, banquets, and musical recitals. As a Barbadian woman explained, the mere fact that they could now be part of this middle-class lifestyle was itself an indication that they had moved up the ladder:

> I used to look around me at all the good people at the parties and piano playing. At such times I see how much progress we have made. As a washerwoman in Bridgetown, I did not take part in these things; I only used to look through the windows into the houses of those White, Malatta [sic] and Bajan men who had studied at Oxford.[14]

Of all the recreational activities, undoubtedly, none was more symbolic of the immigrants' new middle-class status than cricket. In Boston, some of them were elated by the fact that they could now fully participate in that sport, as the statement of a Barbadian woman who moved to Boston in 1938 illustrates:

Until I came here I never really knew the game. But as soon as I got here I started attending the matches at Franklin Field, even though for some time I did not understand or even like the game. But I wanted to be there, to feel the joy of actually being a part of cricket, and for other people to know that I was there. That is why after the weekend I would always announce to my mistress that I was at a cricket match. I would even tell the old Jewish butcher standing behind the counter in the store on Blue Hill Avenue. You see, I wanted them to know that I was somebody. But they were never really glad for me. To this day, I still wonder if they were jealous or what.[15]

Here is a good example of the value standards of the home society at work. So embedded in that culture was the woman cited above that she could not understand that others were not excited for her, perhaps because they had their own criteria for measuring success. Membership in an all-White golf country club would probably have caused heads to turn, but given the racial climate of the time, a group of Black people, foreign or not, who played cricket in the "Black Section" of Franklin Field would not.

The above quote also suggests that it bothered some West Indians that other Bostonians did not acknowledge what they saw as signs of upward mobility. Nevertheless, for the majority of the immigrant generation, acknowledgment from the home society was the "crowning glory." Emphasis on validation from the sending society has always been a common feature among immigrant groups. By the early 1900s, the phrases "goin' foreign" and "making good abroad" had begun to appear in the lexicon of the societies of the British West Indian colonies. People who "went foreign," especially to Western societies like Canada, the United States, and Britain, were viewed by many West Indians at home as middle-class almost immediately upon their departure.[16] This automatic, unearned elevation notwithstanding, the immigrants were still anxious to provide evidence that they had really "made good." They wrote letters home affirming their success. This message was disseminated by word of mouth and even in print media. For example, the editor of the *Jamaica Daily Gleaner* in the May 6, 1915, edition referred to a letter from a "dear friend in Boston" in his commentary on "the great wealth and amazing strides in prosperity" made by West Indians in the United States.

Clear visual support for this success abroad was conveyed in photographs, often carefully selected. These photographs showed happy, healthy individuals and families, with some of their material acquisitions—a facade of their house, lovely furniture, or modern/American amenities—in the background. Such documentation had the desired effect, as illustrated by the impact of five-year-old Elma Lewis's picture of 1926 that was sent to her aunt, Amy Lewis of Christ Church. Amy showed the picture to relatives and friends so that they could see how good life was for her brother and his family in Boston. Explaining this to her brother, she wrote: "Everybody surprise over your nice daughter Christmas photograph. She is so fat and lovely. I show a few friends around, they say you have a very nice daughter and the photograph take nice."[17]

Stories of success were also often substantiated with monetary remittances. Money sent home to relatives (and sometimes to friends) came to be as much a status symbol as it was practical financial assistance. As early as 1900, remittances had become such a significant component of revenue in the British West Indian colonies that they were routinely addressed in the governors' annual reports. Even though much of the money sent to relatives and friends came from Panama, the total money orders from the United States were quite substantial. For example, the value of monetary remittances to Barbados alone from the United States from 1910 to 1920 totaled over half a million pounds.[18] Often, remittances were not made quietly. The remitters bragged about how much and how often they sent money, clothes, provisions, and other necessities to family and friends in the homeland. Jamaican Vere E. Johns, correspondent and lifestyle reporter of the *Chronicle,* tackled the subject of remittance in his column "Through My Spectacles." Emphasizing the role of remittance in status ascription, Johns explained that from what he gathered from his research for the article, he suspected that some West Indians who did not even offer any economic assistance to families at home claimed they did, just "to get the respect."[19]

The efficacy of remittances notwithstanding, some of the first generation still envisioned a visit home, where their physical presence testified to their having "made good." But frequent visits home were highly uncommon. Travel in the first half of the twentieth century was not what it later became in the second half, which witnessed marked improvements in air travel. The passenger steamers, whose fares were prohibitively high for most of the immigrants, were the main means of travel. Moreover, the travel time onboard these steamers, which stopped at several ports, also had to be factored into the already short vacation time that most of the immigrants got from their jobs. Therefore, it is not surprising that many did not go back until many decades after their departure. David Nelson sums up the situation astutely: "Much of the time, any travel money was to get people here [Boston], not to go over there. That was how my parents reasoned and that is why my mother did not set foot on her island again until over twenty-five years after she left.[20] Indeed, practical considerations prevailed in so many of the decisions involving going back. For example, some people who went back did so not for "vacations" but to accompany their American-born children home to relatives who would mind them while the parents returned to "make good" in America. Still, in spite of the financial constraints, nostalgia and sheer determination brought some of the first generation home on "vacation." While it is hard to determine the exact proportion of Boston's West Indians who actually went home on vacation before 1950, it is safe to surmise that it was small. More evident, though, is how vacations to the homeland were interpreted as significant signs of upward mobility and manipulated to demonstrate success.

Many of those who went back had left their homeland as working-class but went back as middle-class. A Jamaican woman illustrates this "reversal of fortunes" in a description of her homecoming:

> Stepping off the S.S. Nelson, seventeen years after I left the Parish of St. Andrew as a poor dressmaker, I was filled with emotion. It was this same port that I used to come with my friends to stare at the people coming from abroad, most of them studying in England. I knew that for me to get the respect they got, I had to go out too. Now, here I was, coming back from Boston. Yes, I did not have any school certificates, but standing right behind me, also getting off the boat, was my son who was studying at Howard University.[21]

Emboldened by the confidence they now possessed because of their new social status, the returnees took pride in visiting places and meeting people with whom they could only have associated hesitantly prior to emigrating. For example, as the August 23, 1947, *Chronicle* reported, one "humble dressmaker" of Boston, who visited her old home in Montego Bay, was the guest of an honorable member of the island's (Jamaica's) legislature. Another insightful case is that of a Barbadian man who described some aspects of his 1940s visit home. During Norris Taylor's visit to Bridgetown, he worshipped in the small church that he used to attend before emigrating. He noted that like those people from Oxford and Cambridge, present in the church were his three children who were all graduates of American universities. He made sure that he and his children sat in one of the front row pews in which the English university graduates used to sit and which, prior to emigrating, he had coveted from his back row pew. The climax of this experience came after the service, when people came over to greet him and meet his children. He was convinced that he saw the admiration and respect in their expressions as they "heard his children speak foreign." He concluded that this experience at the church convinced him more than ever that his decision to move to Boston was a wise one.[22]

It did not matter that when these vacationing West Indian immigrants returned to Boston they came back to haul cargo on the docks or to scrub floors and take care of White people's children. What mattered was that in their reckoning, they were now middle-class and their fellow countrymen and women knew it. In Boston they reported on their trips in the society column of the *Chronicle*. So significant were the trips as an index of success that they were sometimes the source of rivalry. For example, a second-generation Barbadian recalled how in 1949 her family sent a detailed notice about their vacation to Bridgetown to the society news section of the *Chronicle*. Somehow, their account was never published. In the meantime, a neighbor, originally from Jamaica, who had been competing with her mother, had her account of her vacation to Jamaica read in church. Her mother had to struggle hard to contain her disappointment, as people went over to the other woman after the service to congratulate her and to be filled in on the details of her Jamaican trip. This incident infuriated the Barbadian mother of the person recounting this incident so much that she (her mother) decided never to patronize the *Chronicle* again.[23]

Unlike scholars, whose preoccupation was with how Black foreigners compared with native Blacks, the immigrants calculated their progress in America based on their attainment of their West Indian dream. Therefore, when they assessed their success, they searched for and highlighted the components of that phenomenon—homeownership, education of their children, and stable, salaried employment. Clairmont Lewis, who did not move out of the unskilled, blue-collar bracket, achieved the West Indian dream. In his own words:

> I own my own home, a two-apartment house, with eight rooms to each apartment. I am an active citizen taking part in the civic affairs of Boston and vicinity. I have a bank account of over $5,000.00 and a job which I have for over 10 years, earning $58.43 weekly . . . One of my sons was a medical doctor who received his B.S. from Harvard and his M.D. from Howard University, Washington, D.C., and served as First Lt. in the U.S. Army Medical Corps. My other son is a graduate of New England Conservatory of Music and is now Musical Director of the Robert Gould Shaw House in Boston, and my daughter is a graduate of Emerson College of Oratory and have [sic] just opened a dancing school of her own.[24]

From their own accounts, therefore, it seemed that the immigrants successfully attained the goals of migration. Newspaper entries and oral histories tell the same story. They paint the picture of an ambitious group of people determined to succeed, a group of people who worked hard, spent wisely, saved diligently, and succeeded tremendously. But were there no failures? What was the rate of failure? Those who failed, why didn't they succeed? And what happened to them? Did they go back home? Or did they remain in Boston, but away from the West Indian subcommunity? These questions are pertinent yet hard to answer. As with almost all immigrant groups, most of the available data are on those West Indians who made positive strides. The oral data suggests that this was the case because only those who were "immigration material" came to Boston. To some extent this is a valid assumption. As this study has shown, West Indians were clearly economic immigrants, a category usually reflective of strongly motivated individuals. But as determined as the immigrants were, the reality of their new situation—unfamiliar, inclement climate, de facto racial barriers, and ethnic tensions in Boston—must have taxed some of them to the point of failure. So a big puzzle in the story of Boston's West Indians is the whereabouts of that segment, however small.

Some of the foregoing analyses clearly make the point that to a large extent, success for the immigrant generation was evaluated within the parameters of their own world. How coethnics in their own subcommunity and, more importantly, how the folks back home perceived their progress was paramount. But even though, as was emphasized earlier, the immigrants' own perceptions are crucial, there are other ways of attempting to understand their socioeconomic mobility. The West Indians did not live in a vacuum. There were other ethnic groups as well with migration goals of their own. It is thus also useful to compare the Black foreigners' experiences and status with those of the other subcultures within Boston's complex plural society.

In the early twentieth century, the major immigrant groups or "other Bostonians" were Irish, Italians, and Jews. Also among the other Bostonians were the ever-increasing numbers of Black migrants from the American South. As shown in chapter 2, race-based discrimination was very much a hallmark of the socioeconomic structure. However, potent religious and ethnic prejudice and discrimination ensured that all the emerging groups were at one time or another affected by injustice. The Irish, the first group to seriously threaten the homogeneity of the New England Puritan society in the nineteenth century, faced blatant horrific rejection, discrimination, and segregation. As the descendants of Puritans and the self-professed chosen people, the Boston White, Protestant Yankees made no secret of their contempt for the Irish. Drawing from some of the notions spun by centuries of acrimonious English-Irish relationships, the Bostonians openly hurled assaults at the physical appearance, disposition, and mental capabilities of the Irish "intruders." There was no shortage of slurs and stereotypes, like the one which described an Irish man and woman: "Paddy, the hopeless, witty Irishman, given to drink and quick to tears and laughter, who loved nothing more than 'rows and ructions,' and Bridget, the chaste and prudent but comically ignorant serving girl."[25] For all their stupidity, the bigoted Yankees contended, the Irish, as agents of the pope, could not be trusted. Given a free rein, they were capable of undermining American democratic institutions. The established Bostonians found this perceived Irish threat handy as vindication for their open economic and social repression of that group. Thomas O'Connor does not mince words as he points out the severity of the Yankee oppression of the Irish in Boston. According to the Boston-born Irish American historian:

> If there had existed in the nineteenth century a computer able to digest all the appropriate data, it would have reported one city in the entire world where an Irish Catholic, under any circumstance should never, ever, set foot. That city was Boston, Massachusetts. It was an American city with an intensely homogeneous Anglo-Saxon character, an inbred hostility toward people who were Irish, a fierce and violent revulsion against all things Roman Catholic, and an economic system that precluded most forms of unskilled labor. Boston was a city that rejected the Irish from the very start and saw no way in which people of that ethnic background could ever be fully assimilated into the prevailing American culture.[26]

Like the Irish, the Catholic Italians were resented by Protestant, Brahmin Boston partly for religious reasons. Contempt for this non–Anglo-Saxon group was further fueled by their rural, agricultural-based background. In Boston they were catapulted into being what Herbert Gans has labeled "urban villagers."[27] Life in this seemingly unnaturally combined urban-rural milieu was not easy. Historian William DeMarco writes extensively about how Boston's Italians by design and partly through bigoted pressure from the dominant society erected their urban villages in the city's North End. Insulated in their enclaves, early twentieth-century Italians lacked access to vital occupational, economic, political, and social opportunities.[28] Yankee Americanizing proponents, observing from the outside, interpreted the situation as ample evidence of the Italians' deficiencies in two fundamental Yankee characteristics—a commitment to achieve citizenship and the Puritan work ethnic. One such Yankee urban reformer, Robert Woods, actually declared the unsuitability of the Italians for the enterprising Boston society when he reminded his audience that without these two qualities, which the Italians lacked, Boston would have remained a wilderness.[29]

The Jews, another prominent "other Bostonians" group, actually began by sharing the North End, which by the late nineteenth century was "Boston's classic land of poverty," with the Italians.[30] As in the case of the Irish and Italians, religious sentiments also worked against the Jews. Even though the majority of the Jews had come from urban settings with capitalistic economies, unlike the other two groups, they were still subjected to blatant discrimination in employment. Newspaper advertisements carried caveats like those issued for the Irish that "no Hebrew need apply."[31]

From the above synopses emerges the point that initial economic, social, and political closure was not unique to West Indians as an immigrant group. While this basic commonality is clear, so too are some of the points of departure. Summed up simply, all these non-Black, non-Anglo-Saxon groups eventually attained tremendous success as collective entities. This is not to say that all Irish men and women prospered or all Jewish men and women opened successful businesses. The European ethnic groups were tiered socioeconomically. No visitor to Boston in the 1920s, 1930s, or 1940s could fail to recognize the Irish or Italian working-class neighborhoods. What visitors may also have grasped quickly was the hierarchical positioning of whole racial and ethnic groups within the social structure. After all, this was Brahminland, a city with an established caste system. The quest for power and privilege was not simply class-based, between the haves and have-nots across racial and ethnic lines, but also between ethnic groups. Even the established White Protestants found their position as the top tier group seriously threatened by the European ethnics.

Unquestionably, Jews emerged as the most successful of the European immigrant groups in spite of, and actually partly because of, the discrimination they faced. By the time the eastern European Jews began to arrive at the turn of the nineteenth century, the small early community, made up mostly of western and central European Jews, had made significant inroads into some economic niches, paving the way for the later waves. The textile and shoe industries, then part of the backbone of Boston's economy, were two main areas where the newer arrivals found relatively steady employment. What the Jews became most remarkable for, however, was their individual and collective success in entrepreneurship. Undeterred by the Yankee monopoly of the financial establishment of early-twentieth-century Boston, they formed their own financial institutions which supported the creation and growth of numerous Jewish-owned businesses.[32] The general Jewish attitude toward success and material wealth, the deep sense of community, which emphasized looking after the welfare of coreligionists, and the successful establishment of alternative sources of credit within the Jewish subcommunity all aided them in their ascent to being the most economically successful ethnic group in the city. By the second half of the twentieth century, this ascendancy was glaring, as Julius Morse, a descendant of one of Boston's oldest Jewish families observed in 1955:

We find 150,000 Jews prominent in all sectors of the commercial life of the city. Sons and grandsons of the immigrant of the 90s are graduating from our colleges and technical schools to become executive heads of many old business houses while the older members of self same families begin to lay aside much of their wealth to endow schools and colleges—professorships, credit unions, homes for the underprivileged, hospitals, etc. Truly, Jews are a moving spirit in the commercial life of Boston.[33]

The Italian "urban villagers," whose suitability and prospects for success had been pronounced bleak, did not register such recognizable, phenomenal success. The obscurity of early-twentieth-century Italian success is partly due to the way that group has been studied. Historians have pointed out that one of the biggest indices of upward mobility by the early 1900s was the mass movement of ethnic groups to the suburbs. According to Boston historians Buni and Rogers: "This steady flow of ethnic groups to the suburbs demonstrated the continued openness of metropolitan society in general and of Boston's ability in particular to provide a middle-class environment for the children of its immigrants."[34] Most of the studies on Italian migration have focused on the original Italian neighborhoods of the North End and the West End. The census records show that up to the 1940s, the North End especially was not only heavily Italian but also glaringly working-class. Most of the inhabitants still engaged in menial, blue-collar jobs.[35] Merely looking at the "special Italian neighborhoods" of the North End gave the impression that Italians, unlike the other European immigrant groups, did not progress significantly. For the other groups the movement of the second and third generation from the crowded tenements of the West End and the North End to single-family homes in the suburbs came to be one of the clearest indications of socioeconomic mobility and the formation of an ethnic middle class. But immigrant and American-born Italians also moved out, even if not on the same scale as the other European groups. As Thernstrom correctly points out, middle-class Italians and those aspiring to become middle-class were least likely to be found in the North End and West End.[36] Successful Italian Bostonians did move to surrounding suburbs like Medford, Malden, and Arlington. The success of this ethnic group as an entity would come out more clearly if the existing studies had focused more on these more mixed, higher-status neighborhoods.

The Irish offer a far different case. So fascinating is their success story that they came to be the classic case of ethnic ascendancy. Indisputably, the route was political empowerment. By the second decade of the twentieth century, the once virtually disenfranchised group had become a formidable competitor of the Yankees in the political arena, previously monopolized by the latter. Irish politicians, who hailed from working-class backgrounds, were practical. "They entered politics as a career because, if successful, politics made possible rapid upward mobility for the ward boss and his Irish neighbors."[37] This pragmatism was well-calculated, for even though Irish economic progress did not for decades quite match the group's political clout, its success in the political arena translated into significant, tangible material gains for its members. Political control facilitated their entry into municipal jobs in areas like the police and fire departments and access to lucrative government contracts. By the time of the Great Depression, although the blueblood Yankee Brahmins still dominated the apex of the financial establishment, the Irish could also boast of some of the wealthiest entrepreneurs. Irish businessmen made inroads particularly in the contracting and liquor businesses. As Dennis Ryan documents through photographs, the contracting business made some Boston Irish families substantially wealthy. Among them were the Nawns, who helped build the Boston subway and the Logues, whose patriarch, Charles Logue, built Fenway Park. In 1900, Irish businessmen owned many of the eighteen or so breweries. Lawrence Logan, president of the Boston Beer Company, was one of the most prominent entrepreneurs of the time.[38]

By the close of the first half of the twentieth century, it was clear that the descendants of the Irish, whom nineteenth-century cartoonist Thomas Nast once described as ignorant and threatening to American democratic institutions, had triumphed.[39] The flamboyant Irish-American Mayor Curley once reflected on this victory with much thrill. "The Brahmins," he gloated, "must learn that the New England of the Puritans and the Boston of rum and codfish and slaves are as dead as Julius Caesar."[40]

The preceding commentaries about the progress of the European immigrant groups should not be seen as an unnecessary digression from the subject of this study. This snapshot is meant to provide a comparative sense of how West Indians fared within the multilayered, heterogeneous Boston society. It will not be unreasonable to conclude that the West Indians' story of progress is generally similar to that of the other immigrant groups. The Irish and Jews moved to better neighborhoods, and so too did West Indians. The second and third generations of the European groups attained far more education than their parents, as did West Indian children. And the second and third generation of the European groups entered professional occupations, which put them by definition in the middle class, as did many of the second-generation West Indians. What, then, is the point of difference between West Indians and the European groups? Significantly, while stories of individual West Indians clearly illustrate substantial progress, unlike the Jews, Irish, and even Italians, Boston's West Indians never gained recognition as a highly mobile entity. Official contempt is amply displayed in the census records and other official statistics, which do not single West Indians out as a category of the foreign-born and of foreign stock. While the statistics are usefully clear on the rate of progress of first-generation and subsequent generations of Europeans, they only provide references for the general Boston Black population.[41] But West Indian community sources—newspaper and association reports and oral history—provide insights into individual success stories which, collectively, might rival those of certain European groups in certain areas. In the absence of direct, official evidence, if one were to deduce from these community sources, one could conclude that by 1950 no less than 40 percent of second-generation West Indians were college-educated. But before one hastily uses this information to advance the argument of a smooth, unqualified, substantial West Indian progress, it is advisable to go back to the official statistics on the bulk Black Bostonian population.

Statistics on the larger Black community tell a story about educational accomplishment that is similar to the particular one on the Black foreigners. Census records demonstrate that Blacks were generally better educated than Irish and Italians. But they also reveal that despite this seeming social advantage, Blacks as a group remained down in the lower rungs of the occupational ladder. The daunting fact was that the Black white-collar class was far smaller than that of White immigrant groups with less schooling. The 1900 census reported that 20 percent of Blacks aged fifteen to twenty attended school, compared to 39 percent of Yankees and 23 percent of second-generation Europeans, indicating that the educational attainment of Blacks and second-generation Europeans was very close. Yet according to the 1910 census, only 10 percent of Blacks had white-collar occupations, while 45 percent of second-generation Europeans did. Only 8 percent of Blacks had skilled jobs, while 21 percent of second-generation Europeans did. Tellingly, 82 percent of Blacks occupied low manual employment, while 34 percent of second-generation Europeans did. The trends were still the same at the start of the second half of the century. The 1950 census revealed that while the percentage of Blacks who held white-collar and skilled occupations had improved, the White groups were still better represented. Nineteen percent of the Irish and Italian had white-collar occupations, compared to 15 percent of Blacks. Twenty-one percent of Irish and 25 percent of Italians were in skilled occupations, compared to 13 percent for Blacks. Finally, the figure for Blacks in low manual positions was 72 percent, while those for Irish and Italians were 60 percent and 56 percent respectively.[42] The incongruity between occupational rewards for Blacks and their level of educational attainment is starkly presented by these official statistics.[43] Even more germane to this study, these results begin to suggest that a fundamental West Indian conviction could be problematic in the Boston setting, namely the connection between education and economic attainment and status ascription.

West Indian immigrants and their children, like it or not, were part of a historically underprivileged group, one that Thernstrom emphasizes "has the longest and bitterest acquaintance with life on the lowest rungs of the American class ladder."[44] Individual successes notwithstanding, the potential for the collective mobility of Boston's West Indians diminishes with the unavoidable severe handicaps of blackness in pre–civil rights America. Still, though, viewed through the lenses of the home society, the economic and social progress of that group remained tremendous. Fortunately for the first generation, they often assessed the outcomes of the migration venture mainly from this angle. But while they reveled in the educational accomplishments of their children and their perceived and real elevation to the middle class, their position and role in society were often perceived differently by others. For instance, in the first decades of the twentieth century, as the debate on the consequences of immigration raged on, members of the U.S. Senate unabashedly considered the exclusion of people of African descent. Responding to the unfolding controversy, the mainstream *Boston Post* pointed out: "The exclusion is all the more offensive because it is in no way needed, even if one agrees that the dark peoples ought to be excluded. Only a few Negroes enter the United States each year. They come from the West Indies and they are generally *useful types of laborers* [my emphasis]." This pronouncement is relevant here for the light it sheds on what may have been a widely held view of the status of the West Indians of that city.

Puritan John Winthrop, who envisioned Boston as the model city on the hill, never contemplated an egalitarian society. He declared that "in all times some must be rich, some poor, some high and eminent in power and dignity, others mean and in subjection."[45] But this seventeenth-century visionary could not have imagined how some extraneous criteria would combine with forces within the society to ascribe status and influence perceptions of mobility. The Caribbean colonial background, race, racism, and racialization in Boston are all potent forces whose implications for the trajectory of West Indian progress must not be ignored. Prior experiences in the British colonial West Indian societies shaped the immigrants' pursuit and evaluation of progress. Similarly, experiences in Boston, where they were demographically squarely positioned within the Black population, linked their progress inextricably with that of the native-born Black Bostonians. Consequently, even as the Black foreigners educated their children, bought homes, sent money home, and played cricket, they were subjected to the challenges of racialized marginalization. The impediments imposed by this reality, though not sufficient to deter the attainment of the West Indian dream, constituted a formidable hindrance to an American variant of socioeconomic mobility for the group as a recognizable entity.

Conclusion

Rhoda Spence, who immigrated to Boston from Jamaica in 1967, was utterly shocked to find out that the parents of prominent Black Bostonian educator and activist Elma Lewis were originally from Barbados. "I did not know that she had any West Indian connections. I thought we [post-1965 cohort] were the first West Indians to stay here permanently," the bewildered Spence remarked.[1] This unfamiliarity with the pre-1960s West Indian community is common among Bostonians. Paradoxically, some of the city's most prominent African American personalities at the end of the twentieth century were the second generation of that immigrant community. These second-generation West Indian leaders are a significant part of the pre-1960s community. This concluding chapter, therefore, will spotlight their lives and careers before reiterating the main features that help wrap up this story. Marked by highly visible activism, the histories of these children of the first-generation protagonists of this work may, at first glance, seem out of place here. Why are they not part of a previous chapter on activism? For one thing, that chapter looked at their parents, specifically in their capacities as immigrants and ex-colonials. Secondly, the activism of their children, more realistically a post-1950s phenomenon, is outside the chronological scope of this work. Nevertheless, it represents the legacy of an understudied first generation and as such is part of a fitting end to their story.

In 1983, anyone who followed Boston politics knew the name Melvin H. King. In the mayoral election that year, King, a second-generation West Indian, made history as the first Black mayoral candidate in Boston. By this time he was already a seasoned politician and activist. King, who had seen his Barbadian father organize his laborer co-workers on the docks, was committed to challenging the power structure.[2] The education of Black children was one of the first areas to which he would direct his activism. There was an urgent need to address school segregation in the cradle of liberty.[3] Convinced that Blacks must have meaningful input in education policy making, he attempted to sit on the Boston School Committee, an institution once monopolized by the Yankees and, by that time, controlled by the Irish. He ran three times unsuccessfully—1961, 1963, and 1965. Also convinced that effective participation in electoral politics was the way to go, not even his tireless work for the Boston branch of the Urban League could keep him away from city and state politics. By the time he vied for mayor, he had already served five times as state representative from Lower Roxbury and the South End. Although Irish American Ray Flynn soundly beat King 66 percent to 34 percent in the mayoral race, his accomplishment as the first Black candidate to win a primary election and run in the general election for control of Boston's City Hall made a strong statement. As he himself saw it, positively: "Blacks loudly affirmed that 'this is our city, too!'"[4] Even outgoing Mayor Kevin White seemed to concur: "How times have changed. A man or woman being black is not a prohibition on being mayor . . . I did not believe that 10 years ago."[5] King's West Indian parents, too, may not have believed that six decades before, when they first arrived.

While King's 1980s challenge of the status quo was spectacular, it was not the first time that a Bostonian of West Indian descent made history. In 1950, Mayor John B. Hynes appointed Victor Bynoe as city commissioner, with what was then a whopping annual salary of $6,500. The *Boston Guardian* of January 7, 1950, stressing the significance of this event, pointed out that "Mr. Bynoe becomes the first colored man to receive an appointment of this kind." Although the paper also implied that the appointment was reward for Bynoe's efforts as an "energetic Democrat supporter," his qualifications must have been partly responsible. By that time he was not only an engineer but a successful attorney as well.

David Nelson made history as the first Black federal judge in Massachusetts. By the time of his appointment in 1979, Nelson, who still recalled his Jamaican-born father's activities as union organizer for the Amalgamated Clothing Workers of America, had accomplished plenty. A staunch Catholic who felt the barriers of bigotry when he could not enroll in Irish-controlled parochial elementary schools, he ended up attending Boston College, that emblem of Irish-inspired quest for higher learning. By 1990 he was not only one of that institution's most illustrious alumnae, he was also its first African American member of the Board of Trustees.

When it came to the struggle for a strong Black presence in Boston in the second half of the twentieth century, few can deny that Ruth Batson was a firebrand. Batson, who grew up attending UNIA meetings and other Garveyite activities with her West Indian parents and other relatives, waged a relentless battle against the city's educational status quo. She started in the late 1940s as one of the founding members of the Parents Federation, an organization formed to demand improvement in the public schools. Agitation through this forum was not effective enough for Batson. Even though she realized from the long history of Black failure in local elections that she would not win, she decided to run for the School Committee in 1951. She did this, she said, to publicize the problems in the public schools.[6] Even though, as she had anticipated, she lost, her bid was not a complete failure. Mel King and John O'Bryant, the two Black men who ran after her, were partly emboldened by her stand. In 1977 O'Bryant actually won, becoming the first African American elected to the Boston School Committee in the twentieth century.

A more tangible impact of Batson's agitational skills can be found in her work with the Boston branch of the NAACP in the 1960s and 1970s. When she could not get on the School Committee and after the Parents Federation collapsed, she thought she would find another conduit in the Education Committee of the NAACP. But initially she was disappointed to find that this committee was exclusively for scholarships and counseling for college. However, Lionel Lindsay, president of the Boston NAACP, soon told her that her inquiries had prompted the executive to consider the formation of an education subcommittee. Moreover, he wanted her to lead it. This was the beginning of the Boston NAACP Public School Committee, which came to be more commonly referred to as "Ruth Batson's committee." Although it began as a subcommittee, soon it became *the* NAACP Education Committee, practically relegating the original one to the status of subcommittee.[7] Through this organ, Batson made some of her greatest contributions to Black progress in Boston. She was at the center of the school desegregation movement which culminated in the busing crisis of the 1970s. No one familiar with the events can deny her role in and commitment to the struggle. She organized, strategized, and agitated. As Victor Bynoe recalled rather sensationally: "The showdown came down to two women. On their side [the Boston School Committee] they had Louise Hicks and we had Ruth!"[8]

ProclaimHer, the newsletter of the Boston Women's Heritage Trail, paying tribute to Batson and fellow second-generation Barbadian Elma Lewis after their deaths, affirmed that an accurate history of twentieth-century Boston would be incomplete without considering the two women.[9] Indeed, it is impossible to talk about Boston's African Americans in the arts without considering the contributions of Elma Lewis, who is already mentioned extensively in this study. Lewis herself became a star in the local Black community at an early age. She was a fixture at a variety of events organized by the West Indian associations at St. Cyprian's and other venues. *The Boston Chronicle* is replete with notices about her performances. The *Boston Guardian* once described her in this way: "one of the youngest and most talented exponents of dance and drama . . . and no stranger to those in and around

Boston, for her brilliant work has made her an outstanding personality in these fields."[10]

This background must have played a big part in stimulating Lewis's commitment to ensuring Black Bostonians' access to the arts. In 1950, with $300 and an old piano, she started the Elma Lewis School of Fine Arts in her home on Homestead Street in Lower Roxbury. She was determined to provide quality education in the arts for Black children, something most Whites could not even begin to concede that Black children deserved, as the *Guardian* of January 21, 1950, pointed out.

The school grew and Lewis had to move it from her house to three other locations by 1967. By that time, she had begun to entertain plans for elaborate expansions. She wanted to establish a performance center and a national center for Afro-American artists. Such ventures were big and needed space, which she readily spotted in the properties that were being vacated by Jews. She set her sights on one temple in particular—the Temple Mishkan Tefila on Seaver Street, just a stone's throw from her home on Homestead. As authors Levine and Harmon related: "with a facility like Mishkan Tefila's, thought Lewis, no black child whose hands were destined for sculpturing or whose feet were made for dancing need use them in the performance of spirit-numbing dead-end tasks. A temple for the arts was certainly a legitimate use for a beautiful building in a neighborhood that Jews had rejected in recent years in favor of suburban lifestyles."[11]

The Lubavitcher Hasidim Orthodox sect, which had owned the temple since 1954 and was adamant about staying, initially stood in Lewis's way. But as Amanda Houston, Lewis's friend, explained, "she drew from her father's pugnaciousness, her mother's cool but firm dignity, years of Garvey teachings, and her own unwavering conviction about what Boston's Blacks deserved, and she put up a stiff fight for that building."[12] Indeed, Lewis demonstrated a combination of effective agitational qualities. She closely followed both local and national events, like the increasing radicalism of the young people of the Student Non-Violent Coordinating Committee (SNCC), the backlash from Whites, and the blatant radical pronouncements and activities of the Black Panthers. While Lewis herself never participated in extreme forms of Black activism, she calculated the implications of their impact for her ongoing struggle with a section of the Jewish community.[13] Although she never concealed her anger at Jews for the way they "disrespected" Blacks by fleeing, she was shrewd enough to work with their leaders. This alliance with them, however, did not prevent her from employing aggressive, actually downright intimidating, tactics. One example will help illustrate this aspect of Lewis's aggressive side. Because Jewish leaders were so concerned about the Jewish image in the volatile racial climate in the wake of Martin Luther King's assassination, they paid off the intransigent Lubavitchers and invited Lewis to present an offer for the temple. She exploded and pointed out:

> You're asking us for money? The greatest black leader in America was just gunned down by a filthy racist, and you're asking us for money. Your people turned and ran from this neighborhood. Your people let the synagogue slip into disgrace, and now you want money from us. You owe us this building. You owe it to us. And we're not paying a dime.[14]

Defiant to the end, Lewis refused to pay anything, not even when her attorney, Larry Shubow, suggested one dollar as a token of the transfer. Still, the transfer took place and Lewis got her building and her arts center. Her statement at the conclusion of the "transfer ceremony" captures the significance of that event beyond the more tangible physical expansion of a school for Blacks. She said: "It seems singularly appropriate that buildings which had symbolized the proud heritage of Boston's Jewish community should now announce to the world the proud heritage of Boston's black community."[15] In this city where even ethnic groups were put into hierarchical tiers, Lewis was claiming equal footing for her group. Not only was this Black activist daughter of West Indian immigrants holding the beacon of American Blacks up to that of the Jews, she was also, by emphasizing the arts and high culture for Blacks, claiming her people's stakes in the genteel, cultured Yankee society. At the time of her death in January 2004, not only was this daughter of Barbadian immigrants known as the "matriarch of Black Boston," she had been elevated to Brahmin status. In her obituary in the *Boston Globe,* music director John Andrew Ross compared her to John Harvard.[16]

The connection of prominent Blacks to the pre-1960s Boston West Indian community has some national dimensions. Many analyses on the West Indian experience in America mention Malcolm X, whose mother, Louise Little, was from the British Caribbean colony of Grenada.[17] Importantly, Malcolm X, who was then Malcolm Little, spent some of his most formative years in Boston. Could the Boston West Indian community of the 1940s have shaped this man, who later became one of the protagonists of the Black struggle of twentieth-century America? There is no evidence that Little was a part of the West Indian enclave, even though he was aware of its existence. When he moved to Boston from Lansing, Michigan, in 1941 at the age of sixteen, he went to live with Ella Collins, his father's daughter from a previous marriage before the one to his mother. Unlike his mother who was foreign-born, his father, the Reverend Earl Little, and his first wife were American-born Blacks from Georgia. Ella, according to Malcolm, was southern to the core; she was "truly a Georgian Negro woman."[18] She was surrounded by numerous relatives and friends whom she had helped migrate north from Georgia. While some of them, like another sister, Mary, lived in the low-status Crosstown section of the South End and Lower Roxbury, Ella lived on the Hill, which, as chapter 3 of this study explains, was the neighborhood of Blacks who had made it. That was where Little first went to live, in a room in Ella's house in the Waumbeck and Humboldt Avenue section.

Living in this upscale Black section, Little was able to observe the southern "strivers and scramblers," the West Indian "Black Jews," and the "snooty" native-born Black New Englanders. He did not like what he saw: "They [the residents of the Hill] prided themselves on being incomparably more 'cultured,' 'cultivated,' 'dignified,' and better off than their black brethren down in the ghetto, which was no further away than you could throw a rock. Under the pitiful misapprehension that it would make them 'better,' these Hill Negroes were breaking their backs trying to imitate white people."[19] Malcolm Little decided, only a short time after he arrived in Boston, that this community was not for him. So even though his mother was British West Indian, even though he lived on the Hill where by the 1940s prominent West Indian families lived, the evidence is clear: he was not affiliated with St. Cyprian's; he did not join any of the West Indian associations; he did not attend their teas, balls, and recitals; and he did not play cricket. He spent more time with the Crosstown Blacks and later he declared: "Even though I did live on the Hill, my instincts were never—and still aren't—to feel myself better than any other Negro."[20]

It is another prominent Black Muslim, not Malcolm X, who was raised within the Boston West Indian subculture. In 1994, Louis Farrakhan stood on the pulpit of St. Cyprian's and declared, "I've come home." The occasion was the dedication of a silver chalice donated to the church by Elma Lewis in memory of her mother, Edwardine Lewis. In his youth, Farrakhan, who was then Eugene Louis Walcot, served as an acolyte in this same church, and the late Edwardine Lewis, whom he had returned to honor, was his godmother. Eugene Walcot's mother Mae Manning Clarke emigrated to New York from the Caribbean island of St. Kitts in the 1920s. A decade later, she moved to Boston with her two American-born children, Eugene and his older brother Alvan. Her husband, who was also a West Indian, had left the family. Although Mae Clarke was a trained seamstress, she worked as a domestic in several Jewish households. As a single mother, she found much support in the small West Indian community. She lived on Shawmut Avenue, among other West Indians of Lower Roxbury and the South End, and she and her sons participated actively in the activities of St. Cyprian's and the West Indian associations. After only one year at Boston Latin, the predominantly White and the most prestigious high school in the city, Eugene transferred to Boston English. Boston English was the second most prestigious high school and had more Black students, although it was also predominantly White. After high school, he went to Winston-Salem Teachers College in North Carolina for two years before he quit to pursue music. By the early fifties, Eugene, a gifted musician, had become Boston's first calypso performer. Going by the show-biz name of the Prince Charmer, Eugene was not only a fixture in the West Indian community, but in the larger Boston Black community as well. The *Chronicle* and *Guardian* are replete with announcements and reviews of his numerous appearances.

After Eugene, Alvan, and their mother converted to Islam, Eugene ceased to be a calypso star. Immersed in the work of the Nation of Islam and later his Boston mosque, Eugene, who would be Louis X and Louis Farrakhan, also withdrew from the West Indian subculture, which had no place in his new life directions. The fact still remains, though, that Louis Farrakhan spent much of his crucial formative years solidly within the Boston British West Indian culture. What, then, is the legacy of that community in the life of one of the twentieth-century's most controversial African American leaders? Remarkably, Farrakhan himself says virtually nothing of life as a second-generation Boston West Indian. Florence Hamlish Levinsohn, who went "looking for Farrakhan," experienced the frustration of not being able to fully assess the impact of the Boston West Indian community on the subject of her biography.[21] How did Mae Clarke's experiences working for those Jewish families in Boston shape Farrakhan's views about relations between Blacks and Jews? To what extent are his pronouncements and rhetoric drawn from Garveyism and other forms of activism as they were expressed and practiced in the Boston West Indian community? How did racism and other prejudices in Boston, and the West Indian reactions to them, chart his course as an African American Muslim leader and his vision for the future of Blacks in America?

People who knew Gene, as he was fondly called, were willing to speculate. His Latin High schoolmate and fellow second-generation West Indian Leonard de Cordova is convinced that Farrakhan's strong defiance of racism and injustice dates back to his high school days. Gene, de Cordova believes, must have left Boston Latin only after one year because he was not comfortable in a school that was heavily White. He was "sensitive about the way blacks got handled and just couldn't take it."[22] John Bynoe, Victor Bynoe's younger brother and one-time friend of Gene, is fully convinced that Farrakhan owes some of his emphasis on hard work and self-improvement to his upbringing in his West Indian family and community.[23] And, similarly, Farrakhan's cousin Gwen Williams stressed Gene's upbringing as she recalled his mother's strictness, her determination to instill love for the church, and confidence in her sons that they had the ability and the right to succeed.[24]

By the close of the twentieth century, it was clear that Farrakhan, an African American who had grown up straddling the foreign Black community of his mother and the larger American community, had little time to look nostalgically to that past. He was now in the business of struggling for the rights of *American* Blacks. Actually, Elma Lewis, Mel King, and Ruth Batson were also focused on their struggle as Black Americans, even if they more willingly addressed their background as the children of Black immigrants.

While these present-day prominent African American Bostonians are easily recognized in many circles, particularly within the Black community, the immigrant community which is such a vital part of their background has remained hidden. The present study has brought it out of obscurity. This work, clearly, is not primarily about great and famous men and women. It is about a hitherto understudied community whose history reveals deep insights into West Indian migration and Boston history. It illustrates the context within which the movement to Boston occurred. The economic woes and an established tradition of seeking progress abroad prompted emigration. Family and other community networks facilitated the migration process; so did the expansion of international shipping.

By the time the immigrants arrived in Boston, whether directly from the Caribbean or as step migrants from other previous U.S., Canadian, and Central American locations, their conception of work and success had developed substantially. Established homeland values and practices would combine with structural and other forces in Boston to determine the migrants' trajectory. A church, associations, and a newspaper confirmed the existence of a foreign Black community within a larger American Black Boston. Numerically, this subcommunity remained very small throughout the first half of the twentieth century, so small that even the British consul, charged with seeking the welfare of British subjects in Boston, was unaware of its viability.

Relative obscurity certainly was not seen as failure by the members of the community, who mostly used their own standards to review progress. Attaining what amounted to their West Indian dream, they saw the migration experience as a huge success. Not even the blatant disadvantages of racialized marginalization could change this assessment. Home ownership and the prominence of their successful children underscored their triumph.

One could say that the Boston West Indian experience was a familiar one. With the exception of the extreme smallness of the community, the same patterns could be recounted about the contemporaneous West Indian community of New York. Yet Boston's West Indians, like the other immigrants in that city, had one big claim to uniqueness—their location. They were in the land of the Brahmins, those Yankees who still clung to the legacies of their forebears, who had established a "city on the hill" like no other. Examining Boston's West Indians within the context of their existence in Yankee Boston is what makes them different. On the one hand, they were overwhelmingly Protestant and their work ethic, thriftiness, and aspirations fit so well with the gospel of Winthrop's vision, that they could have been the new Puritans. On the other hand, although they emphasized their affiliation with Britain, the same origins of Yankee civilization, their race made them a different kind of British, and the realities of their existence were squarely in a marginalized Black Boston.

Like the Irish before them and the Italians and eastern European Jews, the West Indians' experience sheds valuable light on the virtues and shortcomings of an American city built on some of the loftiest ideals. The West Indians of the early twentieth century are important for understanding many aspects of the workings of what, historically, had been one of America's most noble metropoli. It is indeed ironic that the historical significance of that community has suffered from intellectual neglect for so long. As early as 1927, when the community was still evolving, demographer Niles Carpenter had predicted the significance of foreign Black immigration to Boston. He noted: "It can but be expected that these people [the West Indian migrants] will react strongly to this new environment, and that this reaction will cause repercussions within the native population, both Negro and white . . ."[25] It is these West Indian "reactions" and native "repercussions" that this work has described and discussed and, in the process, unearthed a significant but understudied community in New England history.

NOTES

Introduction

1. In 1900, 714 Black immigrant aliens were admitted into the United States. In 1910, the number had risen to 4,966, and by 1914, the year of the outbreak of the First World War, as many as 8,447 Black immigrants were admitted. Blacks from the Caribbean consistently constituted more than half of the numbers. For example, in 1900, 703 new arrivals, 98.5 percent, were from the Caribbean. In 1916, they were 5,769, or 67.8 percent.

Between 1913 and 1919, 47.1 percent of the Black immigrants reported that New York was their intended state of residence, 18 percent indicated Florida, and 15.6 percent said Massachusetts. It must be noted that the overwhelming majority of these immigrants invariably settled in the principal cities of these states—New York City, Miami, and Boston.

These figures are computed from. U.S. Department of Labor, Bureau of Immigration, *Annual Report of the Commissioner General of Immigration to the Secretary of Labor*, [1900–1920] (Washington, D.C.: Government Printing Office [1901–1921]).

2. John Winthrop is etched in the history of Boston as the chief organizer of the English settlement in Massachusetts Bay in 1630. John Cotton, a prominent Puritan minister, worked closely with Winthrop and the political establishment to mold a community to be governed by divinely inspired laws and values.

3. Thomas H. O'Connor, *Bibles, Brahmins and Bosses: A Short History of Boston*. 2nd ed. (Boston: Boston Public Library, 1984), p. 74.

4. Ibid., p. 76.

5. See Adelaide Cromwell, *The Other Brahmins: Boston's Black Upper Class, 1750–1950* (Fayetteville: University of Arkansas Press, 1994).

6. Demographers have pointed out that Boston was distinctive among major northern cities in attracting far fewer southern migrants during the Great Migration. This observation, although accurate, tends to belie the significance of Black southern migration to the development of the Black population of that city. Since the nineteenth century, Blacks, who had already begun to leave the South in trickles, arrived and settled in Boston. According to U.S. census reports, as far back as 1870, the percentage of southern Blacks had begun to climb above that of the Boston-born—38 percent to 37 percent. By 1900, southern-born Blacks constituted more than half of the Black population. Interestingly, during the peak years of the Great Migration, 1914–1929, the proportion of southern-born Blacks actually declined.

The above analysis is interpreted from figures for 1870 and 1900 cited in John Daniels, *In Freedom's Birthplace: A Study of Boston Negroes* (Boston: Houghton Mifflin, 1914), pp. 468–469, and from the census reports for 1910, 1920, and 1930, U.S.

Bureau of Census, *Negroes in the United States, 1920–1932* (Washington, D.C.: U.S. Government Printing Office, 1935), pp. 74, 75, 216–218.

For a general survey of Black migration from the South to the North, Florette Henri's work, though somewhat dated, remains a useful classic. See Florette Henri, *Black Migration Movement North, 1900–1920: The Road from Myth to Man* (Garden City, N.Y.: Anchor Books, 1976).

7. Since the early 1970s, scholars had begun to point to this imbalance in ethnic and immigration historiography. One of those pioneers was Simon Roy Bryce-Laporte, who urged researchers to study the diverse facets of the Black immigrant experience in the United States. See Simon R. Bryce-Laporte, "Black Immigrants: The Experience of Invisibility and Inequality," *Journal of Black Studies* 3 (September 1972): 29–56.

Although some noteworthy works have come out since Laporte's challenge, a lot more research needs to be done. As Marilyn Halter explained, while historians have studied the forced migrations of thousands of Africans in the slave trade, they virtually overlook voluntary migrations of persons of African descent to the United States from the late eighteenth century to the present. See Marilyn Halter, "Studying Immigrants of African Descent in the Twentieth Century," *The Immigration History Newsletter* 30, no. 1 (1998): 1.

8. For example, Roger Daniels' book, attractively titled *Coming to America: A History of Immigration and Ethnicity in America,* thoroughly analyzes several aspects of European immigration and only glosses over aspects of immigration of Blacks from the Caribbean. Similarly, Ronald Takaki's work *A Different Mirror: A History of Multicultural America,* which is excellent in its consideration of the complexity of the intersection of race, ethnicity, gender, and class, neglects to show how voluntary Black immigration is featured in a multicultural America. Encouragingly, David Reimers' recent book *Other Immigrants,* which he correctly points out could not have been written thirty-five years ago, pays more direct attention to Black immigrants than they have ever received in a general history. Although his focus is post–World War II, in discussing the state of the historiography in the introduction and pertinent aspects like arrival, settlement, and adaptation in a chapter on "the New Black Immigrants," he offers valuable insights into the experiences of immigrants from Jamaica, Haiti, and, refreshingly, from African countries like Nigeria, Senegal, Ethiopia, and Ghana. For more, see Roger Daniels, *Coming to America: A History of Immigration and Ethnicity in America* (New York: Harper Collins, 1990); Ronald Takaki, *A Different Mirror: A History of Multicultural America* (New York: Back Bay Books, 1993); and David M. Reimers, *Other Immigrants: The Global Origins of the American People* (New York: New York University Press, 2005).

9. The terms "British West Indians" and "West Indians" will be used interchangeably in this study to refer to people of African descent from British colonies of the Caribbean and South America. Such colonies are Jamaica, Barbados, Montserrat, Trinidad, St. Kitts-Nevis, St. Vincent, Antigua, the Virgin Islands, and the South American mainland colony of Guyana. In so doing, this work is following the tradition of focusing on these immigrants as a collective entity under the desig-

nation West Indian. However, this collective term can be problematic, and it is used with caution. Although the shared experiences of slavery, British colonialism, and endemic emigration went a long way in creating striking uniformity among the colonies, there were differences and nuances which created variations in the colonial and premigration experiences. Therefore, while this study is looking at the immigrants as a community of West Indians, it will highlight idiosyncrasies wherever necessary.

10. Center for Afro-American and African Studies, The University of Michigan, *Black Immigration and Ethnicity in the United States: An Annotated Bibliography* (Westport, Conn.: Greenwood Press, 1985). Of particular relevance are the sections on "West Indians in the United States," pp. 85–94, and "Caribbeans in the U.S.: General," pp. 81–84.

11. Studies which advance this "cultural heritage superiority" perspective are numerous. One of its most prominent proponents is Thomas Sowell, who, anxious to downplay the salience of race in economic mobility in the U.S., used West Indians as his example of Blacks who succeeded in spite of the structural barriers. See Thomas Sowell, *Race and Economics* (New York: David Mackay, 1975); and Sowell, "Three Black Histories," in *Essays and Data on American Ethnic Groups,* ed. Thomas Sowell (Washington, D.C.: The Urban Institute, 1975), pp. 7–64.

12. For more on the political rivalry between the two Black groups, see David J. Hellwig, "Black Meets Black: Afro-American Reactions to West Indian Immigrants in the 1920s," *South Atlantic Quarterly* 77 (Spring 1978): 373–385; Keith Henry, "The Black Political Tradition in New York: A Conjunction of Political Cultures," *Journal of Black Studies* 7 (June 1977): 455–484; and Violet Johnson, "The Ambivalent Role of West Indian Immigrants in the Black Struggle in America in the 1920s and 1930s," in *In Celebration of Black History Month: Colloquium Papers* (Chestnut Hill, Mass.: Boston College Press, 1992), pp. 23–29.

13. Wilfredo A. Domingo, "Gift of the Black Tropics," in *The New Negro,* ed. Alain Locke (New York: Charles Boni, Inc., 1925; reprint, New York: Arno Press, 1968), pp. 341–349.

14. George Edmund Haynes, *The Negro at Work in New York City* (New York: Arno Press, 1912; reprint, New York: Arno Press, 1968).

15. See for example, Ira De A. Reid, *The Negro Immigrant: His Background, Characteristics and Social Adjustment, 1899–1937* (New York: Columbia University Press, 1939); and Reed Ueda, "West Indians," in *Harvard Encyclopedia of American Ethnic Groups,* ed. Stephan Thernstrom (Cambridge, Mass.: Harvard University Press, 1980), pp. 1020–1027.

16. Milton Vickerman, *Crosscurrents: West Indian Immigrants and Race* (New York: Oxford University Press, 1999); Irma Watkins-Owens, *Blood Relations: Caribbean Immigrants and the Harlem Community, 1900–1930* (Bloomington: Indiana University Press, 1996); Ransford W. Palmer, *Pilgrims from the Sun: West Indian Migration to America* (New York: Twayne Publishers, 1995); Winston James, *Holding Aloft the Banner of Ethiopia: Caribbean Radicalism in Early Twentieth Century America* (London: Verso, 1998); Mary Waters, *Black Identities: West Indian Immigrant*

Dreams and American Realities (New York: Russell Sage Foundation, 1999); Holger Henke, *The West Indian Americans* (Westport, Connecticut: Greenwood Press, 2001); Rachel Buff, *Immigration and the Political Economy of Home: West Indian Brooklyn and American Indian Minneapolis, 1945–1992* (Los Angeles: University of California Press, 2001); Percy C. Hintzen, *West Indian in the West: Self Representations in an Immigrant Community* (New York: New York University Press, 2001).

17. Andrew Buni and Alan Rogers, *Boston: City on a Hill* (Boston: Windsor Publications, 1984), p. 6.

18. See Oscar Handlin, *Boston's Immigrants: A Study in Acculturation* (Cambridge, Mass.: Harvard University Press, 1941; reprint, 1979); Thomas H. O'Connor, *The Boston Irish: A Political History* (Boston: Northeastern University Press, 1995); William M. DeMarco, *Ethnics and Enclaves: Boston's Italian North End* (Ann Arbor: UMI Research Press, 1981); and Jonathan D. Sarna and Ellen Smith, eds., *The Jews of Boston* (Boston: Combined Jewish Philanthropies of Greater Boston, Inc., 1995).

19. Leon F. Litwack, *North of Slavery: The Negro in the Free States, 1790–1860* (Chicago: University of Chicago Press, 1961); John Daniels, *In Freedom's Birthplace;* Elizabeth Hafkin Pleck, *Black Migration and Poverty: Boston, 1865–1900* (New York: Academic Press, 1979).

20. John Daniels, *In Freedom's Birthplace,* p. 170.

21. Ibid., 169.

22. For more on the history of the United Fruit Company, especially in relation to its passenger steamship operations, see John Melville, *The Great White Fleet* (New York: Vantage Press, 1976).

23. For a well-researched social history of the Costa Rican West Indian community, see Aviva Chomsky, *West Indian Workers and the United Fruit Company in Costa Rica, 1870–1940* (Baton Rouge: Louisiana State University Press, 1996). See also Lara Putnam, *The Company They Kept: Migrants and the Politics of Gender in Caribbean Costa Rica, 1870–1960* (Chapel Hill: University of North Carolina Press, 2002).

24. Several of the *Passenger Lists* note the arrest of stowaways. Even the West Indian dailies like the *Daily Gleaner* frequently reported on this practice.

25. Robert Hill, ed. *The Marcus Garvey and the Universal Negro Improvement Association Papers,* Vol. 1, Appendix 1 (Berkeley: University of California Press, 1983–1987), "W.A. Domingo," p. 528; Watkins-Owens, *Blood Relations,* pp. 25, 104.

26. Computed from the census reports for 1910–1950. Full citation for each volume is included in the bibliography of this work.

1. Origins of Migration

1. I observed this map in the living room of one of the respondents interviewed for this study, Ms. Clara Williams. She was born in Bridgetown, Barbados, in 1912 and emigrated to Boston in 1932. In 1987, when she traveled to Barbados to celebrate her seventy-fifth birthday, the map was custom-made for her as a birthday present from her sisters and nieces and nephews who still lived on the island.

2. There are numerous studies which deal more specifically and in great depth with the migration tradition of the West Indies. See, for example, Dawn Marshall, "Toward an Understanding of Caribbean Migration," in *United States Immigration and Refugee Policy,* ed. Mary M. Kritz (Lexington, Mass.: D.C. Heath, 1983). Two useful anthologies are Robert A Pastor, ed., *Migration and Development in the Caribbean: The Unexplored Connection* (Boulder, Colo.: Westview Press, 1985) and Ransford Palmer, ed., *In Search of a Better Life: Perspectives on Migration from the Caribbean* (New York: Praeger, 1990).

3. The economic problems of the West Indies across epochs have been investigated and explained by economists, geographers, historians, sociologists, political scientists, and anthropologists. The following are just a few examples of their endeavors: Ransford Palmer, *The Jamaican Economy* (New York: Praeger, 1968); Ransford Palmer, *Caribbean Dependence on the United States Economy* (New York: Praeger, 1979); Gisela Eisner, *Jamaica, 1830–1930: A Study in Economic Growth* (Manchester, England: Manchester University Press, 1961); Alan H. Adamson, *Sugar Without Slaves: The Political Economy of British Guiana, 1838–1904* (New Haven, Conn.: Yale University Press, 1972); and R. W. Beachey, *The British West Indies Sugar Industry in the Late 19th Century* (Westport, Conn.: Greenwood Press, 1978).

4. Computed from the 1946 census report, *West Indian Census, 1946* (Kingston: Government Printer, 1950). A useful source for analytical summaries of some of the demographic trends of this period is Malcolm J. Proudfoot, *Population Movements in the Caribbean* (New York: Negro Universities Press, 1970).

5. In 1938, for example, the governor of Jamaica in frustration sent a dispatch to the Foreign Office in England lamenting the fact that unemployed persons would rather be stranded in Kingston than work in the country. FO598/15: "Report of the Governor on Labour in Jamaica," May 5, 1938.

6. For example, the 1946 census reported 31.48 percent of working-age males as skilled and 16.54 percent of females.

7. Fitzroy L. Ambursley, "The Working Class in the Third World: A Study in Class Consciousness and Class Action in Jamaica, 1919–1952," B.A. dissertation, Birmingham University, 1978, p. 16.

8. Computed from a report in the Jamaica *Daily Gleaner,* March 15, 1938.

9. Researchers have analyzed and emphasized the enormous significance of the disparity between wages and cost of living in shaping West Indian life in general and specifically in contributing to a migration culture. See for example, Ambursley, "Study of Class in the Third World"; Richard Lobell, "Emigration and the Cost of Living in Jamaica, 1897–1938: An Exploratory Essay," unpublished paper delivered at the 4th Annual Conference of Caribbean Historians, University of the West Indies, Mona, Kingston, Jamaica, 1972; Bonham C. Richardson, *Panama Money in Barbados, 1900–1920* (Knoxville: University of Tennessee Press, 1985); and Peter Fraser, "Nineteenth Century West Indian Migration to Britain," in Palmer, *In Search of a Better Life.*

10. Eric Williams, *The Negro in the Caribbean* (Albany, N.Y.: The Williams Press, Inc., 1942), pp. 32–34.

11. *Blackman* was the newspaper published in Jamaica by Marcus Garvey after his deportation from the United States in the late 1920s.

12. Gladys Lewis to Clairmont Lewis, August 12, 1939, Elma Lewis Papers, M38, Box 3/12, File 12.

13. Olga Lewis to Elma Lewis, February 26, 1976, Elma Lewis Papers, M38, Box 6/12, File 14.

14. Richardson, *Panama Money*, p. 45.

15. Cited in ibid.

16. For more on cricket as a genteel sport which helped define status in the West Indies during colonial times, see Maurice St. Pierre, "West Indian Cricket—A Socio-Historical Appraisal," *Caribbean Quarterly* 19, no. 2 (June 1973): 7–18.

17. Proudfoot, *Population Movements*, p. 1.

18. Richardson, *Panama Money*, p. 43.

19. *Daily Gleaner*, January 21, 1925.

20. *The West Indian Review*, September 1934, p. 8.

21. *Report of the Swaby Education Commission, 1907–1909* (Government Printer, 1909), p. 2.

22. For more on the educational system of the British West Indies in the first half of the twentieth century and its socioeconomic implications, see E. L. Miller, "Education and Society in Jamaica," in *Sociology of Education*, ed. P. Figueroa and G. Persaud (London: Oxford University Press, 1976); Shirley Gordon, *A Century of West Indian Education* (London: Longmans, 1963); and Emmanuel W. Riviére, *Roots of Crisis in the Caribbean* (New York: Bohiyo Enterprises Inc., 1987). Chapter 6, "Education for Black Colonies," is particularly useful.

23. A comprehensive case study which clearly demonstrates this gender-based discrimination in education is Janice Mayers, "Access to Secondary Education for Girls in Barbados, 1907–43," in *Engendering History: Caribbean Women in Historical Perspective*, ed. Verne Shepherd et al. (Kingston, Jamaica: Ian Randall Publishers, 1995), pp. 258–275. Other useful studies on the subject are Joyce Cole, *Official Ideology and the Education of Women in the English-speaking Caribbean, 1834–1945* (Kingston, Jamaica: ISER, University of the West Indies, 1982) and Carl Campbell, "Good Wives and Mothers: A Preliminary Survey of Women and Education in Trinidad, 1834–1981," Unpublished paper from the Social History Workshop, Department of History, University of the West Indies, Mona, Kingston, Jamaica, November 1985.

24. From an unpublished manuscript of an interview of Ms. Lewis by Diana Korzemik, chair of Art Education Department, Massachusetts College of Art, Boston, "Elma Lewis, A Blend of Marcus Garvey and the 92nd Street 'Y', p. 2, Elma Lewis Papers, Box 3/12, File 29.

25. This fact has been emphasized and discussed by several specialists of Caribbean migration history and sociology. See, for example, Charles V. Carnegie, "A Social Psychology of Caribbean Migrations: Strategic Flexibility in the West Indies," in *The Caribbean Exodus*, ed. Barry B. Levine (New York: Praeger, 1987), pp. 32–43; Dawn I. Marshall, "A History of West Indian Migration: Overseas Opportu-

nities and 'Safety-Valve' Policies," in Levine, ed., *Caribbean Exodus;* and Orlando Patterson, "Migration in Caribbean Societies: Socioeconomic and Symbolic Resource," in *Human Migration: Patterns and Policies,* ed. William H. McNeill and Ruth S. Adams (Bloomington: Indiana University Press, 1978), pp. 106–145.

26. Bonham C. Richardson, *Caribbean Migrants and Human Survival on St. Kitts and Nevis* (Knoxville: University of Tennessee Press, 1983), p. 6.

27. Richardson, *Panama Money,* pp. 244–245.

28. W. K. Marshall, Trevor Marshall, and Bently Gibbs, "The Establishment of a Peasantry in Barbados, 1840–1920," Unpublished paper, Department of History, University of the West Indies, Cave Hill, Barbados, 1976, pp. 26–28.

29. Richardson, *Caribbean Migrants,* pp. 129–130.

30. Paule Marshall, "Black Immigrant Women in *Brown Girl Brownstones,*" in *Caribbean Life in New York City: Sociocultural Dimensions,* ed. Constance R. Sutton and Elsa M. Chaney (New York: Center for Migration Studies of New York, Inc., 1987), p. 88.

31. Douglas Kent Midgett, "West Indian Migration and Adaptation in St. Lucia and London," Ph.D. dissertation, University of Illinois at Urbana-Champaign, 1977, p. 132.

32. Isa Maria Soto, "West Indian Child Fostering: Its Role in Migrant Exchanges," Sutton and Chaney, eds., *Caribbean Life,* p. 137.

33. Melville, *The Great White Fleet,* p. 42; Nicholas Williams, *United Fruit Company: Nature and Scope of Its Activities* (Boston: Publicity Department, United Fruit Company, 1931), p. 12.

34. Heather Hathaway, *Caribbean Waves: Relocating Claude McKay and Paule Marshall* (Bloomington: Indiana University Press, 1999), p. 2. In this valuable work on the Caribbean American experience, Hathaway takes a literary approach to explaining some salient themes in the history of African Caribbeaners, as she often referred to the immigrants from the Caribbean. Using two Caribbean American iconic literary figures, Claude McKay and Paule Marshall, she describes and analyzes immigrant generational theses, including the classic "Hensen law," dislocation, relocation, and dual location in shaping the complex experiences of Caribbean immigrants and their children in the United States.

35. Hathaway, *Caribbean Waves.* Chapter 4 is particularly useful. It discusses Marshall's *Brown Girl Brownstones* and what that work and other facets of Marshall's life and career reveal about her experiences with dual location as a member of the second generation. That chapter also contrasts Marshall with first-generation McKay, who, according to Hathaway, displayed some of the "typical" characteristics of dislocation—estrangement from both home and host societies (p. 87).

2. Work and Housing in "Freedom's Birthplace"

1. Amy Maud King to Ida Williams, March 15, 1928.

2. Diane Mei Lin Mark and Ginger Chih, *A Place Called Chinese America* (Dubuque: Kendall/Hunt Publishing Company, 1982), p. 5; Hamilton Holt, ed., *The Life*

Stories of Undistinguished Americans as Told By Themselves (New York: Routledge Press, 1906, reprint 1990), pp. 287–288; Ewa Morawska, *For Bread With Butter* (Cambridge, England: Cambridge University Press, 1985); Kazuo Ito, *Issei: A History of the Japanese in North America* (Seattle, Wash.: Japanese Community Service, 1973), pp. 27–29. High hopes for unlimited prosperity, a tendency displayed by both immigrants and American-born, is encapsulated in the "American Dream," which has been an ubiquitous phenomenon in American society since colonial times. For useful, recent studies on this subject, see Jim Cullen, *The American Dream: A Short History of an Idea That Shaped a Nation* (New York: Oxford University Press, 2003); and Cal Jillson, *Pursuing the American Dream* (Lawrence: University of Kansas Press, 2004).

3. Thomas Kessner and Betty Cardi, *Today's Immigrants: Their Stories* (New York: Oxford University Press, 1981), p. 205.

4. John Bodnar, *The Transplanted: A History of Immigrants in Urban America* (Bloomington: Indiana University Press, 1985), p. 57.

5. *Bay State Banner*, September 8, 1988.

6. The *Boston Chronicle*, the weekly publication founded by West Indian immigrants, constantly reported on Boston's "high culture" and how impressed visitors from the islands were and how they were eager to share their observations with the folks back home. In one such report the paper acknowledged that "no distinction is conferred on us Boston Negroes if we live in an atmosphere of culture and do not breathe it" (*Boston Chronicle*, December 30, 1933).

7. These perceptions came out clearly in several anecdotal accounts from oral history collected for this study.

8. Computed from *Passenger Lists or Manifest of Alien Passengers* of ships arriving at Boston from ports in the West Indies and Costa Rica from 1900 to 1950.

9. This literacy level of the incoming West Indians was confirmed by the examining U.S. immigration officials, who noted their ability to read and write English on the literacy column of the *Passenger Lists*.

10. O'Connor, *Bibles, Brahmins and Bosses*, pp. 167–168.

11. *Boston Looks Seaward: The Story of the Port, 1630–1940.* The WPA Federal Writers' Project, Boston: B Humphries, 1941; reprinted, Boston: Northeastern University Press, 1985.

12. Thomas F. Anderson, "Boston: The Industrial Heart of New England," in *Fifty Years of Boston* (Boston: Tercentenary Committee, 1932), p. 175.

13. Ibid.

14. *Boston Globe*, October 22, 1925.

15. Stephan Thernstrom, *The Other Bostonians* (Cambridge, Mass.: Harvard University Press, 1973), pp. 176–219.

16. The two Black newspapers, the *Boston Guardian* and the *Boston Chronicle*, covered these developments extensively. Also, anecdotal accounts from oral history collected for this study speak to these trends.

17. *Guardian*, March 25, 1939.

18. Charles Trout, *Boston: The Great Depression and the New Deal* (New York: Oxford University Press, 1977), p. 193

19. *Boston Chronicle,* April 29, 1933.

20. Ibid., May 6, 1933.

21. *Boston Guardian,* January 6, 1910.

22. Unfortunately, most of the written, official sources did not distinguish British West Indians in the data on the occupations of Blacks in the city. Therefore, this study relies on disparate accounts by the immigrants themselves in their newspaper, association records, and oral history.

23. For more on African Americans and the Pullman Company, see Joseph F. Wilson, *Tearing Down the Color Bar: An Analysis and Documentary History of the Brotherhood of Sleeping Car Porters* (New York: Columbia University Press, 1989); Jack Santino, *Miles of Smiles, Years of Struggle: Stories of Black Pullman Porters* (Urbana: University of Illinois Press, 1989); Melinda Chateauvert, *Marching Together: Women of the Brotherhood of Sleeping Car Porters* (Urbana: University of Illinois Press, 1998).

24. Obituary of Clairmont Lewis, May 1976, Elma Lewis Papers, Box 3/12, File 10.

25. "Biographical Sketch of Edwardine Jordan, 1897–1951," Lewis Papers, Box 3/12, File 28.

26. All three of these second-generation West Indian Americans are prominent figures in Boston. Activist Mel King made history in 1983 as the first African American to run in the general election for mayor of Boston. He recounted his parents' experiences in a personal interview conducted by the author in Cambridge, Mass., on May 7, 1989. See also, Mel King, *Chain of Change: Struggles for Black Community Development* (Boston: South End Press, 1981). Chapter 1, "Growing Up in the South End," is particularly useful. Elma Lewis was also a well-known activist and educator. As founder of the Elma Lewis School for the Performing Arts, she has been recognized with many awards and honors for her contributions toward identifying and enhancing talent among Black youths in the city. She told her parents' stories in an interview in Roxbury, Mass., on July 8, 1997. David Nelson became the first African American federal judge in Massachusetts in 1979. He talked about the West Indian immigrant community in which he grew up in an interview in Boston on December 6, 1990.

27. Colin Allen, personal interview, South End, Boston, March 17, 1987. Allen was born in Plymouth, Montserrat, in 1910. He joined his mother who was a domestic in Boston in 1923. His father, also a Montserratian, moved from Venezuela and joined the family three years later.

28. Testimonial letter for Clairmont Lewis written by the manager of Waldorf System, Inc., May 24, 1933, Lewis Papers, Box 3/123, File 10.

29. For more on Irish women and work in America, see Hasia R. Diner, *Erin's Daughters in America: Irish Immigrant Women in the Nineteenth Century* (Baltimore: Johns Hopkins University Press, 1983).

30. Mrs. Wiltshire's comments and activities were reported in the *Chronicle* of August 3, 1935, and those of Mrs. Chandler appeared in the August 23, 1947, issue.

31. Many of the West Indian women who emigrated had lived for varying lengths of time in urban areas like Kingston, Jamaica; Bridgetown, Barbados; Plymouth, Montserrat; and Limon, Costa Rica, where they had held jobs as household workers.

32. Victor Bynoe, personal interview, South End, Boston, August 6, 1990.

33. Ivy Smith, personal interview, South End, Boston, February 17, 1989. Born in Plymouth, Montserrat, in 1911, Ms. Smith left two kids and her common-law husband to come to Boston in 1941. The children later joined her.

34. Mrs. Gertrude Warner, personal interview, Roxbury, Mass., June 4, 1990.

35. When I discovered this intragroup rivalry while researching, I decided to try and balance my assessment by getting the other side of the story. So I interviewed some African American women and their children, especially those who had migrated from the South in the same period that the West Indians came.

36. *Boston Chronicle,* February 15, 1936.

37. Mrs. Lily Mae Wilson (originally from Georgia), personal interview, Roxbury, Mass., January 15, 1987.

For more on this "Black xenophobia" since the nineteenth century, see Lawrence Fuchs, "The Reactions of Black Americans to Immigration," in *Immigration Reconsidered,* ed. Virginia Yans-McLaughlin (Ithaca, N.Y.: Cornell University Press, 1977).

38. Sadie Wilson, personal interview, Newton, Mass., September 14, 1990.

39. M. S. Stuart, *An Economic Detour* (New York: Wendell Malliett and Company, 1940).

40. Adalberto Aguirre, Jr., and Jonathan H. Turner, *American Ethnicity: The Dynamics and Consequences of Discrimination* (New York: McGraw-Hill, Inc., 1995), p. 15.

41. For analyses of this assessment of West Indians see, for example, Gilbert Osofsky, *Harlem: The Making of a Ghetto* (New York: Harper and Row, 1968), p. 133; Ueda, "West Indians," p. 1023; David Hellwig, "Black Meets Black"; and Nancy Foner, "West Indians in New York City and London: A Comparative Analysis," *International Migration Review,* Vol. 13, No. 2, 1979, p. 287.

42. Watkins-Owens, *Blood Relations,* p. 127.

43. Unfortunately there is a paucity of published studies on Black business enterprise in Boston. Even a well-received work like Shelly Green and Paul Pryde's *Black Entrepreneurship in America* (New Brunswick, N.J.: Transactions Publishers, 1990), neglects the Boston scene. Still, important conclusions can be gleaned from oral histories and reports in the two Black newspapers.

44. Aguirre and Turner, *American Ethnicity,* p. 15.

45. For more on the middleman minority theory, which examines how immigrant minority groups capitalize on certain factors in their economic and social adaptation, see, for example, Edna Bonacich, "A Theory of Middleman Minorities," *American Sociological Review,* Vol. 38 (1973): 583–594; and Suzanne Model, "The Ethnic Niche and the Structure of Opportunity: Immigrants and Minorities in New York City," in *The Underclass Debate: Views from History,* ed. Michael B. Katz (Princeton, N.J.: Princeton University Press, 1993).

46. For much of the twentieth century, Chinese involvement in the grocery trade was widely seen as a monopoly of that economic sector. This perception, also held by many of the Black emigrants of the early twentieth century, helped to foster resentment against the Chinese and resulted, in some instances, in explosive encounters between the Chinese and other racial groups. Increasingly, however, revisionist studies are being conducted which aim to show that the Chinese control of the grocery business, especially in Jamaica, had been exaggerated. Following new approaches to examining the statistics and narratives, such studies affirm that in spite of their visibility in that business arena, the Chinese never monopolized the grocery retail industry. See, for example, Gail Bouknight-Davis, "Chinese Economic Development and Ethnic Identity Formation in Jamaica," in *The Chinese in the Caribbean,* ed. Andrew Wilson (Princeton, N.J.: Markus Wiener, 2004), pp. 69–70.

47. Carl Stone, "Race and Economic Power in Jamaica," in *Garvey: His Work and Impact,* ed. Rupert Lewis and Patrick Bryan (Trenton, N.J.: Africa World Press, Inc., 1991), pp. 243–264. For more on the history of intermediary groups in the West Indies, especially in the economic arena, see Stephan Alexander Fortune, *Merchants and Jews: The Struggle for British West Indian Commerce, 1650–1750* (Gainesville: University of Florida Press, 1984); Jacqueline Levy, "The Economic Role of the Chinese in Jamaica: The Grocery Retail Trade," *The Jamaican Historical Review,* Vol. 15, 1986: 117–138; and David Nicholls, "The Syrians of Jamaica," *The Jamaican Historical Review,* Vol. 15, 1986.

48. For more on the development of Boston's ethnic neighborhoods, see O'Connor, *Bibles and Brahmins,* pp. 119–152; and Buni and Rogers, *Boston, City on a Hill,* pp. 88–95.

49. For some important facts about the migration of southern Blacks to Boston in the first half of the twentieth century, see J. Anthony Lukas, *Common Ground: A Turbulent Decade in the Lives of Three American Families* (New York: Alfred A. Knopf, 1985), p. 60.

50. Lukas, *Common Ground,* p. 60. To reconstruct the face of early twentieth-century Black Boston, I relied on articles and advertisements in the two Black publications of the period—the *Guardian* and *Chronicle*—and on oral history collected for this study.

51. *U.S. Census, 1920.* The Dunbar Associates, a West Indian–African American social club, estimated the figure much higher at 12 percent.

52. King, *Chain of Change,* p. 10.

53. William A. Leahy, "The Population Gains and Losses," in *Fifty Years of Boston,* a volume commemorating the tercentenary of 1930 (Boston: Tercentenary Committee, 1932). pp. 63–64.

54. This picture of West Indian concentration was retraced from oral history and disparate newspaper reports, especially those from the West Indian–owned *Chronicle.*

55. *Chronicle,* December 21, 1940.

56. For more on the process and ramifications of the demographic ethnic succession of Jews by Blacks, see Yona Ginsberg, *Jews in a Changing Neighborhood: The Study of Mattapan* (London: The Free Press, 1975) and Hillel Levine and Lawrence

Harmon, *The Death of an American Jewish Community: A Tragedy of Good Intentions* (New York: The Free Press, 1992).

57. *Chronicle*, December 21, 1940.

58. Bynoe, interview.

59. Nelson, interview.

3. Identity, Culture, and Community

1. Report of the British Embassy, Washington, D.C., to the Foreign Secretary, March 1934. Public Record Office, Kew (PRO) FO 598/15.

2. Judith E. Smith, *Family Connections: A History of Italian and Jewish Immigrant Lives in Providence, Rhode Island, 1900–1940* (Albany: State University of New York Press, 1985), p. 1.

3. The following are some of the studies on family and community in the West Indies done in the first half of the twentieth century: T. S. Simey, *Welfare and Planning in the West Indies* (London: Oxford University Press, 1946); Madeline Kerr, *Personality and Conflict in Jamaica* (Liverpool: Liverpool University Press, 1951); M. J. and F. S. Herskovits, *Trinidad Village* (New York: Alfred A. Knopf, 1947); R. T. Smith, *The Negro Family in British Guiana* (London: Routledge and Kegan Paul, 1956); and Fernando Henriques, *Family and Colour in Jamaica* (London: Eyre and Spottiswoode, 1953).

4. One of the first studies to show the positive aspects of community organization was Edith Clarke's classic study *My Mother Who Fathered Me* (London: Allen and Unwin, 1957). Interestingly, Clarke was one of the scholars appointed by the Colonial Science Research Council in Britain to investigate the problems uncovered by the 1938 Royal Commission. Another important contribution is M. G. Smith's *West Indian Family Structure* (Seattle: University of Washington Press, 1962). Smith also discusses the historiography of West Indian family and community studies in "A Survey of West Indian Family Studies," in *Work and Family Life,* ed. Lambros Comitas and David Lowenthal (Garden City, N.Y.: Anchor Press/Doubleday, 1973). For a more recent study which summarizes past studies and assesses the current state and future directions of Caribbean family studies, see Marietta Morrissey, "Explaining the Caribbean Family: Gender, Ideologies and Gender Relations," in *Caribbean Portraits: Essays on Gender Ideologies and Identities,* ed. Christine Barrow (Kingston, Jamaica: Ian Randle, 1998).

5. Gleaned from entries of several volumes of the *Passenger Lists* of the U.S. Immigration Services.

6. Perhaps the most famous second-generation West Indian to exemplify this trend is Shirley Chisholm, the first Black woman elected to the Congress of the United States. Born in Brooklyn, Chisholm (then St. Hill) and her two younger sisters were sent to live with grandparents in Barbados when she was three. After spending seven years there, they reunited with their parents in New York. Chisholm talks about this formative period and other experiences in her autobiography *Unbought and Unbossed* (New York: Houghton Mifflin, 1970).

7. Unfortunately, concrete statistical evidence to substantiate the high inci- · dence of marriage between people from the same or different West Indian societies is hard to find. What would have been the most valuable source, the St. Cyprian's (the West Indian church) marriage register, was destroyed in a fire. In this circumstance, the conclusions for this study come from anecdotal evidence from oral history, newspaper reports, and naturalization petitions.

8. Nelson, interview.

9. Glenis Williams, personal interview, South End, Boston, June 4, 1989. Mrs. Williams was born in Spanish Town, Jamaica, in 1925. After elementary school, she worked as a washerwoman. A vacationing Boston white family brought her to Boston to work as a domestic in 1946.

10. See for example, Bodnar, *The Transplanted,* pp. 57–84; Smith, *Family Connections,* pp. 23–82; John Bodnar, Roger Simon, and Michael Weber, *Lives of Their Own: Blacks, Italians and Poles in Pittsburgh, 1900–1960* (Urbana: University of Illinois Press, 1982); Robert C. Ostregren, "Kinship Networks and Migration: A Nineteenth Century Swedish Example," *Journal of American Ethnic History* 3, no. 2, 1984.

11. See, for example, Irma Watkins-Owens, "Early Twentieth-Century Caribbean Women: Migration and Social Networks in New York City," in *Islands in the City: West Indian Migration to New York,* ed. Nancy Foner (Berkeley: University of California Press, 2001).

12. Higglering is an economic activity in the West Indies that has existed since slavery, whereby women functioned as itinerant suppliers of produce to market vendors. Such wholesale produce traders were called higglers. A good analysis of the correlation between economic stability and family and kindred cohesiveness is R. T. Smith, *The Negro Family in British Guiana,* especially chapter IV.

13. George Commissiong, personal interview, Mattapan, Mass., November 20, 1989. George Commissiong was born in Grenada in 1909. His family moved to Trinidad in 1915. In 1942, an "American military man" he met in Trinidad arranged for him to come to Boston.

14. One of the main theses of Herbert Gutman's classic work *The Black Family in Slavery and Freedom* is the enduring kinship support among American Blacks, despite the destructive effects of slavery. See Herbert Gutman, *The Black Family in Slavery and Freedom, 1850–1925* (New York: Pantheon, 1976). Other studies which substantiate kinship support in occupational endeavors among African American migrants from the south are Henri, *Black Migration;* Bodnar, Weber, and Simon, *Lives of Their Own* and John Sibley Butler, *Entrepreneurship and Self-Help Among Black Americans* (New York: State University of New York Press, 1991).

15. John Bodnar, Michael Weber, and Roger Simon, "Migration, Kinship and Urban Adjustment: Blacks and Poles in Pittsburgh, 1900–1930," *Journal of American History* 66 (1979): 554.

16. For more on women and work in the British West Indies, see Sidney Mintz, "Black Women, Economic Roles and Cultural Traditions," in *Caribbean Freedom: Economy and Society from Emancipation to the Present,* ed. Hilary Beckles and Verene Shepherd (Kingston: Ian Randle Publishers, 1993); Keith Hart, ed., *Women and Sex-*

ual Division of Labour in the Caribbean (Kingston, Jamaica: Consortium Graduate School, University of the West Indies, 1989); and Verene A. Shepherd, *Women in Caribbean History* (Kingston, Jamaica: Ian Randle, 1999). Chapter 5, "Adjustments to Emancipation and Socio-Economic Life," is particularly useful.

17. See Bodnar, *The Transplanted,* pp. 78–80; Leslie Woodcock Tentler, *Wage-Earning: Industrial Work and Family Life in the United States, 1900–1930* (New York: Oxford University Press, 1979), pp. 137–138, 142; Joan Younger Dickinson, *The Role of Immigrant Women in the U.S. Labor Force, 1890–1910* (New York: Arno Press, 1980), pp. 1, 58, 122; Smith, *Family Connections,* pp. 44–51.

18. Patrice G., personal interview, Roxbury, Mass., June 4, 1990. Born in Kingston, Jamaica, in 1915, she joined her mother, a domestic, and stepfather, a laborer, in Boston in 1931.

19. Bynoe, interview.

20. At my very first meeting with Ms. Lewis, September 20, 1985, she proudly recalled how she started contributing to the family income at an early age. She told of how she, a gifted performer, performed as a dramatic reader at St. Cyprian's church from the age of eleven. Earnings were given to her parents to augment funds for her education. In several articles on her performances, the *Chronicle* substantiates Lewis's remarkable career.

21. Bodnar, *The Transplanted,* p. 193. See also Smith, *Family Connections,* pp. 52–58; Alice Kessler-Harris, *Out to Work: A History of Wage-Earning Women in the United States* (New York: Oxford University Press, 1982), pp. 123–124.

22. Robert Campbell, personal interview, Waltham, Mass., February 15, 1989. Mr. Campbell was born in Montego Bay, Jamaica, around 1912. He worked on a United Fruit steamer as a painter and decided to "just disappear" in Boston in 1937.

23. For examples of attempts by other immigrant/ethnic groups to preserve homeland cultures even as they negotiated various forms of Americanisms, see Dennis Clark, *Erin Heirs: Irish Bonds of Community* (Lexington: University of Kentucky Press, 1991). Chapter 1 is particularly useful. See also Robert C. Ostergren, *A Community Transplanted: The Trans-Atlantic Experience of a Swedish Immigrant Settlement in the Upper Middle West, 1835–1915* (Madison: University of Wisconsin Press, 1988).

24. William Sandiford, personal interview, Boston, January 17, 1990.

25. Statement on the life of Edwardine Lewis, on the occasion of the dedication of a memorial chalice in her honor to St. Cyprian's Church, June 20, 1982. Lewis Papers, Box 3/12, File 28.

26. Many visitors to the islands commented on the strong presence of Christianity. For example, in the late 1930s, a visitor researching Jamaica observed: "Jamaica is or has been well evangelized . . . churches and chapels have been provided in almost every valley and almost every hamlet . . . Jamaica is probably better churched and 'Christianized' than parts of the world more commonly known as 'Christian.'" Cited in John M. Davis, *The Church in the New Jamaica: A Study of the Economic and Social Basis of the Evangelical Church in Jamaica* (New York: International Missionary Council, 1942), p. 39.

Holger Henke uncovered similar claims. As he put it: "Whether it is true or not, many people in Jamaica will tell you that their country boasts the greatest number of church buildings per square mile in the world. Baptists, Methodists, Anglicans, Roman Catholics, and dozens of other mainly Protestant Christian churches punctuate the urban and rural landscape in the English-speaking Caribbean with their church buildings, and many communal activities and initiatives . . . continue to have the churches as the organizational support and operational base." See Henke, *West Indian Americans*, p. 9.

27. *General Report of the Census of the Population of the British West Indies* (Kingston, Jamaica: Government Printing Office, 1946). For more background into church history in Barbados, see Kortright Davis, *Cross and Crown in Barbados: Caribbean Political Religion in the Late 19th Century* (Frankfurt: Verlag Peter Lang, 1983).

28. Davis, *Cross and Crown*, p. iii. See also Robert Stewart, "A Slandered People—Views on 'Negro Character' in the Mainstream Christian Churches in Post-Emancipation Jamaica," in *Crossing Boundaries: Comparative History of Black People in the Diaspora*, ed. Darlene Clark Hine and Jacqueline McLeod (Bloomington: Indiana University Press, 1999), pp. 179–201.

29. Stewart aptly summarizes this material attractiveness of the church in the case of Jamaica: "The church allegiances of Afro-Jamaicans after emancipation tended to be pragmatically flexible and simultaneous: they would shift their attachments for what European preachers saw as secular reasons, or they would belong to one of the Euro-Christian congregations for the access to land, housing, education and political influence that such membership might provide. . . . ," Stewart, "A Slandered People," p. 182.

30. This tabulation of West Indian church affiliation was contained in a paper presented by Gerald Vincent, graduate student at Harvard, on "Blacks and the Church," at St. Marks Congregational Church in April 1940. A summary of this paper was published in the *Chronicle*, May 11, 1940.

31. King, *Chain of Change*, pp. 10–11.

32. For a concise history of St. Cyprian's, see Robert C. Hayden, *Faith, Culture and Leadership: A History of the Black Church in Boston* (Boston: Boston Branch of the NAACP, 1983), pp. 50–53.

33. It is significant that the Black foreigners named their church for Thascius Caecilius Cyprianus (c. 200–258), who was an outstanding theologian and, very importantly, was African. Pastor Henderson Brome points to the founders' choice of a name as "a profound affirmation of their common African roots." See Henderson L. Brome, *Voices and Victors in the Struggle* (n.p., n.d.), p. 16, a pamphlet on a brief history of St. Cyprian's Church and the Black heroes painted on the church's stained glass windows. By the time of the founding of Boston's St. Cyprian's, there seemed to have developed a Black Episcopalian tradition around the celebration of St. Cyprian with which many of the immigrants were already conversant. A St. Cyprian's Anglican Church was already in existence in St. Michael, Barbados. Importantly, similar West Indian communities elsewhere in the United States also established St. Cyprian

Episcopalian churches. For example, New York's Caribbean immigrants and African American migrants from the South, with financial help from the Protestant Episcopalian Mission Society, formed St. Cyprian Episcopal Church in San Juan Hill in 1905 (Watkins-Owens, *Blood Relations*, p. 58). Similarly, in 1923, around the time of the founding of Boston's St. Cyprian's, "twice dispersed" West Indians, who had migrated to San Francisco from the Panama Canal Zone, collaborated with Black American migrants to form a Black Episcopal Church they named St. Cyprian's. A concise history of St. Cyprian's Episcopal Church, San Francisco, can be found on the church's website at

http://www.saintcyprianssf.org/history.htm.

34. The figures here are sketchy because vital records were lost in the fire. Some of these rough estimates were provided by Dr. Henderson Brome, pastor of the church, in an informal interview with the author, Roxbury, May 4, 1989.

35. These figures from church records are cited in Hayden, *Faith, Culture and Leadership*, p. 52.

36. Bynoe, interview.

37. Hayden, *Faith, Culture and Leadership*, p. 51; Bynoe, interview; and Delroy Johnson, personal interview, Roxbury, Mass., April 17, 1990.

38. Bynoe, interview; *Chronicle*, September 25, 1937.

39. From excerpts of Fergusson's sermon at St. Cyprian's, April 22, 1939. Cited in *Boston Chronicle*, April 28, 1939.

40. John Higham, "Leadership," in Stephan Thernstrom, ed., *Harvard Encyclopedia of American Ethnic Groups;* Victor Green, *American Immigrant Leaders, 1800–1910: Marginality and Identity* (Baltimore: Johns Hopkins University Press, 1987); and John Higham, ed., *Ethnic Leadership in America* (Baltimore: Johns Hopkins University Press, 1978).

41. Studies which conveyed this kind of assessment have already been discussed in the introduction to this book.

42. Watkins-Owens, *Blood Relations*, pp. 56–57.

43. Elma Lewis, interview, July 8, 1997.

44. For more on Marcus Garvey and the Universal Negro Improvement Association, see Judith Stein, *The World of Marcus Garvey: Race and Class in Modern Society* (Baton Rouge: Louisiana State University Press, 1986); and Jeannette Smith-Irvin, *Marcus Garvey's Footsoldiers of the Universal Negro Improvement Association* (Trenton, N.J.: Africa World Press, 1989).

45. Vital records of the Boston UNIA perished when the UNIA building burned to the ground in 1952. Therefore, this study relies on local newspaper reports, oral history, and, very importantly, pertinent reports in the "News from Branches" section of the UNIA publication, *Negro World*, to help reconstruct the history of Garveyism in Boston.

46. For discussions on how some immigrants balanced work and leisure, see Roy Rosenzweig, *Eight Hours for What We Will: Workers and Leisure in an Industrial City, 1870–1920* (Cambridge and New York: Cambridge University Press, 1983); and Bodnar, *The Transplanted*, pp. 185–188.

47. For more on the socioeconomic ramifications of cricket in the British West Indies, see St. Pierre, "West Indian Cricket: A Sociohistorical Appraisal"; C. L. R. James, *Beyond a Boundary* (London: Hutchinson, 1969); Michael Manley, *History of West Indies Cricket* (London: Andre Deutsch, 1988); and Frank E. Manning, "Celebrating Cricket: The Symbolic Construction of Caribbean Politics," in *Blackness in Latin America and the Caribbean* Vol. II. ed. Arlene Torres and Norman E. Whitten, Jr. (Bloomington: Indiana University Press, 1998), pp. 460–482.

48. For example, the February 11, 1933 *Chronicle* reported: "The ladies of the West India A Cricket Team are forging ahead by giving entertainment to assist the club in procuring proper outfit for the coming of cricket." Similarly, Elma Lewis proudly pointed out, "Hand in hand with the men, the women made cricket what it became in the recreational scene." Lewis, interview.

49. See Robert E. Park's classic on this subject, *The Immigrant Press and Its Control* (New York: Harper & Brothers, 1922); and Sally M. Miller, ed., *The Ethnic Press in the United States: A Historical Analysis and Handbook* (Westport, Conn.: Greenwood Press, 1987); Rudolph J. Vecoli, "The Italian Immigrant Press and the Construction of Social Reality, 1850–1920," in *Print Culture in a Diverse America.* ed. James P. Danky and Wayne A. Wiegand (Urbana: University of Illinois Press, 1998).

50. Stephen R. Fox, *The Guardian of Boston: William Monroe Trotter* (New York: Atheneum, 1970), p. 267.

51. *Chronicle*, July 23, 1932, and March 30, 1935, respectively.

52. It is important to point out that African American–owned and operated newspapers like the *Chicago Defender* and the *Pittsburgh Courier* also reported on events in Africa. But this was most clearly visible with these papers during highly publicized international developments like the Italian invasion of Ethiopia, while the *Chronicle's* attention on Africa and other Black communities outside the U.S. was more constant.

For more on the dynamics of a Black Atlantic world born out of slavery and the slave trade and sustained by the migration of people and ideas in transnational contexts, see Paul Gilroy, *The Black Atlantic: Modernity and Double Consciousness* (Cambridge, Mass.: Harvard University Press, 1993).

53. *Chronicle*, March 15, 1941.

54. *Daily Gleaner*, April 30, 1930; June 21, 1930.

55. Walter Rodney, "Barbadian Immigration Into British Guiana, 1863–1924," in *Proceedings of the 9th Conference of Caribbean Historians* (Kingston, Jamaica: University of the West Indies, 1977), p. 78.

56. Cited in the *Daily Gleaner,* June 13, 1935.

57. See, for example, Katharine W. Jones, *Accent on Privilege: English Identities and Anglophilia in the U.S.* (Philadelphia: Temple University Press, 2001); Noel Ignatiev, *How the Irish Became White* (New York: Routledge, 1995); and Marilyn Halter, *Between Race and Ethnicity: Cape Verdean American Immigrants* (Urbana: University of Illinois Press, 1993).

58. Mrs. Betty Williams, personal interview, Roxbury, Mass., June 15, 1990. Williams, born in Bridgetown, Barbados, in 1920, came to Boston in 1938.

59. Bynoe, interview; Commissiong, interview; and Elfreda E., personal interview, Mattapan, Mass., June 7, 1987.

60. Many who contributed oral histories to this study explained that they were proud of their accent and clung to it largely because it drew attention to the fact that they were foreign.

In a recently published study, sociologist Katharine Jones describes and discusses similar experiences among white upper-middle-class English immigrants in America, who draw on anglophilia as a cultural capital. See Jones, *Accent on Privilege.*

61. Holger Henke talks about the enduring anglophilia in the English-speaking Caribbean in his recent study. As he put it: "the colonial British culture set the standard for what was regarded as respectable and civilized. In many instances this remains so. . . . In many countries, the British monarch has remained the titular head of state." See Henke, *West Indian Americans,* p. 13.

62. Circular from Edmund Gray, Esq, consul general of Boston, September 16, 1922. PRO FO 620/1.

63. R. L. Lindsay, British ambassador to the United States, to the Foreign Office, January 17, 1934. PRO FO 598/15.

64. Address of the president of Jamaica Associates at the first meeting of the Sons and Daughters of the Associates, April 17, 1940. From excerpts in the *Chronicle,* May 11, 1940.

65. From the "Psychologist's Report," by V. T. Graham, Ph.D., November 7, 1924, Lewis Papers, Box 3/12, File 6.

66. Nelson, interview. Nelson's experiences in this area are also explored in Brian Doyle, "The Passion of Dave Nelson," *Boston College Magazine,* Fall 1988, p. 54.

67. King, *Chain of Change,* p. 10.

68. Amanda Houston, personal interview, Chestnut Hill, Mass., March 14, 1992. Mrs. Amanda Houston, first director of the Black Studies Program of Boston College, was until her death in 1995 one of the prominent African Americans of the city of Boston. With strong roots in the Humboldt Avenue Roxbury neighborhood, where many of the West Indian families lived, Mrs. Houston was instrumental in identifying sources and making contacts for some of the interviews used for this study.

69. Bynoe, interview.

70. "Elma Lewis, Blend of Marcus Garvey and the 'Y,'" p. 10.

71. Yvonne Mason, personal interview, Roxbury, Mass., February 2, 1988. Ms. Mason was born in Bridgetown, Barbados, in 1920, came to New Bedford in 1939, and later moved to Boston in 1942. The son of whom she speaks was born in the West Indies but joined her in New Bedford in 1940 at the age of five.

For more on the second-generation experience with identity, race, and racism, see Mary C. Waters, "Growing Up West Indian and African American: Gender and Class Differences in the Second Generation," in Foner, ed., *Islands in the City;* Waters, "Ethnic and Racial Identities of Second-Generation Black Immigrants in New York City," *International Migration Review* XXVIII, no. 4, 1994, pp. 795–820. For analyses of West Indian identity and race consciousness, see Waters, *Black Identities*; Milton Vickerman, "Tweaking a Monolithic: The West Indian Immigrant Encounter with 'Blackness,'" in Foner, ed., *Islands in the City*; and Vickerman, *Crosscurrents*.

72. *Chronicle*, November 16, 1935; December 21, 1940.

73. Edward Cooper, manager of First National Store, South End, and first president of the Progressive Credit Union. This quote is taken from an address at a membership drive meeting, cited in the *Chronicle*, March 9, 1940.

74. Bynoe, interview.

75. *Chronicle*, April 2, 1948.

76. *Boston Guardian*, December 2, 1944. Crispus Attucks, one of the heroes in African American history, is remembered for being the first person to die in the American Revolution.

4. Militant Immigrants and Relentless Ex-colonials?

1. Several issues of the *Guardian* and the *Chronicle* carried extensive coverage of the incident and the developments which followed. Remarkably, a mainstream newspaper like the *Boston Globe* was silent.

2. *Chronicle*, July 21, 1934.

3. Domingo, "Gift of the Black Tropics," p. 349.

4. *Plain Talk*, December 28, 1935.

5. Dennis Forsythe, "West Indian Radicalism in America: An Assessment of Ideologies," in *Ethnicity in the Americas*, ed. Frances Henry (The Hague: Mouton Publishers, 1976), p. 301.

6. Marcus Garvey to Major R. R. Moton, February 1916, in Robert Hill, ed., *The Marcus Garvey and Universal Negro Improvement Association Papers* (Berkeley: University of California Press, 1983), p. 180.

7. For more on the complex racial climate in the sending societies of the West Indies, particularly Jamaica, see Vickerman, *Crosscurrents*. Chapter 1 is particularly useful.

8. Albert J. Von Frank, *The Trials of Anthony Burns: Freedom and Slavery in Emerson's Boston* (Cambridge, Mass.: Harvard University Press, 1998), p. xii.

9. The Black newspapers, especially the *Guardian*, were effective conduits for echoing Blacks' agreement with perceptions of Black progress. Many letters to the editor of the *Guardian* in the early 1900s bear testimony to this fact. The classic study of Boston's Black upper class is Hill, *The Other Brahmins*.

10. Thernstrom, *The Other Bostonians*, p. 258. Chapter 8, "Blacks and Whites," is particularly useful.

11. Mark Schneider, *Boston Confronts Jim Crow, 1890–1920* (Boston: Northeastern University Press, 1997), p. 4.

12. For more on Boston and the Depression, see Trout, *Boston: The Great Depression and New Deal*.

13. For the rationale, strategies, strengths, and weaknesses of the don't-buy-where-you-can't-work campaign of the Depression era, see August Meir, Elliot Rud-

wick, and Francis L. Broderick, *Black Protest Thought in the Twentieth Century* (Indianapolis, Ind.: Bobbs-Merrill, 1983), pp. 122–131; Darlene Clark Hine, "The Housewives' League of Detroit: Black Women and Economic Nationalism," in *Visible Women: New Essays on American Activism,* ed. Nancy A. Hewitt and Suzanne Lebsock (Urbana: University of Illinois Press, 1993), pp. 223–241.

14. For more on the origins, tenets, and expressions of Uplift, see Kevin Gaines, *Uplifting the Race: Black Leadership, Politics, and Culture in the Twentieth Century* (Chapel Hill: University of North Carolina Press, 1996).

15. Nat Hentoff, *Boston Boy* (New York: Knopf, 1986). Many anecdotal accounts in the oral history conducted for this study also speak to the volatile situation.

16. See Lance Carden. *Witness: An Oral History of Black Politics in Boston, 1920–1960* (Boston: Boston College Press, 1989); Levine and Harmon, *Death of an American Jewish Community,* pp. 19–22.

17. *Chronicle,* May 4, 1935.

18. Bynoe, interview; Carden, *Witness,* p. 53.

19. *Chronicle,* April 26, 1947.

20. Since the early 1900s, American-born Black leaders, including William Monroe Trotter, had unsuccessfully tried to have police officers prosecuted. Some vivid accounts of these attempts are related in Carden, *Witness,* p. 5.

21. In April 1931, the trial of nine Black youths began in Scottsboro, Alabama. They were accused of raping two White women in a freight train. The charges, which were controversial from the beginning, elicited rage among Blacks around the country and the world. See James Goodman, *Stories of Scottsboro* (New York: Vintage Books, 1994).

22. This pledge was made by the founders and editors of *Freedom's Journal,* Samuel E. Cornish and John B. Russwurm, in the first edition (March 16, 1827). Cited in Lerone Bennett, Jr., *Before the Mayflower: A History of Black America* (New York: Penguin, 1984), p. 174.

23. For an example of ward bossism in Boston, see O'Connor, *The Boston Irish.*

24. John F. Fitzgerald, boss of Ward 6 in the North End and today perhaps best known as the maternal grandfather of President John F. Kennedy, was the first Boston-born, Irish American, Catholic mayor.

25. *Boston Guardian,* November 30, 1905.

26. In August 1906, African American soldiers stationed in Brownsville, Texas, were involved in a riot. The White residents, who had resented their presence there, blamed the Black soldiers for all the trouble. Siding with the residents, President Theodore Roosevelt summarily dismissed the entire battalion without honor and disqualified its members for service in either the military or the U.S. Civil Service. This incident, which happened ironically in the height of the Progressive movement, enraged African Americans across the nation.

27. *Boston Guardian,* December 7, 1907.

28. The Good Government Association was formed at the turn of the century through the initiative of old Bostonians who were alarmed by the imminent Irish political ascendancy. *Guardian,* January 6, 1910; January 8, 1910.

29. Cited in Carden, *Witness*, p. 15.

30. *Guardian*, September 19, 1942.

31. *Chronicle*, April 23, 1932.

32. Carden, *Witness*, p. 16.

33. Nelson, interview.

34. From excerpts of the minutes of the meeting of the Jamaica Associates on October 10, 1934. Printed in the *Chronicle*, October 20, 1934.

35. Williams, interview; *Chronicle*, October 20, 1934.

36. *Chronicle*, July 23, 1932.

37. *Guardian*, January 23, 1943.

38. Many scholars have described and discussed the harsh and contemptuous treatment the Irish endured in Boston. See, for example, O'Connor, *The Boston Irish*, XV.

39. This starkly racist film met with opposition from Blacks throughout the nation. For more on the protest in Boston, see Buni and Rogers, *Boston, City on a Hill*, pp. 120–121.

40. Bynoe. interview; Carden, *Witness*, p. 16.

41. Ignatiev, *How the Irish Became White*, pp. 178–179.

42. Diner, *Erin's Daughters in America: Irish Immigrant Women in the Nineteenth Century*.

43. *Chronicle*, September 17, 1932.

44. James Jennings, *The Politics of Black Empowerment: The Transformation of Black Activism in Urban America* (Detroit: Wayne State University Press, 1992), p. 11.

45. *Chronicle*, November 16, 1935; Bynoe, interview.

46. For a general history of the National Association for the Advancement of Colored People (NAACP), see Minnie Finch, *The NAACP, its Fight for Justice* (Metuchen, N.J.: Scarecrow Press, 1981); Charles Flint Kellogg, *NAACP, a History of the National Association for the Advancement of Colored People* (Baltimore: Johns Hopkins University Press, 1967). For the specific history of the Boston branch, see Robert C. Hayden, *Boston's NAACP History, 1910–1982* (Boston: Boston Branch of the NAACP, 1982).

47. Carden, *Witness*, pp. 28–29. The issue of leadership of the Boston NAACP in the early twentieth century has been a controversial and sometimes distorted subject. So convinced were some about the strong influence of Whites over the leadership that the erroneous impression that the presidents, including Butler Wilson, were Whites found its way into the scholarship. In a much earlier work of mine, "Relentless Ex-Colonials and Militant Immigrants: Protest Strategies of Boston's West Indian Immigrants," in Patrick Miller et al., *The Civil Rights Movement Revisited: Critical Perspectives on the Struggle for Racial Equality in the United States* (Munster, Germany: LIT VERLAG, 2001) p. 12, quoting from Carden's *Witness*, I identified Wilson as White. Unfortunately, I had used a copy of Carden's book which was missing the erratum he had issued correcting the error, which, it turns out, he had picked up from Charles Trout's work on Boston and the Great Depression.

48. Hayden, *Boston's NAACP*, pp. 4–5.

49. Bynoe, interview.

50. Elma Lewis, interview; Bynoe, interview; King, interview.

51. Carden, *Witness,* p. 9.

52. Ibid. Lewis also gave similar accounts in her interview. Her father's obituary proudly proclaimed that he was "one of the first investors in Garvey's Black Star Line," Lewis Papers, M38. Box 3/12, File 10.

53. Carden, *Witness,* p. 10.

54. Bynoe, interview.

55. For concise yet analytical accounts of the upheavals in colonial British West Indies in the 1930s, see Richard Hart, "Labour Rebellions of the 1930s," in *Caribbean Freedom: Economy and Society From Emancipation to the Present,* ed. Hillary Beckles and Verene Shepherd (Princeton, N.J.: Markus Wiener, 1996), pp. 370–375; and Arthur W. Lewis, "The 1930s Social Revolution," in Beckles and Shepherd, eds., *Caribbean Freedom,* pp. 376–392.

56. *Chronicle,* June 4, 1938.

57. Ibid., May 22, 1943.

58. Ibid., June 2, 1943.

59. See Joyce Moore Turner and Burghardt Turner, *Richard B. Moore: Caribbean Militant in Harlem* (Bloomington: Indiana University Press, 1996).

60. *Guardian,* July 7, 1939.

61. Confidential dispatch from the governor of the colony of Jamaica to Rt. Honourable W. Ormsby Gore, M.P., Secretary of State for the Colonies, April 11, 1938. PRO FO 598/15.

62. *Chronicle,* February 15, 1936.

63. Report of R. E. Barclay, British Ambassador, to the Consular Department of the Foreign Office. June 16, 1943. PRO FO 369/2916.

64. Minutes of the Meeting of Consular Officers, February 14, 1944. PRO FO 369/3049.

65. James B. Nelson, personal interview, South End, Boston, August 17, 1989.

66. For more on the Black Women's Club Movement, see Stephanie J. Shaw, "Black Club Women and the Creation of the National Association of Colored Women," in *We Specialize in the Wholly Impossible: A Reader in Black Women's History,* ed. Darlene Clark Hine, Wilma King, Linda Reed (New York: Carlson Publishing, Inc., 1995), pp. 433–447.

67. Bynoe, interview.

68. *Chronicle,* April 26, 1947.

5. "Making Good in America" and Living the West Indian Dream

1. References to some of the studies on the progress of Afro-Caribbeans in America can be found in the introduction to this study.

2. It is instructive to note that West Indians were not the only immigrant group that continually used the homeland as a point of reference in how they pursued and interpreted progress in America. See, for example, Leonard Dinnerstein

and David M. Reimers, *Ethnic Americans: A History of Immigration* (New York: Harper Collins, 1988), Chapter 8, "Pilgrims Progress: Ethnic Mobility in Modern America," pp. 147–171; Joy K. Lintelman, "'America is the Woman's Promised Land': Swedish Immigrant Women and American Domestic Service," *Journal of American Ethnic History* 8, no. 2, 1989, pp. 9–23; and M. Mark Stolarik and Murray Friedman, eds., *Making it in America: The Role of Ethnicity in Business Enterprise, Education and Work Choices* (Lewisburg, Pa.: Bucknell University Press, 1986).

3. Victor Bynoe related this account about his father. John Leo Bynoe was born in Bridgetown, Barbados, in 1895. He first moved to Nova Scotia, Canada, before he moved to Boston in 1919. Bynoe, interview; Naturalization Petition #360359, General Records of the Department of Justice, National Archives of the United States.

4. Many people who provided the oral history for this study made references to the "daalar" catch word.

5. Stephan Thernstrom emphasizes this general effect of the occupational structure on Boston's Blacks—Boston-born and transplanted Blacks alike. See Thernstrom, *The Other Bostonians*. Chapter 8, "Blacks and Whites," is particularly useful.

6. Sample earnings for the West Indies were pulled from Ambursley, "The Working Class in the Third World." Sample rates for Boston were computed from Help Wanted advertisements in the *Boston Globe*. Earnings in these occupations in Boston were well within the national average. See Scott Derks, *The Value of a Dollar: Prices and Incomes in the United States, 1860–1989* (Detroit: Gale Research Inc., 1994), p. 150. At the outbreak of World War I the exchange value of the pound to the dollar was £1 to \$4.76, in 1939 it was £1 to \$4.03 and £1 to \$2.80 in 1949. Information on exchange rates was acquired from the *Funk and Wagnall's New Encyclopedia* Vol. 21 (Funk and Wagnall's Corporation, 1993), p. 229.

7. Elvin James, personal interview, South End, Boston, April 17, 1987. James, a bricklayer in Barbados, was born in Christ Church in 1920. He emigrated to Boston in 1938 with the help of a cousin who had migrated three years earlier.

8. Education and socioeconomic mobility in the West Indies has already been discussed in chapter 1.

9. David Nelson, interview; Elma Lewis, interview; Mavis Sinclair, personal interview, Roxbury, May 28, 1990. Sinclair was born and raised in Boston. Her mother, Rhoda Ingram, arrived in Boston on the *Admiral Dewey* from Port Morant on June 28, 1911. The oral history collected for this study contains several other similar anecdotes about the resolve of the foreign-born parents to educate their children.

10. King, *Chain of Change*, pp. 32–33; Bynoe, interview.

11. The detailed description of Elma Lewis's graduation from Emerson with a Bachelor of Literary Interpretation (*Guardian*, June 26, 1943) is exemplary of this trend. The list of guests, more than twenty, mentioned in the notice, read like a who's who of the emerging Black middle-class zone of the Hill. Recognition of educational achievement by the ethnic press was displayed by other groups as well. For example, around the same time, the Jewish newspaper the *Boston Advocate* published the names of all Jewish graduates of Boston high schools and local colleges

who had distinguished themselves with honors. See William Braverman, "The Emergence of a Unified Community, 1880–1917," in Sarna and Smith, eds., *Jews of Boston*, p. 83.

12. Bynoe, interview.

13. Researchers Hillel Levine and Lawrence Harmon in their study *The Death of an American Jewish Community* shed light on some of the underhanded tactics used by money-hungry, unscrupulous realtors to accelerate the departure of the Jewish residents of the Hill. The main objective of such realtors was to drive fear into the Jewish residents about the repercussions of a fast-spreading "criminal" Black community.

14. Merna Johnson, interview. Roxbury, Mass., May 17, 1988. Merna Johnson was born in Bridgetown, Barbados, in 1915. She was a washerwoman there when one of her sisters used her "Panama money" to help her emigrate to live with a cousin in Boston in 1934.

15. "C.M.," personal interview, South End, Boston, June 17, 1989.

16. Sociologist Bernard D. Headley tackled this phenomenon in his essay "Gone Foreign!" *The Jamaica Mirror*, April 1989; July–August 1989.

17. Amy Lewis to Clairmont Lewis, May 3, 1927, Lewis Papers, Box 3/12, File number 12. Rob Kroes offers a concise and fascinating example of how this phenomenon works. Focusing on photographs sent home by a cross-section of individuals from selected European countries, he describes and discusses how pictures were used not only to maintain vital ties but to convey the immigrants' desired representations of their productive lives in America. Rob Kroes, *Questions of Citizenship in a Globalizing World: Them and Us* (Urbana: University of Illinois Press, 2000), chapter 4, "Immigrants and Transnational Localism: A Focus on Photography," pp. 43–56.

18. "Sources and Values of Money Orders Paid in Barbados." From Reports on the Post Office of Barbados, 1901–1920.

19. *Chronicle*, May 17, 1930.

20. David Nelson, interview.

21. Elsa B., interviewed by Elsa Williams for a school project entitled "Researching Your Family History," Baltimore, Maryland, December 1977. Elsa B. was born in Jamaica in 1902. She came to Boston in 1921 at age nineteen, leaving behind the son she mentions in the quote. He was about five years old when he joined her in Boston.

22. Norris Taylor, interviewed by Mavis Taylor Wilson (his granddaughter) "around" May 1970. Mavis Taylor Wilson recounted Norris Taylor's story to the present author in an interview, Roxbury, June 4, 1990.

23. Carol Johnson, personal interview, Mattapan, Mass., May 17, 1989. Johnson is an American-born second-generation Barbadian. Her parents were born in Barbados and migrated to Boston in 1920.

24. Statement of Financial Support from Clairmont Lewis to Mr. Perry N. Jester, U.S. consul general, petitioning a visa to enable his nephew, Glenfield Lewis, to emigrate from Barbados to Boston, December 27, 1961. Lewis Papers, Box 3/12, File

#10. George Clarence Corbin is the deceased son Lewis refers to in this statement. Corbin, Lewis's wife Edwardine's son from her first marriage, was the first Black doctor on the staff of Beth Israel Hospital in Boston.

25. Thomas Brown, *Irish-American Nationalism 1870–1890* (Philadelphia: J. P. Lippencott Co., 1966), pp. 44–45.

26. O'Connor, *The Boston Irish*, xv–xvi. For more on the Irish plight, see the classic study, Oscar Handlin, *Boston's Immigrants, 1790–1880: A Study in Acculturation* (Cambridge, Mass.: Harvard University Press, 1959). Also useful and concise is chapter V, "The Coming of the Irish," in Buni and Rogers, *Boston, City on a Hill*. Useful for a concise yet broader understanding of the Irish experience beyond Boston is an excellent review essay by Patrick Blessing. In that piece Blessing discusses three works on the Irish experience: Dale T. Knoble, *Paddy and the Republic: Ethnicity and Nationality in Antebellum America* (Middletown, Conn.: Wesleyan University Press, 1986); Timothy J. Meagher, ed., *From Paddy to Studs: Irish American Communities in the Turn of the Century Era, 1880 to 1920* (Westport, Conn.: Greenwood Press, 1986); and Lawrence J. McCaffrey, Ellen Skerrett, Michael F. Funchion, and Charles Fanning, *The Irish in Chicago* (Urbana: University of Illinois Press, 1987). See Patrick J. Blessing, "Paddy: The Image and Reality of Irish Immigrants in the American Community," *Journal of American Ethnic History* 9, no. 1, 1989: 112–119.

27. Herbert J. Gans, *The Urban Villagers: Group and Class in the Life of Italian Americans* (New York: Free Press, 1962).

28. DeMarco, *Ethnics and Enclaves: Boston's Italian North End.*

29. Buni and Rogers, *Boston, City on a Hill*, p. 95.

30. Ibid. p. 93.

31. For more on the waves of Jewish immigration to Boston, bigotry from Yankees as well as from the Irish and Italians, and community and success, see Jonathan Sarna, "The Jews of Boston in Historical Perspective," in Sarna and Smith, eds., *Jews of Boston*, pp. 3–17.

32. For examples, see Braverman, "The Emergence of a Unified Community, 1880–1917," in ibid., pp. 78–79.

33. *Boston Advocate*, January 27, 1955. Cited in Leon A. Jick, "From Margin to Mainstream, 1917–1967," in Sarna and Smith, *Jews of Boston*, p. 106. For more on the success of Boston's Jews, also see Buni and Rogers, *Boston, City on a Hill*, pp. 91–92.

34. Buni and Rogers, *Boston, City on a Hill*, p. 103. For an in-depth study of nineteenth-century demographic developments and their socioeconomic implications, see Sam Bass Warner, Jr., *Streetcar Suburbs: The Process of Growth in Boston, 1870–1900* (Cambridge, Mass.: Harvard University Press, 1978).

35. O'Connor, *Bibles, Brahmins and Bosses*, p. 151.

36. Thernstrom, *The Other Bostonians*, p. 169.

37. Buni and Rogers, *Boston, City on a Hill*, p. 108; O'Connor, *Bibles, Brahmins and Bosses*, pp. 132–133. The Irish patronage system reached its zenith during the heyday of Mayor James Michael Curley. In the early 1900s, Curley went on a con-

struction frenzy which provided employment for his supporters, most of whom were Irish. See Buni and Rogers, *Boston, City on a Hill,* pp. 112–115.

38. Dennis P. Ryan, *Images of America: A Journey Through Boston Irish History* (Charleston, S.C.: Arcadia Publishing, 1990), pp. 28–30.

39. Thomas Nast's cartoon entitled "Ignorant Vote—Honors Are Easy" is a good example of his berating of the Irish. A copy can be found in O'Connor, *Boston Irish,* p. 155.

40. Ibid., p. 188.

41. Thernstrom computed some figures from various census reports, which he used to create some useful tables, for example one that illustrates the occupational distribution of first- and second-generation European immigrants, 1890, 1910, and 1930. He compares these statistics with those of the general Black population. Thernstrom, *The Other Bostonians,* p. 196.

42. The figures used to make the points here are drawn from published U.S. Census data for the censuses of 1900, 1910, 1940, and 1950. Also see Thernstrom, *The Other Bostonians,* pp. 196–207.

43. This situation went beyond Boston. Several scholars have pointed to the paradox in the relationship between education and socioeconomic mobility among African Americans. One of the best concise studies on this subject is David Hogan's article on ethnicity and education. Hogan emphasizes that for much of the Black experience, education has had limited use in upward mobility. See David Hogan, "Ethnicity and Education," in Stolarik and Friedman, eds., *Making it in America.*

44. Thernstrom, *The Other Bostonians,* p. 176.

45. Cited in Peter Medoff and Holly Sklar, *Streets of Hope: The Fall and Rise of an Urban Neighborhood* (Boston: South End Press, 1994), pp. 7–8.

Conclusion

1. Rhoda Spence, informal conversation with the author, Newton, Mass., August 2, 1992.

2. King, *Chain of Change,* pp. 9, 212.

3. This was not the first time that Boston's Blacks confronted the issue of racial segregation in education. In 1844, they organized to challenge the separate and unequal educational system. "They petitioned, investigated, publicized, demonstrated, and finally in 1849 brought suit against the city." Although the court decided that the Boston School Committee had the right to set its educational policy, the Massachusetts legislature abolished separate schools in 1855. Much of the change was only in theory. One hundred years later, King and other activists were still confronted with the problem of school segregation. For a concise account of the school desegregation struggle of the nineteenth century, see Buni and Rogers, *Boston, City on a Hill,* p. 75.

4. King, interview.

5. This Kevin White quote is cited in Buni and Rogers, *Boston, City on a Hill,* p. 152.

6. Carden, *Witness*, p. 58.

7. Ibid., p. 59.

8. Bynoe, interview. Louise Day Hicks was the chair of the Boston School Committee at the time. Indeed, an incident resembling a "showdown" between the two women occurred at a meeting. Hicks had agreed to meet with representatives of the NAACP on the condition that there be absolutely no discussion of de facto segregation, an odd stipulation since for the Black protesters this issue was at the heart of the problem. Most probably, Batson consciously and defiantly mentioned the term and Hicks promptly ended the meeting. See Ronald P. Formisano, *Boston Against Busing: Race, Class, and Ethnicity in the 1960s and 1970s* (Chapel Hill: University of North Carolina Press, 1991), p. 29.

9. *ProclaimHer,* Spring 2004, p. 1.

10. *Guardian,* May 6, 1939.

11. Levine and Harmon, *Death of an American Jewish Community,* p. 131.

12. Houston, interview.

13. Lewis explained this to the present author in an interview. SNCC demonstrated its extreme activism, specifically toward Jews, in early 1968 when young radical Black leaders demanded reparations from Jewish institutions operating in Black communities.

14. Levine and Harmon, *Death of an American Jewish Community,* p. 150.

15. Ibid., 151.

16. *Boston Globe,* January 18, 2004. Interestingly, during her lifetime, Lewis thought the label "Matriarch of the Black community" was problematic. According to her, "There's something derogatory about it. I'm black and I'm not running away from it, but my work as an educator and artist is not limited to the black community in Boston . . . I may sleep nights in Boston but I live in the world." This quote is from an interview with Lewis in the *Bay State Banner,* January 26, 1984.

17. See, for example, Henke's *West Indian Americans,* which puts Malcolm X on the list of "Notable Caribbean Americans." Henke, *West Indian Americans,* p. 171, James, *Holding Aloft the Banner,* p. 268, and Waters, *Black Identities,* p. 94.

18. Alex Haley and Malcolm X, *The Autobiography of Malcolm X* (New York: Ballantine Publishing Group, 1999), p. 41.

19. Ibid., p. 42.

20. Ibid., p. 45.

21. Florence Hamlish Levinsohn, *Looking for Farrakhan* (Chicago: Ivan R. Dee, Inc., 1997).

22. Ibid., p. 196.

23. Ibid., p. 210.

24. Ibid., p. 192

25. Niles Carpenter, *Immigrants and Their Children: 1920* (Washington, D.C.: U.S. Government Printing Office, 1927), p. 104.

BIBLIOGRAPHY

Archival Collections

National Archives of the United States

Passenger Lists of Manifest of Alien Passengers Arriving at Boston (From ports in
the West Indies and Costa Rica from 1900–1948)
General Records of the Department of Justice (Selected Naturalization Petitions)

Jamaica Archives, Spanish Town, Jamaica

Annual Reports of the Governors
Reports on the Post Office
Census of Jamaica
Register of Dispatches

British Public Record Office, Kew, England

Colonial Office Records
—CO 318/393/1: Report of Arbour Stephens, M.D., ex-chairman, Swansea Educa-
tion Committee, on Education in the British West Indies and Wales. October
1928.
—CO 318396/12: Correspondence between J. Maxton, Esq., M.P. and Rt. Hon. Lord
Passfield, M.P., Secretary of State for the Colonies on "Native Conditions in the
West Indies." November 1929.

Foreign Office Records

FO 620/1: Circular from the Consul General of Boston. September 16, 1922.
FO 598/15: Report of the British Embassy, Washington, D.C. to the Foreign Secre-
tary. March 1934.
FO 369/2379: Sir R. Lindsay, "Reports on West Indian Groups in the United States."
March 8, 1934.
FO 598/15: Confidential Dispatch from the Governor of the Colony of Jamaica to
Rt. Honourable W. Ormsby Gore, M.P., Secretary of State for the Colonies.
April 11, 1938.
FO 598/15: Report of the Governor on Labour in Jamaica. May 5, 1938.
FO 369/2916: Report of R.E. Barclay, British Ambassador, to the Consular Depart-
ment of the Foreign Office. June 16, 1943.
FO 369/3049: Minutes of the Meeting of Consular Officers. February 14, 1944.

Northeastern University, Boston, Archives and Special Collections

Elma Ina Lewis Papers

Newspapers and Magazines

Bay State Banner
Boston Chronicle
Boston Globe
Boston Guardian
Jamaica Daily Gleaner
Jamaica Mirror
Negro World
Plain Talk
West Indian Review

Oral Histories and Interviews

Allen, Colin. South End, Boston, Mass., March 17, 1987.
B., Elsa. Interviewed by Elsa Williams, South End, Boston, Mass., December 1977.
Bynoe, Victor. South End, Boston, Mass., August 6, 1990.
Campbell, Robert. Waltham, Mass., February 15, 1990.
"C.M." South End, Boston, Mass., June 17, 1989.
Commissiong, George. Mattapan, Mass., November 20, 1989.
"E," Elfreda. Mattapan, Mass., June 7, 1987.
"G," Patrice. Roxbury, Mass., June 4, 1990.
Houston, Amanda. Chestnut Hill, Mass., March 14, 1992.
James, Elvin. South End, Boston, Mass., April 17, 1987.
Johnson, Carol. Mattapan, Mass., May 17, 1987.
Johnson, Merna. Roxbury, Mass., May 17, 1988.
King, Mel. Cambridge, Mass., May 7, 1989.
Lewis, Elma. Roxbury, Mass., July 8, 1997.
Mason, Yvonne. Roxbury, Mass., February 2, 1988.
Nelson, David. Boston, Mass., December 6, 1990.
Sandiford, William. Boston, Mass., January 17, 1990.
Sinclair, Mavis. Roxbury, Mass., May 28, 1990.
Smith, Ivy. South End, Boston, Mass., February 17, 1989.
Spence, Rhoda. Newton, Mass., August 2, 1992.
Taylor, Norris. Interviewed by Mavis Taylor Wilson, May 1970.
Warner, Gertrude. Roxbury, Mass., June 4, 1990.
Williams, Betty. Roxbury, Mass., June 15, 1990.
Williams, Glenis. South End, Boston, Mass., June 4, 1989.
Wilson, Lily Mae. Roxbury, Mass., January 15, 1987.

Wilson, Mavis Taylor. Roxbury, Mass., June 4, 1990.
Wilson, Sadie. Newton, Mass., September 14, 1990.

Government and Official Publications

Census of Jamaica, 1943. Kingston, Jamaica: Government Printer, 1945.

General Census of the Population of the British West Indies. Kingston, Jamaica: Government Printing Office, 1946.

Handbook of Jamaica (various years from 1920–1945). Kingston, Jamaica: Government Printing Office.

The Swaby Education Commission, 1907–1909. Kingston, Jamaica: Government Printer, 1909.

United States Bureau of the Census. *Negroes in the United States, 1920–1932.* Washington, D.C.: United States Government Printing Office, 1935.

United States Department of Commerce, Bureau of the Census. *Thirteenth Census of the United States: 1910.* Washington, D.C.: Government Printing Office, 1913.

United States Department of Commerce, Bureau of the Census. *Fourteenth Census of the United States: 1920.* Washington, D.C.: Government Printing Office, 1922.

United States Department of Commerce, Bureau of the Census. *Fifteenth Census of the United States: 1930.* Washington, D.C.: Government Printing Office, 1932.

United States Department of Commerce, Bureau of the Census. *Sixteenth Census of the United States: 1940.* Washington, D.C.: Government Printing Office, 1943.

United States Department of Commerce, Bureau of the Census. *A Report of the Seventeenth Decennial Census of the United States: 1950.* Washington, D.C.: Government Printing Office, 1952.

United States Department of Labor, Bureau of Immigration. *Annual Report of the Commissioner General of Immigration to the Secretary of Labor,* 1900–1920. Washington, D.C.: Government Printing Office, 1901–1921.

Dissertations, Theses, and Unpublished Papers

Ambursley, Fitzroy L. "The Working Class in the Third World: A Study in Class Consciousness and Class Action in Jamaica, 1919–1952." B.A. dissertation, University of Birmingham, 1978.

Campbell, Carl. "Good Wives and Mothers: A Preliminary Survey of Women and Education in Trinidad, 1834–1981." Unpublished paper from the Social History Workshop, Department of History, University of the West Indies, Mona, Kingston, Jamaica, November 1985.

Dunbar, Barrington. "Factors in the Cultural Background of the American Southern Negro and the British West Indian Negro That Condition Their Adjustment in Harlem." Master's thesis, Columbia University, 1935.

Goddard, Lawford Lawrence. "Social Structure and Migration: A Comparative Study of the West Indies." Ph.D. dissertation, Stanford University, 1976.

Haynes, Elizabeth Ross. "Negroes in Domestic Service in the United States." Master's thesis, Columbia University, 1923.

Hunter, Gary. "Don't Buy from Where You Can't Work: Black Urban Boycott Movements During the Depression." Ph.D. dissertation, University of Michigan, 1977.

Lewis, Rupert. "A Political Study of Garveyism in Jamaica and London: 1914–1940." Master's thesis, University of the West Indies, Kingston, Jamaica, 1971.

Lobell, Richard. "Emigration and the Cost of Living in Jamaica, 1897–1938: An Exploratory Essay." Unpublished paper delivered at the 4th Annual Conference of Caribbean Historians. University of the West Indies, Mona, Kingston, Jamaica, 1972.

Marshall, W. K., Trevor Marshall, and Bently Gibbs. "The Establishment of a Peasantry in Barbados, 1840–1920." Unpublished paper, Department of History, University of the West Indies, Cave Hill, Barbados, 1976.

Massiah, Joycelin. "The Population of Barbados: Demographic Development and Population Policy in a Small Island State." Ph.D. dissertation, University of the West Indies, Mona, Kingston, Jamaica, 1981.

Midgett, Douglas Kent. "West Indian Migration and Adaptation in St. Lucia and London." Ph.D. dissertation, University of Illinois at Urbana-Champaign, 1977.

Newton, Velma. "British West Indian Emigration to the Isthmus of Panama, 1850–1914." Master's thesis, University of the West Indies, Kingston, Jamaica, 1968.

Noguera-Devers, Aurora. "The Factors Responsible for the Economic Success of West Indian Migrants." Senior thesis, University of California at Berkeley, 1992.

Pastor, Robert A. "Caribbean Emigration and U.S. Immigration Policy: Cross Currents." Paper presented at the Conference on International Relations of the Contemporary Caribbean, San Germán, Puerto Rico, April 22–23, 1983.

White, Noel A. "The Contribution of West Indian Immigrants to the Negro Community in the United States." Master's thesis, Columbia University Teachers College, 1963.

Articles

Anderson, Thomas F. "Boston: The Industrial Heart of New England." In *Fifty Years of Boston*. Boston: Tercentenary Committee, 1932.

Barrow, Christine. "Ownership and Control of Resources in Barbados, 1834 to the Present." *Social and Economic Studies* 32, no. 3 (1983): 83–120.

Blackett, Richard. "Some of the Problems Confronting West Indians in the Black American Struggle." *Black Lines* 1 (1971).

Best, Tony. "West Indians and Afro-Americans: A Partnership." *The Crisis* 82 (1975): 389–393.

Blessing, Patrick J. "Paddy: The Image and Reality of Irish Immigrants in the American Community." *Journal of American Ethnic History* 9, no. 1 (1989): 112–119.

Bonacich, Edna. "A Theory of Middleman Minorities." *American Sociological Review* 38 (1973): 583–594.

Bouknight-Davis, Gail. "Chinese Economic Development and Ethnic Identity Formation in Jamaica." In *The Chinese in the Caribbean*. Ed. Andrew Wilson. Princeton, N.J.: Markus Wiener, 2004.

Bodnar, John, Michael Weber, and Roger Simon. "Migration, Kinship, and Urban Adjustment: Blacks and Poles in Pittsburgh, 1900–1930." *Journal of American History* 66 (1979): 548–565.

Braverman, William. "The Emergence of a Unified Community, 1880–1917." In *The Jews of Boston*. Ed. Jonathan Sarna and Ellen Smith. Boston: Combined Jewish Philanthropies of Greater Boston, Inc., 1995.

Butcher, Kristin F. "Black Immigrants in the United States: A Comparison with Native Blacks and Other Immigrants." *Industrial and Labor Relations Review* 47 (1994): 265–285.

Bryce-Laporte, Simon Roy. "Black Immigrants: The Experience of Invisibility and Inequality." *Journal of Black Studies* 3 (September 1972): 29–56.

Campbell, Horace. "Garveyism, Pan-Africanism and African Liberation in the Twentieth Century." In *Garvey: His Work and Impact*. Ed. Rupert Lewis and Patrick Bryan. Trenton, N.J.: Africa World Press, Inc., 1991.

Carnegie, Charles V. " A Social Psychology of Caribbean Migrations: Strategic Flexibility in the West Indies." In *The Caribbean Exodus*. Ed. Barry B. Levine, 32–43. New York: Praeger, 1987.

Clarke, J. H. " West Indian Partisans in the Fight for Freedom." *Negro Digest* 15 (1966).

Clarke, John Henrick. "J. A. Rogers: In Search of the African Personality in World History." *Black History is no Mystery* 1, no. 2 (1991).

Comitas, Lambros. "Occupational Multiplicity in Rural Jamaica." In *Work and Family Life: West Indian Perspectives*. Ed. Lambros Comitas and David Lowenthal. New York: Anchor Books, 1973.

Conzen, Kathleen Neils. "Immigrants, Immigrant Neighborhoods, and Ethnic Identity: Historical Issues." *Journal of American History* 66 (1979).

Coombes, Orde. "West Indians in New York: Moving Beyond the Limbo Pole." *New York* 3, no. 28 (1970).

Dodoo, F. Nil-Amoo. "Earnings Differences among Blacks in America." *Social Science Research* 20 (1991): 93–108.

Domingo, Wilfredo A. "Gift of the Tropics." In *The New Negro*. Ed. Alain Locke, pp. 341–349. New York: Charles Bond, Inc., 1925. Reprint. New York: Arno Press, 1968.

Doyle, Brian. "The Passion of Dave Nelson." *Boston College Magazine*. Fall 1988.

Drayton, Kathleen. "Racism in Barbados." *Bulletin of Eastern Caribbean Affairs* 9, no. 2 (1983): 1–5.

Foner, Nancy. "West Indians in New York City and London: A Comparative Analysis." *International Migration Review* 13, no. 2 (1979).

Forsythe, Dennis. "West Indian Radicalism in America: An Assessment of Ideologies." In *Ethnicity in the Americas*. Ed. Frances Henry. The Hague: Mouton Publishers, 1976.

Fraser, Peter. "Nineteenth Century West Indian Migration to Britain." In *In Search of a Better Life: Perspectives on Migration from the Caribbean*. Ed. Ransford Palmer. New York: Praeger, 1990.

Fuchs, Lawrence. "The Reactions of Black Americans to Immigration." In *Immigration Reconsidered*. Ed. Virginia Yans-McLaughlin. Ithaca, N.Y.: Cornell University Press, 1977.

Hall, Douglas. "The Colonial Legacy in Jamaica." *New World Quarterly* 4, no. 1 (1968).

Hall, Stuart. "Cultural Identity and Diaspora." In *Identity, Community, Culture, Difference*. Ed. Jonathan Rutherford. London: Lawrence and Wishart, 1990.

———. "Negotiating Caribbean Identities." *New Left Review* 209 (1995): 3–14.

Halter, Marilyn. "Studying Immigrants of African Descent in the Twentieth Century." *The Immigration History Newsletter* 30, no. 1 (1998).

Hart, Richard. "Labour Rebellions of the 1930s." In *Caribbean Freedom: Economy and Society From Emancipation to the Present*. Ed. Hillary Beckles and Verene Shepherd, pp. 370–375. Princeton, N.J.: Markus Wiener, 1996.

Headley, Bernard D. "Gone Foreign!" *The Jamaica Mirror,* April 1989.

Hellwig, David J. "Black Meets Black: Afro-American Reactions to West Indian Immigrants in the 1920s." *South Atlantic Quarterly* 77 (Spring 1978): 373–385.

Henry, Keith. "The Black Political Tradition in New York: A Conjunction of Political Cultures." *Journal of Black Studies* 7 (1977): 455–484.

Higham, John. "Leadership." In *Harvard Encyclopedia of American Ethnic Groups*. Ed. Stephen Thernstrom. Cambridge, Mass.: Harvard University Press, 1983.

Hine, Darlene Clark. "The Housewives' League of Detroit: Black Women and Economic Nationalism." In *Visible Women: New Essays on American Activism*. Ed. Nancy Hewitt and Suzanne Lebsock, pp. 223–241. Urbana: University of Illinois Press, 1993.

Hoetink, H. "'Race' and Color in the Caribbean." In *Caribbean Contours*, 4th ed. Ed. Sidney W. Mintz and Sally Price, pp. 55–84. Baltimore: Johns Hopkins University Press, 1992.

Jennings, James. "Race, Class and Politics in the Black Community of Boston." In *From Access to Power: Black Politics in Boston*. Ed. James Jennings and Mel King. Cambridge, Mass.: Schenkman Books, Inc., 1986.

Jick, Leon A. "From Margin to Mainstream, 1917–1967." In *The Jews of Boston*. Ed. Jonathan Sarna and Ellen Smith. Boston: Combined Jewish Philanthropies of Greater Boston, Inc., 1995.

Johnson, Violet. "The Ambivalent Role of West Indian Immigrants in the Black Struggle in America in the 1920s and 1930s." In *In Celebration of Black History Month: Colloquium Papers*. Chestnut Hill, Mass.: Boston College Press, 1992.

Karch, Cecilia. "Class Formation and Class and Race Relations in the West Indies." In *The Middle Class in Dependent Countries*. Ed. Dale Johnson. New York: Sage Foundation, 1985.

Katzin, M. F. " Partners: An Informal Savings Institution in Jamaica." *Social and Economic Studies* 8 (1959).

Leahy, William A. "The Population Gains and Losses." In *Fifty Years of Boston*. Boston: Tercentenary Committee, 1932.

Levy, Jacqueline. "The Economic Role of the Chinese in Jamaica: The Grocery Retail Trade." *The Jamaican Historical Review* 15 (1986).

Lewis, Arthur W. "The 1930s Social Revolution." In *Caribbean Freedom: Economy and Society From Emancipation to the Present*. Ed. Hillary Beckles and Verene Shepherd, pp. 376–392. Princeton, N.J.: Markus Wiener, 1996.

Lewis, Gordon K. "The Contemporary Caribbean: A General Overview." In *Caribbean Contours*, 4th ed. Ed. Sidney W. Mintz and Sally Price, pp. 219–250. Baltimore: Johns Hopkins University Press, 1992.

Lintelman, Joy K. "'America is the Woman's Promised Land': Swedish Immigrant Women and American Domestic Service." *Journal of American Ethnic History* 8, no. 2 (1989): 9–23.

Lowenthal, David. "The Population of Barbados." *Social and Economic Studies* 6, no. 4 (1957): 445–501.

Lobell, Richard. "British Officials and the West Indian Peasantry, 1842–1938." In *Labour in the Caribbean*. Ed. Malcolm Cross and Gad Heuman, pp. 195–207. London: Macmillan Caribbean, 1988. Reprint 1992.

Manning, Frank E. "Celebrating Cricket: The Symbolic Construction of Caribbean Politics." In *Blackness in Latin America and the Caribbean* Vol. II. Ed. Arlene Torres and Norman E. Whitten, Jr., pp. 460–482. Bloomington: Indiana University Press, 1998.

Marshall, Dawn I. "A History of West Indian Migration: Overseas Opportunities and 'Safety-Valve' Policies." In *The Caribbean Exodus*. Ed. Barry B. Levine. New York: Praeger, 1987.

———. "Emigration as an Aspect of the Barbadian Social Environment." *Migration Today* 9 (1980): 6–14.

———. "Toward an Understanding of Caribbean Migration." In *United States Immigration and Refugee Policy*. Ed. Mary M. Kritz. Lexington, Mass.: D.C. Heath, 1983.

Marshall, Paule. "Black Immigrant Women in *Brown Girl Brownstones*." In *Caribbean Life in New York City: Sociocultural Dimensions*. Ed. Constance R. Sutton and Elsa M. Chaney. New York: Center for Migration Studies of New York, Inc., 1987.

Mayers, Janice. "Access to Secondary Education for Girls in Barbados, 1907–43." In *Engendering History: Caribbean Women in Historical Perspective*. Ed. Verene Shepherd et al., pp. 258–275. Kingston, Jamaica: Ian Randall Publishers, 1995.

Miller, E. L. "Education and Society in Jamaica." In *Sociology of Education*. Ed. P. Figueroa and G. Persaud. London: Oxford University Press, 1976.

Mintz, Sidney. "Black Women, Economic Roles and Cultural Traditions." In *Caribbean Freedom: Economy and Society from Emancipation to the Present*. Ed. Hillary Beckles and Verene Shepherd. Kingston, Jamaica: Ian Randall Publishers, 1993.

Mintz, Sidney W. "From Plantations to Peasantries in the Caribbean." In *Caribbean Contours*, 4th ed.. Ed. Sidney W. Mintz and Sally Price, pp. 127–153. Baltimore: Johns Hopkins University Press, 1992.

Model, Suzanne. "The Ethnic Niche and the Structure of Opportunity: Immigrants and Minorities in New York City. In *The Underclass Debate: Views from History*. Ed. Michael B. Katz. Princeton, N.J.: Princeton University Press, 1993.

Momsen, Janet Henshall. "Gender Roles in Caribbean Agricultural Labour." In *Labour in the Caribbean*. Ed. Malcolm Cross and Gad Heuman, pp. 141–158. London: Macmillan Caribbean, 1988. Reprint 1992.

Morrissey, Marietta. "Explaining the Caribbean Family: Gender, Ideologies and Gender Relations." In *Caribbean Portraits: Essays on Gender Ideologies and Identities*. Ed. Christine Barrow. Kingston, Jamaica: Ian Randle, 1998.

Nicholls, David. "The Syrians of Jamaica." *The Jamaican Historical Review* 15 (1986).

Nunes, Fred. "Social Values and Business Policy in the Caribbean." *Caribbean Quarterly* 19, no. 3 (1973).

Ostregen, Robert C. "Kinship Networks and Migration: A Nineteenth Century Swedish Example." *Journal of American Ethnic History* 3, no. 2 (1984).

Patterson, Orlando. "Migration in Caribbean Societies: Socioeconomic and Symbolic Resource." In *Human Migration: Patterns and Policies*. Ed. William H. McNeil and Ruth S. Adams, pp. 106–145. Bloomington: Indiana University Press, 1978.

Peach, Ceri. "The Force of West Indian Identity in Britain." In *Geography and Ethnic Pluralism*. Ed. Colin Clarke, David Ley, and Ceri Peach, pp. 214–230. London: George Allen and Urwin, 1984.

Ramesar, M. "The Role of British West Indian Immigrant Labourers in Trinidad, 1870–1921." In *Proceedings of 9th Conference of Caribbean Historians*, pp. 87–119. Mona, Kingston, Jamaica: University of the West Indies, 1977.

Raphael, Lennox. "West Indians and Afro-Americans." *Freedomways* (1964): 438–445.

Roberts, George. "Emigration from the Island of Barbados." *Social and Economic Studies* 4, no. 3 (1955): 245–288.

Rodney, Walter. "Barbadian Immigration into British Guiana, 1863–1924." In *Proceedings of the 9th Conference of Caribbean Historians*. Kingston, Jamaica: University of the West Indies, 1977.

Sarna, Jonathan. "The Jews of Boston in Historical Perspective." In *The Jews of Boston*. Ed. Jonathan Sarna and Ellen Smith. Boston: Combined Jewish Philanthropies of Greater Boston, Inc., 1995.

Shaw, Stephanie J. "Black Club Women and the Creation of the National Association of Colored Women." In *We Specialize in the Wholly Impossible: A Reader in Black Women's History.* Ed. Darlene Clark Hine, Wilma King, and Linda Reed, pp. 433–447. New York: Carlson Publishing, Inc., 1995.

Smith, J. Owens. "The Politics of Income and Educational Differences Between Blacks and West Indians." *Journal of Ethnic Studies* 13 (1985).

Smith, M. G. "A Survey of West Indian Family Studies." In *Work and Family Life.* Ed. Lambros Comitas and David Lowenthal. Garden City, N.Y.: Anchor Press/Doubleday, 1973.

Soto, Isa Maria. "West Indian Child Fostering: Its Role in Migrant Exchanges." In *Caribbean Life in New York City: Sociocultural Dimensions.* Ed. Constance R. Sutton and Elsa M. Chaney. New York: Center for Migration Studies of New York, Inc., 1987.

Sowell, Thomas. "Three Black Histories." In *Essays and Data on American Ethnic Groups.* Ed. Thomas Sowell, pp. 7–64. Washington, D.C.: The Urban Institute, 1975.

St. Pierre, Maurice. "West Indian Cricket: A Sociohistorical Appraisal." *Caribbean Quarterly* 19, no. 2 (1973): 7–27.

Stewart, Robert. "A Slandered People—Views on 'Negro Character' in the Mainstream Christian Churches in Post-Emancipation Jamaica." In *Crossing Boundaries: Comparative Historyof Black People in the Diaspora.* Ed. Darlene Clark Hine and Jacqueline McLeod. Bloomington: Indiana University Press, 1999.

Stone, Carl. "Race and Economic Power in Jamaica." In *Garvey: His Work and Impact.* Ed. Rupert Lewis and Patrick Bryan, pp. 243–264. Trenton, N.J.: Africa World Press, Inc., 1991.

Ueda, Reed. "West Indians." In *Harvard Encyclopedia of American Ethnic Groups.* Ed. Stephan Thernstrom, pp. 1020–1027. Cambridge, Mass.: Harvard University Press, 1980.

Vecoli, Rudolph J. "The Italian Immigrant Press and the Construction of Social Reality, 1850–1920." In *Print Culture in a Diverse America.* Ed. James P. Danky and Wayne A. Wiegand. Urbana: University of Illinois Press, 1998.

Vickerman, Milton. "Tweaking a Monolithic: The West Indian Immigrant Encounter with Blackness." In *Islands in the City: West Indian Migration to New York.* Ed. Nancy Foner. Berkeley: University of California Press, 2001.

Walter, John C. "West Indian Immigrants: Those Arrogant Bastards." *Contributions on Black Studies* 5 (1981–82).

Waters, Mary C. "Ethnic and Racial Identities of Second-Generation Black Immigrants in New York City." *International Migration Review* XXVII, no. 4 (1994): 795–820.

———. "Growing up West Indian and African American: Gender and Class Differences In the Second Generation." In *Islands in the City: West Indian Migration to New York.* Ed. Nancy Foner. Berkeley: University of California Press, 2001.

Watkins-Owens, Irma. "Early Twentieth-Century Caribbean Women: Migration and Social Networks in New York City." In *Islands in the City: West Indian Migration to New York.* Ed. Nancy Foner. Berkeley: University of California Press, 2001.

Books

Adams, Frederick Upham. *Conquest of the Tropics: The Story of the Creative Enterprises Conducted by the United Fruit Company.* Garden City, N.Y.: Doubleday, Page & Co., 1914.

Adamson, Alan H. *Sugar Without Slaves: The Political Economy of British Guiana, 1838–1904.* New Haven, Conn.: Yale University Press, 1972.

Aguirre, Adalberto, Jr., and Jonathan H. Turner. *American Ethnicity: The Dynamics and Consequences of Discrimination.* New York: McGraw-Hill, Inc., 1995.

Beachey, R. W. *The British West Indies Sugar Industry in the Late 19th Century.* Westport, Conn.: Greenwood Press, 1978.

Bennett, Lerone, Jr. *Before the Mayflower: A History of Black America.* New York: Penguin, 1984.

Blackwell, J. E. *The Black Community: Diversity and Unity.* New York: Harper Collins, 1991.

Bodnar, John. *The Transplanted: A History of Immigrants in Urban America.* Bloomington: Indiana University Press, 1985.

Bodnar, John, Roger Simon, and Michael Weber. *Lives of Their Own: Blacks, Italians and Poles in Pittsburgh, 1900–1960.* Urbana: University of Illinois Press, 1982.

Bonnett, Aubrey. *Institutional Adaptation of West Indian Immigrants to America: An Analysis of Rotating Credit Associations.* Washington, D.C.: University Press of America, 1981.

Brome, Henderson L. *Voices and Victors in the Struggle.* N.p. n.d.

Brown, Thomas. *Irish-American Nationalism, 1870–1890.* Philadelphia: J. P. Lippencott Co., 1966.

Bryce-Laporte, Roy Simon, and D. Mortimer, eds. *Caribbean Immigration in the United States.* Washington, D.C.: Smithsonian Institution, 1976.

Buff, Rachel. *Immigration and Political Economy of Home: West Indian Brooklyn and American Indian Minneapolis, 1945–1992.* Los Angeles: University of California Press, 2001.

Buni, Andrew, and Alan Rogers. *Boston: City on a Hill.* Boston: Windsor Publications, 1984.

Butler, John Sibley. *Entrepreneurship and Self-Help Among Black Americans.* New York: State University of New York Press, 1991.

Carden, Lance. *Witness: An Oral History of Black Politics in Boston, 1920–1960.* Boston: Boston College Press, 1989.

Carpenter, Niles. *Immigrants and Their Children: 1920.* Washington, D.C.: U.S. Government Printing Office, 1927.

Center for Afro-American and African Studies, the University of Michigan. *Black Immigration and Ethnicity in the United States: An Annotated Bibliography.* Westport, Conn.: Greenwood Press, 1985.

Chisholm, Shirley. *Unbought and Unbossed.* New York: Houghton Mifflin, 1970.

Clark, Dennis. *Erin Heirs: Irish Bonds of Community.* Lexington: University of Kentucky Press, 1991.

Clarke, Edith. *My Mother Who Fathered Me.* London: Allen and Unwin, 1957.

Craig, Suzan. *Contemporary Caribbean: A Sociological Reader.* Maracas, Trinidad: College Press, 1982

Cromwell, Adelaide. *The Other Brahmins: Boston's Black Upper Class, 1750–1950.* Fayetteville: University of Arkansas Press, 1994.

Chateauvert, Melinda. *Marching Together: Women of the Brotherhood of Sleeping Car Porters.* Urbana: University of Illinois Press, 1998.

Chomsky, Aviva. *West Indian Workers and the United Fruit Company in Costa Rica, 1870–1940.* Baton Rouge: Louisiana State University Press, 1996.

Cole, Joyce. *Official Ideology and the Education of Women in the English-speaking Caribbean, 1834–1945.* Kingston, Jamaica: ISER, University of the West Indies, 1982.

Conzen, Michael P., and George K. Lewis. *Boston, a Geographical Portrait.* Cambridge: Ballinger, 1976.

Cullen, Jim. *The American Dream: A Short History of an Idea that Shaped a Nation.* New York: Oxford University Press, 2003.

Daniels, John. *In Freedom's Birthplace: A Study of Boston Negroes.* Boston: Houghton Mifflin, 1914.

Daniels, Roger. *Coming to America: A History of Immigration and Ethnicity in America.* New York: Harper Collins, 1990.

Darrett, Rutman. *Winthrop's Boston: Portrait of a Puritan Town.* Chapel Hill: University of North Carolina Press, 1965.

Davis, John M. *The Church in the New Jamaica: A Study of the Economic and Social Basis of the Evangelical Church in Jamaica.* New York: International Missionary Council, 1942.

Davis, Kortright. *Cross and Crown in Barbados: Caribbean Political Religion in the Late 19th Century.* Frankfurt: Verlag Peter Lang, 1983.

DeMarco, William M. *Ethnics and Enclaves: Boston's Italian North End.* Ann Arbor: UMI Research Press, 1981.

Derks, Scott. *The Value of a Dollar: Prices and Incomes in the United States, 1860–1989.* Detroit: Gale Research Inc., 1994.

Dickinson, Joan Younger. *The Role of Immigrant Women in the U.S. Labor Force, 1890–1910.* New York: Arno Press, 1980.

Diner, Hasia R. *Erin's Daughters in America: Irish Immigrant Women in the Nineteenth Century.* Baltimore: Johns Hopkins University Press, 1983.

Dinnerstein, Leonard, and David Reimers. *Ethnic Americans: A History of Immigration.* New York: Harper Collins, 1988.

Eisner, Gisela. *Jamaica, 1830–1930: A Study in Economic Growth.* Manchester, England: Manchester University Press, 1961.

Fergus, Howard A. *Montserrat: A History of a Caribbean Colony.* New York: Macmillan Caribbean, 1994.

Finch, Minnie. *The NAACP, its Fight for Justice.* Metuchen, N.J.: Scarecrow Press, 1981.

Fisher, Sethard. *From Margin to Mainstream: the Social Progress of Black Americans.* New York: Russell Sage Foundation, 1992.

Formisano, P. *Boston Against Busing: Race, Class, and Ethnicity in the 1960s and 1970s.* Chapel Hill: University of North Carolina Press, 1991.

Fortune, Stephan Alexander. *Merchants and Jews: The Struggle for British West Indian Commerce, 1650–1750.* Gainesville: University of Florida Press, 1984.

Fox, Stephen R. *The Guardian of Boston: William Monroe Trotter.* New York: Atheneum, 1970.

Gaines, Kevin. *Uplifting the Race: Black Leadership, Politics, and Culture in the Twentieth Century.* Chapel Hill: University of North Carolina Press, 1996.

Gans, Herbert J. *The Urban Villagers: Group and Class in the Life of Italian Americans.* New York: Free Press, 1962.

Gilroy, Paul. *The Black Atlantic: Modernity and Double Consciousness.* Cambridge, Mass.: Harvard University Press, 1993.

Ginsberg, Yona. *Jews in a Changing Neighborhood: The Study of Mattapan.* London: The Free Press, 1975.

Gmelch, G. *Double Passage: The Lives of Caribbean Migrants Abroad and Back Home.* Ann Arbor: University of Michigan Press, 1992.

Goodman, James. *Stories of Scottsboro.* New York: Vintage Books, 1994.

Gordon, Shirley. *A Century of West Indian Education.* London: Longmans, 1963.

Green, Shelley, and Paul Pryde. *Black Entrepreneurship in America.* New Brunswick, N.J.: Transactions Publishers, 1990.

Green, Victor. *American Immigrant Leaders, 1800–1910: Marginality and Identity.* Baltimore: John Hopkins University Press, 1987.

Gutman, Herbert. *The Black Family in Slavery and Freedom, 1850–1925.* New York: Pantheon, 1976.

Haley, Alex, and Malcolm X. *The Autobiography of Malcolm X.* New York: Ballantine Publishing Group, 1999.

Halter, Marilyn. *Between Race and Ethnicity: Cape Verdean American Immigrants.* Urbana: University of Illinois Press, 1993.

Handlin, Oscar. *Boston's Immigrants: A Study in Acculturation.* Cambridge, Mass.: Harvard University Press, 1959.

Hart, Keith, ed. *Women and Sexual Division of Labour in the Caribbean.* Kingston, Jamaica: Consortium Graduate School, University of the West Indies, 1989.

Hathaway, Heather. *Caribbean Waves: Relocating Claude McKay and Paule Marshall.* Bloomington: Indiana University Press, 1999.

Hayden, Robert C. *African Americans in Boston: More than 350 Years.* Boston: Boston Public Library, 1991.

————. *Boston's NAACP History, 1910–1982.* Boston: Boston NAACP Branch, 1982.

————. *Faith, Culture and Leadership: A History of the Black Church in Boston.* Boston: Boston Branch of the NAACP, 1983.

Haynes, George Edmund. *The Negro at Work in New York City.* New York: Arno Press, 1912. Reprint. New York: Arno Press, 1968.

Henke, Holger. *The West Indian Americans.* Westport, Conn.: Greenwood Press, 2001.

Henri, Florette. *Black Migration Movement North, 1900–1920: The Road from Myth to Man.* Garden City, N.Y.: Anchor Books, 1976.

Henriques, Fernando. *Family and Colour in Jamaica.* London: Eyre and Spottis-woode, 1953.

Herskovits, M. J., and F. S. Herskovits. *Trinidad Village.* New York: Alfred A. Knopf, 1947.

Hentoff, Nat. *Boston Boy.* New York: Alfred Knopf, 1986.

Higham, John, ed. *Ethnic Leadership in America.* Baltimore: Johns Hopkins University Press, 1978.

Hill, Robert, ed. *The Marcus Garvey and Universal Negro Improvement Association Papers.* Berkeley: University of California Press, 1983–1987.

Hintzen, Percy C. *West Indian in the West: Self Representation in an Immigrant Community.* New York: New York University Press, 2001.

Holt, Hamilton, ed. *The Life Stories of Undistinguished Americans as Told by Themselves.* New York: Routledge Press, 1906. Reprint 1990.

Ignatiev, Noel. *How the Irish Became White.* New York: Routledge, 1995.

Ito, Kazuo. *Issei: A History of the Japanese in North America.* Seattle, Wash.: Japanese Community Service, 1973.

James, C. L. R. *Beyond a Boundary.* London: Hutchinson, 1969.

James, Winston. *Holding Aloft the Banner of Ethiopia: Caribbean Radicalism in Early Twentieth-Century America.* London: Verso, 1998.

Jennings, James. *The Politics of Black Empowerment: the Transformation of Black Activism in Urban America.* Detroit: Wayne State University Press, 1992.

Jennings, James, and Mel King, eds. *From Access to Power: Black Politics in Boston.* Cambridge, Mass.: Schenkam Books, Inc., 1986.

Jillson, Cal. *Pursuing the American Dream.* Lawrence: University of Kansas Press, 2004.

Jones, Katharine W. *Accent on Privilege: English Identities and Anglophilia in the U.S.* Philadelphia: Temple University Press, 2001.

Kasinitz, Phillip. *Caribbean New York: Black Immigrants and the Politics of Race.* Ithaca, N.Y.: Cornell University Press, 1992.

Kellogg, Charles Flint. *NAACP: A History of the National Association for the Advancement of Colored People.* Baltimore: Johns Hopkins University Press, 1967.

Kerr, Madeline. *Personality and Conflict in Jamaica.* Liverpool: Liverpool University Press, 1951.

Kessler-Harris, Alice. *Out to Work: A History of Wage-Earning Women in the United States.* New York: Oxford University Press, 1982.

Kessner, Thomas, and Betty Cardi. *Today's Immigrants: Their Stories.* New York: Oxford University Press, 1981.

King, Mel. *Chain of Change: Struggles for Black Community Development.* Boston: South End Press, 1981.

Krieger, Alex, David Cobb, and Amy Turner, eds. *Mapping Boston.* Cambridge, Mass.: MIT Press, 2001.

Kroes, Rob. *Questions of Citizenship in a Globalizing World: Them and Us.* Urbana: University of Illinois Press, 2000.

Lemelle, Sidney J., and Robin D. G. Kelley. *Imagining Home: Class, Culture and Nationalism in the African Diaspora.* New York: Verso, 1996.

Lewis, Gordon. *The Growth of the Modern West Indies.* London: MacGibbon & Kee, 1968.

Levine, Barry B. *The Caribbean Exodus.* New York: Praeger, 1987.

Levine, Hillel, and Lawrence Harmon. *The Death of an American Jewish Community: A Tragedy of Good Intentions.* New York: The Free Press, 1992.

Levinsohn, Florence Hamlish. *Looking for Farrakhan.* Chicago: Ivan R. Dee, Inc., 1997.

Litwack, Leon F. *North of Slavery: The Negro in the Free States, 1790–1860.* Chicago: University of Chicago Press, 1961.

Lukas, J. Anthony. *Common Ground: A Turbulent Decade in the Lives of Three American Families.* New York: Alfred A. Knopf, 1985.

Lupo, Alan, Frank Colcord, and Edmund P. Fowler. *Rites of Way: The Politics of Transportation in Boston and the U.S. City.* Boston: Little Brown, 1971.

Manley, Michael. *History of West Indies Cricket.* London: Andre Deutsch, 1988.

Mark, Diane Mei Lin, and Ginger Chih. *A Place Called Chinese America.* Dubuque, Iowa: Kendall/Hunt Publishing Company, 1982.

Medoff, Peter, and Holly Sklar. *Streets of Hope: The Fall and Rise of an Urban Neighborhood.* Boston: South End Press, 1994.

Meir, August, Elliot Rudwick, and Frances Broderick. *Black Protest Thought in the Twentieth Century.* Indianapolis, Ind.: Bobbs-Merrill, 1983.

Melville, John. *The Great White Fleet.* New York: Vantage Press, 1976.

Miller, Sally M., ed. *The Ethnic Press in the United States: A Historical Analysis and Handbook.* Westport, Conn.: Greenwood Press, 1987.

Morawska, Ewa. *For Bread With Butter.* Cambridge, England: Cambridge University Press, 1985.

Morison, Samuel Eliot. *Maritime History of Massachusetts, 1783–1860.* N.p. 1921. Reprint. Northeastern University Press, 1980.

Nettleford, Rex Milton. *Identity, Race and Protest in Jamaica.* New York: Morrow, 1972.

O'Connor, Thomas H. *Bible, Brahmins and Bosses: A Short History of Boston,* 2nd ed. Boston: Boston Public Library, 1984.

———. *The Boston Irish: A Political History.* Boston: Northeastern University Press, 1995.

Osofsky, Gilbert. *Harlem: The Making of a Ghetto.* New York: Harper and Row, 1968.

Ostregren, Robert C. *A Community Transplanted: The Trans-Atlantic Experience of a Swedish Immigrant Settlement in the Upper Middle West, 1835–1915.* Madison: University of Wisconsin Press, 1988.

Palmer, Ransford. *Caribbean Dependence on the United States Economy.* New York: Praeger, 1979.

———. *The Jamaican Economy.* New York: Praeger, 1968.

———. *Pilgrims from the Sun: West Indian Migration to America.* New York: Twayne Publishers, 1995.

Palmer, Ransford, ed. *In Search of a Better Life: Perspectives on Migration from the Caribbean.* New York: Praeger, 1990.

Park, Robert E. *The Immigrant Press and Its Control.* New York: Harper & Brothers, 1922.

Pastor, Robert A., ed. *Migration and Development in the Caribbean: The Unexplored Connection.* Boulder, Colo.: Westview Press, 1985.

Pleck, Elizabeth Hafkin. *Black Migration and Poverty: Boston, 1865–1900.* New York: Academic Press, 1979.

Proudfoot, Malcolm J. *Population Movements in the Caribbean.* New York: Negro Universities Press, 1970.

Putnam, Lara. *The Company They Kept: Migrants and the Politics of Gender in Caribbean Costa Rica, 1870–1960.* Chapel Hill: University of North Carolina Press, 2002.

Reid, Ira De Augustine. *The Negro Immigrant, His Background, Characteristics, and Social Adjustment, 1899–1937.* New York: Columbia University Press, 1939.

Reimers, David. *Other Immigrants: The Global Origins of the American People.* New York: New York University Press, 2005.

Richardson, Bonham C. *Caribbean Migrants and Human Survival on St. Kitts and Nevis.* Knoxville: University of Tennessee Press, 1983.

———. *Panama Money in Barbados, 1900–1920.* Knoxville: University of Tennessee Press, 1985.

Riviére, Emmanuel, W. *Roots of Crisis in the Caribbean.* New York: Bohiyo Enterprises, Inc., 1987.

Rosenzweig, Roy. *Eight Hours for What We Will: Workers and Leisure in an Industrial City, 1870–1920.* Cambridge: Cambridge University Press, 1983.

Ryan, Dennis P. *Images of America: A Journey Through Boston Irish History.* Charleston, S.C.: Arcadia Publishing, 1990.

Santino, Jack. *Miles of Smiles, Years of Struggle: Stories of Black Pullman Porters.* Urbana: University of Illinois Press, 1989.

Sarna, Jonathan D., and Ellen Smith, eds. *The Jews of Boston.* Boston: Combined Jewish Philanthropies of Greater Boston, Inc., 1995.

Schneider, Mark. *Boston Confronts Jim Crow, 1890–1920.* Boston: Northeastern University Press, 1997.

Shepherd, Verene A. *Women in Caribbean History.* Kingston, Jamaica: Ian Randle, 1999.

Simey, T. S. *Welfare and Planning in the West Indies.* London: Oxford University Press, 1946.

Smith, Judith E. *Family Connections: A History of Italian and Jewish Immigrant Lives in Providence, Rhode Island, 1900–1940.* Albany: State University of New York Press, 1985.

Smith-Irvin, Jeannette. *Marcus Garvey's Footsoldiers of the Universal Negro Improvement Association.* Trenton, N.J.: Africa World Press, 1989.

Smith, M. G. *West Indian Family Structure.* Seattle: University of Washington Press, 1962.

Smith, Raymond T. *Kinship and Class in the West Indies: A Genealogical Study of Jamaica and Guyana.* Cambridge: Cambridge University Press, 1998. Reprint 1990.

————. *The Negro Family in British Guiana.* London: Routledge and Kegan Paul, 1956.

Sowell, Thomas. *Race and Economics.* New York: David Mackay, 1975.

Stein, Judith. *The World of Marcus Garvey: Race and Class in Modern Society.* Baton Rouge: Louisiana State University Press, 1986.

Stolarik, Mark M., and Murray Friedman, eds. *Making it in America: The Role of Ethnicity in Business Enterprise, Education and Work Choices.* Lewisburg, Pa.: Bucknell University Press, 1986.

Stuart, M. S. *An Economic Detour.* New York: Wendell Malliett and Company, 1940.

Takaki, Ronald. *A Different Mirror: A History of Multicultural America.* New York: Back Bay Books, 1993.

Tentler, Leslie Woodcock. *Wage Earning: Industrial Work and Family Life in the United States, 1900–1930.* New York: Oxford University Press, 1979.

Thernstrom, Stephan. *The Other Bostonians.* Cambridge, Mass.: Harvard University Press, 1973.

Trout, Charles. *Boston: The Great Depression and the New Deal.* New York: Oxford University Press, 1977.

Turner, Joyce Moore, and Burghart Turner. *Richard G. Moore: Caribbean Militant in Harlem.* Bloomington: Indiana University Press, 1996.

Vickerman, Milton. *Crosscurrents: West Indian Immigrants and Race.* New York: Oxford University Press, 1999.

Von, Frank, Albert J. *The Trials of Anthony Burns: Freedom and Slavery in Emerson's Boston.* Cambridge, Mass.: Harvard University Press, 1998.

Warner, Sam Bass, Jr. *Streetcar Suburbs: The Process of Growth in Boston, 1870–1900.* Cambridge, Mass.: Harvard University Press, 1978.

Waters, Mary C. *Black Identities: West Indian Immigrant Dreams and American Realities.* New York: Russell Sage Foundation, 1999.

Watkins-Owens, Irma. *Blood Relations: Caribbean Immigrants and the Harlem Community, 1900–1930.* Bloomington: Indiana University Press, 1996.

Williams, Eric. *The Negro in the Caribbean.* Albany, N.Y.: The Williams Press, 1942.

Williams, Nicholas. *United Fruit Company: Nature and Scope of Its Activities.* Boston: Publicity Department, United Fruit Company, 1931.

Wilson, Andrew, ed. *The Chinese in the Caribbean.* Princeton, N.J.: Markus Wiener, 2004.

Wilson, Joseph F. *Tearing Down the Color Bar: An Analysis and Documentary History of the Brotherhood of Sleeping Car Porters.* New York: Columbia University Press, 1989.

WPA Federal Writers' Project. *Boston Looks Seaward: The Story of the Port, 1630–1940.* Boston: B Humphries, 1941. Reprint. Boston: Northeastern University Press, 1985.

INDEX

Page numbers in italics refer to illustrations.

VIOLET SHOWERS JOHNSON
is Professor of History at Agnes Scott College.